Smart Girls

(Revised Edition)

A New Psychology of Girls, Women, and Giftedness

Barbara Kerr, Ph.D.
Arizona State University

Smart Girls (Revised Edition)—A New Psychology of Girls, Women, and Giftedness

Cover Design\Interior Design: Spring Winnette
Indexer: Joan K. Griffitts

Published by
Gifted Psychology Press
P.O. Box 5057
Scottsdale, AZ 85261

Formerly
Ohio Psychology Press
P.O. Box 90095
Dayton, OH 45490

First published in 1985 under the title, *Smart Girls, Gifted Women*,
Revised and enlarged in 1995 under the title, *Smart Girls Two*, revised and
enlarged.

Printed and bound in the United States of America

Library of Congress Cataloging-in-Publication Data

Kerr, Barbara A.
    Smart Girls: A New Psychology of Girls, Women, and Giftedness
    / Barbara Kerr.
        p. cm.
    Rev. ed. of: *Smart Girls Two*. 1994.
    Includes bibliographical references (p.   ) and index.
    ISBN 0-910707-26-X (pbk.)
    1. Gifted girls. 2. Gifted women. 3. Gifted women—Longitudinal studies.
4. Gifted Women—Biography. 5. Gifted Women—Employment. 6. Self-actualization (Psychology) 7. Achievement motivation in women—Case studies.
8. Success—Psychological aspects—Case studies. I. Kerr, Barbara A. *Smart
Girls Two*.
BF723.G52K48 1997

155.6'33'0879—dc21   97-23100
                                        CIP

ISBN 0-910707-26-X

This book is dedicated to my family:

*Chuck Claiborn,
my loving husband
and my most respected colleague.*

*My son Sam,
who must wonder when I'll ever get around
to writing a book about boys.*

*My daughter Grace, whose first five years
have taught me more about smart little girls
than all my research.*

Acknowledgments

Thank you to my classmates in the Track IA classes who responded to two questionnaires ten years apart with openness, rich feeling, and wit. Also, thank you to the teachers, parents, and students who have shared my book with each other, and shared their reactions with me. A warm thanks to Audrey Julian and Sheila Saunders, who helped me with word processing in their evening hours and Susan Maresh, who did research for me and became an expert in her own right on girls and giftedness. Many graduate students gave their time and energy to the counseling research laboratories where bright girls received guidance and told us about their lives; thanks for the many insights. Thank you to Jim Webb, editor and publisher, who kept *Smart Girls, Gifted Women* in print for ten years, and whose persuasiveness made *Smart Girls (Revised Edition)—A New Psychology of Girls, Women, and Giftedness* possible. Fond thanks to Linder Senter, the editor who made my words say exactly what I meant and who became a friend. The work for these two books on smart girls was performed while I was a professor at three different universities: University of Nebraska, University of Iowa, and Arizona State University. At each of thse universities, I encountered varying degrees of support from colleagues and administrators. To those wonderful mentors, men and women, who found funding for my research, collaborated with me on projects, and who made a place for me and my work at those institutions, my profoundest gratitutde.

Table of Contents

Foreword

What began as a simple question—why had certain gifted women failed to fulfill the rich promise of childhood?—became a research project, then a counseling program for gifted girls and women, and finally, a book: *Smart Girls, Gifted Women*. Identified as gifted soon after the launch of Sputnik in 1957, these girls (and myself as well, since I too was so singled out) were given, for the next seven years, a special curriculum designed to foster leadership and success. When we met for a reunion ten years after graduation from high school, their stories intrigued me, and my studies of their lives became the basis for *Smart Girls, Gifted Women. Smart Girls (Revised Edition)—A New Psychology of Girls, Women, and Giftedness* continues with a twenty-year follow-up of the group; neither a second edition nor a sequel, it is rather, a transformation and extension of the original material, based on a new understanding of the lives of gifted women. This transformation took place with the help of my classmates, my colleagues in this field, and the readers of my first book.

The definition of giftedness has changed greatly over the last two decades. Once, "the gifted" were those who scored in the upper 3 to 5 percent on standardized intelligence (I.Q.) tests. However, while they predict school performance fairly well for white, middle-class children, these I.Q. tests often cannot identify creativity and unusual talents, and they furthermore are not complete measures of the abilities of children who are members of minority groups or are handicapped. New theories of intelligence, such as Howard Gardner's (1983) theory of multiple intelligences, suggest that specific, extraordinary talents are the mark of giftedness, and so new procedures have been developed for identifying gifted children. In my work I have found I.Q. test scores helpful but often unnecessary in labeling both children and adults as gifted. (In fact, my experience has been that parents who suspect their child is gifted are correct 99 percent of the time, making parental judgment one of the best assessments around.) The definition of giftedness in this book embraces exceptional academic ability as well as creative and specific talents, and its range includes "high-potential" girls (the upper 25 percent on school achievement tests) as well as the near-genius Presidential Scholars. Therefore, it includes almost all who have the potential for excellence in their chosen fields.

I hope this book will be interesting to bright women as well as to the men who care about or work with them. *Smart Girls, Gifted Women* has been the basis for workshops with gifted girls and for women's studies courses in high schools and colleges, and I hope that this *Smart Girls (Revised Edition)—A New Psychology of Girls, Women, and Giftedness* will be useful in the same way. I hope, too, that it will help parents and grandparents of girls with great potential for intellectual and creative achievement.

As I travel around the country lecturing on giftedness and achievement in women, I have often been dismayed by the defensive postures of many gifted women in regard to their lifestyles. The seemingly simple question "Why don't gifted girls achieve more in their careers?" has drawn angry questions and hostile retorts: "So what's wrong with not having a career?" argue women who consider themselves traditional. "You're measuring women by masculine standards of achievement!" insist certain feminists. Some women have been offended because they believed I was devaluing home-making; others, because I referred to research showing that gifted women earn less and have lower-status jobs than gifted men. They thought such data suggested that women should act more like men. But I now realize that, gifted or not, most women in America—including myself—have felt defensive at one time or another about lifestyle choices and self-definitions. *Smart Girls (Revised Edition)—A New Psychology of Girls, Women, and Giftedness* offers a solution to this dilemma with its new perspectives on achievement and career. Research studies have traditionally defined achievement in terms of school grade-point averages or occupational status and salary, and career has usually meant income-producing employment, most often at a professional level. While these definitions are retained when I discuss such studies, a different meaning for achievement and career nonetheless evolves in this book. New definitions of these terms are needed if we are to help gifted girls and women understand and plan their lives meaningfully and effectively.

In this book and in my counseling and teaching, I have re-defined achievement to be the use of one's gifts and talents, as one understands them, to the fullest. Achievement means being all that one can be, according to one's deeply-held values.

Achievement then is not tied to grades or salary, but to a woman's fulfillment of her own dreams; not to a particular environment, because women can operate at peak capacity in many settings; not to academic honors, titles, and offices, since these by-products or signs of achievement are not the equivalent of achievement.

What do you call a series of goal-directed activities that exercise a woman's talents to the utmost and give meaning to her life? I call it a vocation. A vocation is not a job. One can think of a vocation as a mission in life and a belief in the fulfillment of, and the urge to exercise, one's energies and talents. Someone can take away your job, but nobody can take away your vocation: whether it is understanding eighteenth-century literature, the search for a cure for AIDS, or advocacy for the rights of gifted children, a vocation in this sense is the passionate, energetic pursuit of a goal that persistently calls to you. By defining achievement and career as the maximum use of talents in the pursuit of a vocation, perhaps women can stop defending their lifestyles and can search for those challenges that will allow fulfillment of potential.

Smart Girls (Revised Edition)—A New Psychology of Girls, Women, and Giftedness builds on theories and findings of research to create a portrait of gifted girls and women, incorporating new theories and research findings. Chapters One and Two describe my ten-year follow-up study of my former classmates, all graduates of the program supposedly designed to train us as "Leaders of Tomorrow." Four patterns of development emerged from this small group: full-time homemaking, in which half of the women were engaged; traditional female occupations, another quarter; dual career couples, only a few; and single professional career women, also just a few.

The third chapter explores the lives and goals of the gifted women twenty years after graduation. A much more complex categorization was now needed, for while some women had continued as before, others had radically transformed their lives; and a new group had emerged, the "overwhelmed," who were having difficulty with the most basic issues of survival and sanity.

As a way of understanding the critical events which can lead to being either satisfied and actualized or overwhelmed, the lives of eminent women are examined in Chapter Four, for such women's stories often reveal more than formal research can about the ways women find fulfillment and surmount barriers to achievement. The information in this chapter has often been controversial, simply because eminence has so frequently been a male-defined category with male-defined attributes. Rather than focusing upon women who simply achieved high honors and recognition, I chose those who seem to have fulfilled their own dreams and goals. I limited myself to names we recognize, yet there are thousands of women who have fulfilled dreams and actualized talents in obscurity. Some of their accomplishments, like Emily Dickenson's posthumously-discovered poems, are yet to be known. Others' work shines through a world more beautiful, more humane, more understandable, thanks to their quiet persistence.

The nine eminent women chosen are Marie Curie, Eleanor Roosevelt, Georgia O'Keeffe, Margaret Mead, Gertrude Stein, Maya Angelou, Beverly Sills, Katherine Hepburn and Rigoberta Menchu, from whose life stories we can derive important principles for guiding gifted girls. Some emerging ideas are the importance of time alone, the effects of feeling "different," and the role of individualized instruction, childhood mentoring, and same-sex educational experiences. We can see also that guidance and encouragement during difficult adolescence are clearly of critical importance. What furthermore is apparent in these women's lives are the determined refusal to acknowledge limitations of gender, an ability to combine roles, a strong sense of one's personal identity, taking responsibility for oneself, and a mission in life.

Chapters Five through Nine explore the major scientific studies on the girlhood, adolescence, college years and adult lives of gifted women. The famous long-range study of the lives of gifted individuals from childhood to old age by Lewis Terman yielded proportions of women in homemaking, traditional occupations, and professional careers surprisingly similar to proportions found in my study of my classmates. Not much difference was found in the patterns of women born in 1912 or in 1952. Society's most highly gifted Presidential Scholars of 1964-1968 were studied by Felice Kaufmann, confirming these women to be accomplished in their crafts but poorly paid. A third research project shows high-potential women lagging behind high-potential men in career achievement; marriage and childbirth prompt them to defer or drop their own goals, with long-term economic disadvantages. A study of bright students at a private school for girls shows them losing confidence in their opinions. A new, long-term study of Illinois' valedictorians by Arnold and Denney reveals frightening changes in women's perceptions of their own intelligence. An ethnographic study by Holland and Eisenhart identifies the "culture of romance" as a major cause of bright women's loss of confidence. Two different research projects emphasize that gifted women seek both love and achievement, which can be integrated in a lifestyle combining family and career, but the task is not easy, nor the path self-evident. More recent studies, like my own twenty-year follow-up, show a picture of gifted girls and women that is even more complex than that of a decade ago. For instance, gifted girls today have higher career goals and less math anxiety than they did ten years ago: a research project I conducted with Nicholas Colangelo, examining career goals of all juniors and seniors in the United States taking the ACT, found that as many gifted girls aspired to careers in law, medicine, and business as gifted boys. Another new understanding, emerging from studies of women who are in competition with and in groups including men, is that these women have less fear of success and less of a tendency to comply with men's ideas and opinions than when studies were first performed in the late eighties. However, many gifted women continue to struggle with waning belief in their abilities, with the need to submerge intellectual goals in the "culture of romance," and most alarming, with a lack of a sense of purpose.

Chapter Ten describes the barriers to accomplishment which still must be overcome by gifted girls and women. First, girls continue to receive a second-class education compared to boys, who are called on three times more often by teachers and receive more informative responses. Most of the characters in children's literature and other media used in the schools are boys. Bright girls continue to take less rigorous coursework than bright boys. Second, a loss of self-esteem and confidence seems to be the fate of most girls in adolescence, according to the Gilligan study and a national survey by the American Association for University Women. Third, the American coeducational colleges and universities remain a chilly, if not hostile, environment for the intellectual and career development of young women. Holland and Eisenhart, in their devastating portrait of women on two college campuses, blame the "Culture of Romance," a system of intense social pressure which channels women's energies almost entirely in the direction of pursuing and maintaining relationships with men. Fourth, despite the addition of a great many women in the professional workplace, sexual harassment and sex discrimination continue to be experienced by even the brightest and most competent women in their fields.

Finally, what is most alarming to me is that many of today's young women who have learned to name high-level career aspirations, to dress for success, and to put together a slick resume have not learned the deeper lesson of the women's movement: that women can find meaning through their work. Bright young women, despite their choice of ambitious goals, may lack a real commitment to those goals. When faced with barriers to achievement, they may falter because they do not have a sense of purpose and identity associated with their choice of work. These deficits are subtle and difficult to recognize, as are the negative expectancies and fears harbored by many bright women. Several theories which seek to explain women's difficulties with achievement—the Fear of Success (or Horner Effect), the Cinderella Complex, the Imposter Phenomenon, and Gilligan's theory of women's moral development—are described in this chapter, along with current thinking about these theories. Paradoxically, gifted women may also be at a disadvantage because they can adjust so well! Their adept coping may be more of a factor in their accepting lower status careers and salaries than any particular syndrome or complex, so this chapter includes my own theory that gifted women may be too "well-adjusted" for their own good.

In the years following the publication of *Smart Girls, Gifted Women*, many events in education, in our society, and in the lives of my classmates and myself came together to add to my knowledge of gifted women and to alter my perspective. First, coinciding with the release of my book, there was a small explosion in the literature of gifted education, and new ideas emerged about the nature of giftedness. An exciting new theory for me was Howard Gardner's Theory of Multiple Intelligences—I stalked him at the

American Psychological Association to insist that he discuss the implications for women! In *Frames of Mind, The Theory of Multiple Intelligences,* Gardner presented persuasive evidence that there are at least seven separate intelligences: linguistic, mathematical-logical, spatial-visual, kinesthetic, musical, and two forms of "personal" intelligence. Gardner's theory opened up whole new ways of understanding how different talents develop, and how personality and talent interact. Chapter Eleven, on girls and women with specific talents, reflects this new approach to giftedness.

Another great change in our understanding of gifts and talents comes from the wave of multiculturalism in gifted education, which has led us to the treasure trove of talent among our nation's minority children. A series of studies I conducted with my colleague, Nicholas Colangelo, of academically talented minority students, as well as my clinical experiences in that most diverse of states, Arizona, led to Chapter Twelve on gifted minority girls and women.

The last decade abounded with new books and articles on guiding and educating bright students, and, even more exciting to me, many new works on gifted girls and women appeared. I read avidly the research of Constance Hollinger and her colleague, Elyse Fleming, whose series of studies on the career development of gifted girls clarified the skills bright girls need to set goals and stick to them. From Linda Silverman, a clinical psychologist who had tested and counseled hundreds of bright girls, I learned about the absolute importance of early identification and guidance. Carol Gilligan's *In a Different Voice* and her longitudinal work on girl's psychological development, while not specifically about gifted girls, confirmed observations I had made in my own studies: first, that girls made many of their most important life decisions based on relationships rather than upon particular principles and goals; and second, that the years between 11 and 17 are, for girls, a time of declining self-esteem and confidence. Although I disagreed with some of Gilligan's conclusions, her work influenced many of my ideas about guiding adolescent gifted girls. The writings of Kate Noble, Deidre Lovecky, and Jane Piirto about gifted adult women taught me about the critical events which seem to determine whether women will lead or follow, achieve or fail.

The International Conference on Girls, Women, and Giftedness at Lethbridge, Alberta, Canada, in the spring of 1987, was a peak experience for many of us who attended. In that mysterious and isolated landscape of vast prairie canyons called "coulees," we hiked, debated, dined, and discussed for four days. Although it cannot re-create the excitement of those days, the book of proceedings edited by the organizers, Julie Ellis and John Willinsky, does convey the wealth of knowledge gained there.

All of these advances—in society, in the psychology of giftedness, in the psychology of women—influenced the chapter called "Is Self-Actualization Optional?", which represents most clearly the transformation in my understanding of the development of talent in women. Since the publication of *Smart Girls, Gifted Women*, I have been torn between the ideas of cultural feminism (that women have a different culture and different goals than men) and equity feminism (that women should strive for the right and the responsibility to achieve the same goals as men). It has taken me ten years to find a synthesis that makes sense for me, and, I hope, for gifted women. I have come to believe, however, that although women's socialization and education do indeed shape them to be more concerned with connectedness and intimacy, that gifted women still bear the responsibility for actualizing their talents. It is not an either/or world, and women do not have to choose between vocation and intimacy. A woman's vocation can provide, at the ultimate stage of personal development, a source of healing and connectedness for all of society, as well as for those she loves. The thesis of this chapter is that the rarer a woman's gift, the greater her responsibility to actualize that gift. Discovering the exact nature and degree of giftedness becomes crucial to understanding the individual's and society's responsibilities for education, guidance, and use of talent.

And with that understanding, the problem of guiding gifted girls becomes much more subtle, for we know that it is not enough simply to raise the aspirations of gifted girls: it is necessary also to help those whose aspirations are already high to be more deeply committed to those dreams. Rather than simply providing gifted girls with excellent role models of women who are engineers and doctors, it is necessary to provide models of women who are passionate about their work. Rather than helping them to live with inequitable educational practices, it is necessary to teach them to demand equality in the classroom and to create equality in their own families.

The new material in the last three chapters not only incorporates the new knowledge on gifted girls and women; it also includes guidance strategies which will help prepare gifted girls for life in the next century. Described are practical programs for gifted girls that have had an impact on math anxiety, inadequate career aspirations, and low self-esteem. A few of the more recent workshops discussed here were based on findings and suggestions presented in *Smart Girls, Gifted Women*. Finally, there are specific suggestions for parents of gifted girls and for gifted women, and a set of guidelines for helping gifted girls "from preschool to professional school"—or to anywhere else that their sense of mission and meaning might take them.

As a psychologist, I have chosen the study of giftedness as my particular mission. My conviction is that people are happiest when they are pushing the limits of personal potential. Freud said the healthy individual is the one who is able to love and to work. In *Smart Girls (Revised Edition)—A New Psychology of Girls, Women and Giftedness* I want to show once again the limitless challenges and opportunities for bright women to work arduously, to love deeply, and to live fully.

References

Colangelo, N., and Zaffran, T. T., Eds. *New Voices in Counseling the Gifted.* Dubuque, Iowa: Kendall/Hunt, 1979.

Ellis, J. L. & Willinsky, J. M. *Girls, women, and giftedness.* Monroe, NY: Trillium Press, 1990.

Kerr, B. A., & Colangelo, N. "The college plans of academic talented students." In *Journal of Counseling and Development 66*, 9: 366-370, 1988.

Noble, K. D. "Counseling gifted women: Becoming the heroes of our own stories." In *Journal for the Education of the Gifted, 12*, 2: 131-141, 1989.

Piirto, J. "Encouraging Creativity and Talent in Adolescents." In J. Genshaft & M. Bircley (Eds.), *The gifted adolescent: Personal and educational issues.* Teachers College Press, 1991.

Silverman, L. K. "What happens to the gifted girl?" In C. J. Maker (Ed.), *Critical Issues in Gifted Education: Programs for the Gifted.* Rockville, MD: Aspen, 1986.

Chapter 1

The Leaders of Tomorrow: A Retelling

I knew only two of the other girls who were to be my classmates, and both had been a half-grade ahead of me at my old school. The taller, five feet at age ten, was Mary Barker; the other, Gina Pasquale. I had often admired Mary on the playground because she was the best softball player in school. She also won all-city prizes in track. And smart! I'd seen her give accurate, instant answers to intricate math problems that other girls had spent hours huddled over in the bathroom, trying desperately to solve before handing in their papers. Sometimes Mary would only help others with homework for money. She had a side that was unscrupulous and fearless, and despite her tender age, her almost insatiable appetite for makeup and earrings required money. Nobody could believe her mother allowed her to use lipstick and wear earrings, but no one would deny that she looked good. The shirtwaist, the long blunt-cut auburn hair, the skeptical brown eyes all made her look mature and intimidatingly attractive.

Gina was so completely opposite in character and values that the two seemed destined to despise one another. A little overweight,

1

heavy-featured and curly-haired, Gina didn't care what she wore, as long as her clothes were neat. For her first day at "gifted school" her parents had given her a genuine leather briefcase for carrying her prized books. Gina, in everybody's opinion, was some kind of genius. She didn't have Mary's facile, smart-aleck intelligence, but her intellect was deep, bottomless, almost weird. Information about everything just floated to the top of her brain whenever she needed it. She had taught herself algebra. She typed long, footnoted essays when a hand-written short composition would have sufficed. When she talked, she sounded forty years old. Mostly, Gina was reserved and distant, yet quick to explode with biting comebacks. Ready to detect any insult, Gina instantly retaliated as though to protect herself from the cruelty so often showered upon plain children by their peers. She terrified me, and I looked away whenever her small, critical eyes examined me appraisingly.

Mary, always one to enjoy combat, stood with Gina that first morning trying to engage her in conversation, inviting me to join in with a generous "Come on over here, Shrimp." Dutifully, as always, I obeyed Big Mary. I would rather have stayed back, though, near another girl who had politely introduced herself as Linda Martin from Norton school.

Linda seemed nice. She talked easily to me about her poodle, Charlie. Her pixie haircut was darling—just what I wanted—and she wore a plaid jumper and new Hushpuppies. She carried a shiny red plaid satchel, but what I envied most of all was her Barbie lunchbox, with containers and compartments for everything. That morning, she seemed the perfect girl: petite, and neither ostentatious nor shy. She was probably really smart, but she didn't like act it, and that of course was good. She was showing me the inside of her lunchbox when the bus came (by which time Mary and Gina were trading insults: "Jerk!" "Barbarian!") and we all scrambled aboard.

The fourth girl at the bus stop that day, I was small, anxious, and eager to please. Sometimes, if I knew the people I was with, I could show off a little. I could think up and write imaginative stories, and I was reasonably good at school work, but looking around me on the bus that morning I felt terribly average—or even below-average. As I admired Mary's determined strength, Gina's uncanny brilliance, and Linda's neat perfection, I began to fear that the people who had scored my entrance exams had made an awful mistake.

The bus took us out of our neighborhood, with its closely-packed brick houses, into a lovely, spacious St. Louis Hills area. Our

2

new school, on the corner of a large park, was a modern, one-story building with tinted windows and spotless entranceways—a far cry from the littered, gloomy schools we had come from.

We took our seats in the fifth-grade classroom, where even our odd-looking desks were new. The teacher, Miss Mary O'Malley, was a small, square-shouldered woman with short, tightly curled red hair. I had already heard about her: the school principal had told my parents that Miss O'Malley was the best teacher in the district, and that's why she had the task of teaching the new class of gifted students. Even the teachers here had been required to take intelligence tests, parents were told, and Miss O'Malley had scored very highly.

She introduced herself and asked us to do the same. There were thirty of us, fifteen boys and fifteen girls. I was surprised to see how tall most of my classmates were. All were Caucasian except for one Japanese-American girl, and most wore new and stylish clothes. (As it turned out, there was a black gifted program in another part of the city, of which we knew nothing. But that's another story.) We came from eight different elementary schools in St. Louis, and almost every one of us knew at least one other person. The impulse to sit near acquaintances was already defeated by a seating system devised by the teacher and based on some unknown principle.

After introductions, Miss O'Malley said, "Now, I expect that you will get to know one another at recess. There will be little time for socializing in the classroom. Today we are going to plunge right into our studies and then have a little talk at the end of the day. You will all be accelerated by at least one grade, some of you by a grade-and-a-half or two because we are confident of your ability to perform at a higher level than your age peers. In addition to studying most subjects a year earlier than you normally would, you will be trained in special subjects you did not have at your old school: French, pre-algebra, rapid reading, and choral reading. You will have more homework than you have ever had before, an average of three hours each week night, with two nights' homework on the weekends. You will have to work very, very hard, and I will accept no excuses other than illness for unfinished homework. If you receive failing grades on your tests and do not perform your homework well, you will be removed from these classes and sent back to your original school. While you are here, you will sit in rows according to your academic performance. We will rearrange the seating every two weeks to reflect changes in your test scores and your oral recitation. Now we will pass out the books."

3

Mute with anxiety, I received my books and carefully wrote my name on the inside cover, as directed. First, an English book, the regular sixth-grade text for spelling and vocabulary. I'd already seen it and decided it wasn't hard. Besides, this was my best subject, and it would be fun not to be bored (for surely these classes would never be boring). Then came the geography book: Europe and the Middle East. Wait a minute, I thought. What about South America and Africa, which were done in fourth and fifth grade? Wasn't I going to study them? How was I supposed to know about those countries if I just skipped over them? Would I have to catch up by getting books from the library? Before I could even clearly form these questions, the math book appeared. Figuring square roots! Again I cringed. I hadn't even gotten through the long division! How was I going to learn this? By the time an abacus was circulated (for figuring math?), along with a French book filled with line drawings and assorted gibberish, my heart had sunk completely.

The morning's lessons began. First, an English assignment: analyze and diagram twenty-five sentences. Next, twenty-five review problems in math. Then French, and a different teacher. Madame Bem, a huge young woman with tiny curls, bounded into the room exclaiming, "Bonjour, mes enfants! Je suis enchantée de faire votre connaissance. Nous parlons seulement Francais, et pas de tout Anglais!" My relief at having an hour with a teacher who was warmer and kinder than Miss O'Malley was tempered by Madame Bem's refusal to speak any English whatsoever. We had to guess that she was greeting us, that she was asking our names, that we were supposed to reply. I hurriedly wrote on a card the phonetic pronunciation of what we were being asked to say—"Ju mop pell Barbara"—and waited for my turn to struggle with the strange sounds and to be corrected, gently but repeatedly.

After the French lesson, we were released to go to lunch. In the new, sterile cafeteria, I missed the smell of tennis shoes, baloney, and old cork floors. I wanted to stay with the few girls I knew, but Mary gulped down her food, grabbed a baseball bat and ball, and left to organize a quick game. Gina had brought one of her books and just scowled at me when I tried to start a conversation. Linda went to sit with the girls who had very neat lunchboxes and pretty dresses. So I spent that first lunch hour observing the girls and boys with whom I would spend the next eight years—if I made it.

The boys seemed more confident and less intimidated by the new school than the girls did. In fact, the morning's lessons had clearly caused some real anxiety for several girls. Molly was nause-ated, and Christy kept wetting the ends of her long hair and twisting them into knots. Little Kathy Nakomura's fingers had trembled in concentration over her work. Even dauntless Mary had twisted her mouth in resentment as assignments were piled on. At lunch the girls who knew one another whispered about the morning in tense indignation and puzzlement. The boys, however, were very lively and excited, not at all preoccupied with the morning's events. It seemed to me that they ought to be showing some effects other than boisterous delight after such a miserably difficult beginning. Could it be that they somehow liked the challenge? Could the same events that caused self-doubt among girls actually spur the boys on to self-affirming competitiveness?

After lunch we had "choral reading," during which we recited poetry in unison, with exaggeratedly precise pronunciation and inflec-tion. "Hot cross buns," we chanted vigorously, and "bells, bells, bells, bells, bells, bells, bells . . ." we repeated emphatically. It was strange but not difficult. After choral reading a Mr. Peel taught the art lesson, lecturing on tapestries and instructing us to create a design for an attractive tapestry. We labored with our colored pencils as he strolled among us. When we had finished, he examined each drawing and flamboyantly tore several in half, exclaiming that they were too sym-metrical and that those kinds of designs quickly became boring. He was intensely and vocally critical of most of our work. Nearly all of us had to redesign our tapestry at least once. What might have been a pleasant lesson was soured by his cutting remarks. He came down hardest on Linda: "Boring! Ordinary! You've simply copied your neighbor, haven't you?" Quickly turning, he profusely praised Richard's underwater scene and laughed at Eddie's "Aliens Eating Their Lunch." He patted Eddie on the back and said, "Good idea! Try to be neater."

For our last lesson that day we had another guest teacher, a "reading specialist" named Mrs. Coffey. She told us that President Kennedy was a rapid reader, able to read five newspapers in the time it took most people to read one. Scientists, she said, needed to read great numbers of books and articles just to find a few needed facts, making rapid reading a necessity. She then turned on her tachis-toscope, a projector that showed one phrase or sentence at a time at a speed controlled by Mrs. Coffey. In order to find our basal reading rate, we were to read as fast as we could, while Mrs. Coffey set the pacer faster and faster. We were to raise our hands when we could no longer read the sentences, which told a story, and our comprehension would be tested afterwards.

We started at 150 words per minute, which seemed rather unnatural and crawly. Nobody raised a hand until the speed reached 250 words per minute; a few hands went up and more followed with each change in speed. I dropped out soon, no longer able even to bluff my way through the coming quiz. Faster and faster the words flew on the screen, until at last, at some eerie pace like 750 words per minute, Gina put up her hand in sullen resignation.

This exercise ended the coursework for the day. Miss O'Malley reviewed our assignments for the next day and then gave us The Little Talk:

> *"Boys and girls, for many of you this has been the most difficult school day you've ever had. You will have many more difficult days. In two years you will be doing high school work. In tenth grade you will do college work. By the time you are in college, you will be able to take advanced courses that will help you to enter your careers.*
>
> *"You were chosen for this program because you are gifted. What does being gifted mean? It does not just mean that you scored 140 or higher on an I.Q. test. It means that each of you has a special gift—yes, a gift from God—of intelligence. Because it is a gift, you must use it well. You must use it to serve your country. For many years the Russians have been training their young people in science and mathematics. Because of their gifted young scientists, they now are ahead of us, for they were able to achieve space flight before we did. The free world must catch up with the Communists. To do this we need many fine scientists and leaders. You must study very hard, not for yourselves but for your family, your school, and your country.*
>
> *"You will have the best books, the best teachers, the most up-to-date curricula—in short, the finest education our country can provide. In return, you are asked to give your best efforts and to commit yourself completely to your education. You are the hope of our nation and the pride of our schools. You are the leaders of tomorrow."*

The boys beamed. The girls looked at their folded hands, embarrassed.

Eighteen years later, soon after I had taken my first position as an assistant professor of educational psychology, I received an invitation to our high school reunion, which was to include the students from our special classes from fifth grade on as well as another group of gifted students who had joined us in high school. Although I had lost track of my classmates after graduation, rumors did reach me: Mandy and Debbie "had to get married" soon after high school graduation. The same fate, I learned, had also befallen Jennie, but no baby turned up after her unexpected marriage. So at least three of the fifteen girls were married in their late teens. To my knowledge, none of the boys had married so young. Word had it that my old boyfriend Eddie was a doctor and that Mike was a lawyer. Jerry had followed his brilliant brother into the foreign service. As for Mary and Gina, I didn't quite believe the things I heard—something about Mary's sanity, and something else about Gina leaving her Ivy League school after an "unhappy experience."

Even though I might already have spotted a pattern in these rumored events, I didn't. I was saddened and worried by some, amused by others. My overwhelming feeling about the reunion was embarrassment for myself. I was certain that the majority of my gifted classmates would have become scientists and leaders of their communities. After all, that had been the goal of our training, which by this time I recognized as exemplary and rare. Generally, only about one-half of gifted children receive any special classes, and some programs are no more than a few hours a week of "enrichment activities," often not very challenging. Our curriculum had been the exception: one that provided a full-time series of challenging academic activities led by trained educators of the gifted. Since I knew from whence I had come, I was ashamed to have entered the "soft" science of psychology. Compared to the lofty careers I imagined for my classmates, psychology seemed frivolous. So with some trepidation I accepted the invitation and prepared to make the best of it.

The reunion was in the same hotel that we'd rented for our prom. Then, it had been a high school senior's notion of elegance, but ten years later, it seemed corny, tacky, a "Starlite Dome" penthouse lounge with too much Atomic Age decor. The summer night was hot, the air conditioning didn't work, and the place was packed. My classmates, the "Track I-A" students (our little group had grown in high school with the addition of students from other districts) were

44 of this class of 630. About two-thirds of the class had returned for the reunion, and the gifted group was well-represented.

At the door I was greeted by the organizers, all three of whom were members of the original, elementary school gifted class: Eddie the doctor, Mike the lawyer, and Jeff the well-to-do businessman. Replying warmly to each in turn, I said that yes, I was married; I was a psychologist; my husband was a psychologist; and no, we had no children yet. Clutching the reunion booklet titled "Where Are They Now?" I then was swept up in a wave of vaguely familiar faces.

In that sea of acquaintances, I found my old friends. First I saw Linda. She was seated at a banquet table, and I could see that she was pregnant. She wore a lacy, pastel maternity blouse; her hair was held loosely back by pink ribbons. She blushed and patted her tummy frequently. Surrounded by other women who seemed, from their gestures, to be comparing pregnancies, she was as popular as ever. As I walked over, I recognized those around her: Kathy, the math wizard; Molly, who'd been the high school newspaper editor as well as a talented singer; and Sherry, a timid and nervous perfectionist who had excelled in French and had taken private Chinese lessons. Linda gave me a pleased squeal of recognition. "How are you? As you can see, I'm expecting! What about you? No? Well! Kathy has two, a boy and a girl, and Molly has a little girl, and Sherry thinks she's expecting." At this everyone laughed. I said that I certainly hoped to have children, but that I wanted to wait until my career was established. "Well, don't wait too long! Hey—sit with us!" I sat down.

It was not the conversation I had expected, though upon reflection, I found it normal enough. In fact, that was the problem: it was *quite* normal. I consulted my booklet under each name. Linda Ackerman: first-grade teacher, retiring now to have a baby, married to Marty Kellerman. Kathy Brown: high school math teacher for the Army, married to Bob Worcester, an Army aerospace engineer (oh, no, I groaned, she married him). Molly Schuster: degree in journalism from University of Missouri, not working at the present time, married to Rick Hanowitz. Sherry Speth: homemaker and volunteer, married to Nick Martin, director of Christian Youth Choir. The entries were not at all what I had expected of gifted women.

At the sight of a tall figure in a flowing white evening gown, I stopped reading. Big Mary had crossed over to my table. "Kerr, a bunch of us want to talk to you." I followed her to some overstuffed chairs near the bar where most of the old volleyball team was seated.

Big, strong, eager girls, they had hung around with Mary throughout high school.

"Kerr, we have a question for you. You're a psychologist, right?"

"Right . . ."

"OK. Well, I'm currently trying to get employed. Hard to get a good job when you've been through what I have. Jeri clerks at the bank. Lori is a nurse. Nan—what are you doing? Oh yeah, she's back in the community college. OK. What I want to know is this: why aren't we the leaders of tomorrow?"

"I don't know—there's sexism, discrimination . . ."

"No, that's not what I mean. I want to know, if we're so smart, why didn't wonderful things happen to us? We want you to find out." Suddenly, Gina was there, too, fixing me in my tracks with her intelligent eyes. *"Mary's right. You're a psychologist. You should be able to study us."*

"Well, that's not my area of research—"

"Kerr! Make it your area, OK? Mary almost shouted. *Look at us! You think it's not important that we're a bunch of has-beens at age 29? Find out what happened."*

I had always done what Big Mary told me to do. This time was no exception.

After the reunion, I went back to the University of Nebraska's educational psychology department and changed my area of research to the career development of gifted and talented. I read every book and article I could find in the field of guiding gifted and talented people of all ages. I read all of the works of Lewis Terman, the "father of gifted education," who traced the lives of gifted children from age 11 through adulthood, as well as the works of Leta Hollingworth, the "mother of gifted education," who wrote about the education and guidance of the highly gifted. Several newer books pointed to an awakening interest in the social, emotional, and career concerns of gifted children; among them was *Guiding the Gifted Child*, by Webb, Meckstroth, and Tolan (1982), which described major problems of the gifted and gave parents and teachers specific strategies to help these children.

Most of the authors were emphatic on one point: that the gifted child will not always "get by" without guidance. Intelligence alone doesn't guarantee a life of smooth sailing. Many authors described the conflicts gifted children experience as a result of unrealistic expectations of others or of themselves. Others delved into the peer relations and social isolation of the gifted child and explored the many strategies gifted children use to cope with being different. All of the authors deplored the lack of knowledge about the complex development of the gifted child, and all pleaded for more research to help in understanding these complexities.

Once I had reviewed books and articles on gifted students, I began reviewing the literature on gifted women, a process that was unexpectedly difficult. Fortunately, I was preceded in my interest in gifted girls by Lynn Fox (Fox, Tobin, & Brody, 1981) at Johns Hopkins University, who was doing important work in career education of mathematically precocious girls in the program developed by Julian Stanley (Stanley, George, & Solano, 1977). Constance Hollinger and Elyse Fleming (1984) had developed a model guidance program for academically talented girls. I wanted not only to learn about what had happened to my classmates, but also to contribute new knowledge through research. Within a month of the reunion, I had designed and mailed a questionnaire to each of the female graduates of my high school's Accelerated Learning Program.

To work with the career development issues affecting gifted young women, I created the Guidance Laboratory for Gifted and Talented at the University of Nebraska. Here, my staff and I could counsel and provide career guidance to gifted adolescents throughout the school year. While learning of their plans and dreams, we could observe their progress toward achievement. We compared girls' and boys' reactions to counselors' questions, and devised interventions that would encourage girls and boys equally in their aspirations. We extended the program to counseling adults, enabling us to study the striking differences in career development of gifted women and gifted men. I used the literature on gifted as well as my own observations in the counseling laboratory to understand the results of my own study. Now, I thought, it might be possible to understand what had happened to the Leaders of Tomorrow.

References

Fox, L. H.; Tobin, D.; and Brody, L. "Career Development of Gifted and Talented Women." In *Journal of Career Education*, 7, 289-298, 1981.

Hollinger, C. L. & Fleming, E. S. "Internal Barriers to the Realization of Potential: Correlates and Interrelationships Among Gifted and Talented Female Adolescents." In *Journal of Youth and Adolescence*, 14, 389-399, 1984.

Stanley, J. C.; George, W. C.; and Solano, C. H. *The Gifted and the Creative: A Fifty-Year Perspective.* Baltimore: The Johns Hopkins University Press, 1977.

Webb, J. T.; Meckstroth, E. A.; and Tolan, S. S. *Guiding the Gifted Child: A Practical Source for Parents and Teachers.* Scottsdale: Gifted Psychology Publishing, 1982.

Chapter 2

Looking for the Leaders of Tomorrow

Developing a fifteen-minute questionnaire that illuminates eighteen years of career development and personal adjustment is no easy task. The newly established Guidance Laboratory for Gifted and Talented ultimately sent only ten carefully selected questions, but plenty of writing space (see FIG. 1). Certain demographics were important: college attended, marital/family status, current location, and employment. More importantly, though, we wanted to know how these gifted women saw themselves, their development, career goals, attainments, and life satisfactions.

To start with, I wanted to understand how parents reacted to their daughter's identification as gifted, so I asked, "What did your parents tell you about participation in the Accelerated Learning Program?" The teachers in the students' original schools surely influenced the girls' perceptions of their giftedness, so I also asked, "What did your teachers tell you?"

Memory records our life experiences inaccurately: we recall the joys of childhood, but tend to alter actual events—as do our parents—to fit with our current world view and self-concept. Thus do we all mend and polish our past until each of us has a "Story of My Life" that can be narrated as a fairly coherent series of events linked by recurring themes. Every psychotherapist knows that this story, this worldview, profoundly affects how we behave on a daily basis and how we make decisions. In fact, our current perceptions of our life events, more than the events themselves, shape actions and reactions. Knowing this, I constructed my questions to reveal how my classmates explained to themselves what being gifted had meant to them.

To find out how the women thought their career goals had been shaped, I asked, "What were your career or life goals at graduation from eighth grade, from high school, and from college?" Also, I asked, "What is your current career goal?" with extra space for explanations.

- *What did your parents tell you about participation in the Accelerated Learning Program?*
- *What did your teachers tell you?*
- *What were your career goals at*
- *. . .graduation from eight grade?*
- *. . .graduation from high school?*
- *. . .graduation from college?*
- *What is your current career goal?*
- *How has your marriage history affected your career goals?*
- *How has the birth of children affected your career goals?*
- *What positive effects did the Accelerated Learning Program have on your life?*
- *What negative effects did the Accelerated Learning Program have on your life?*
- *In order to qualify for the Accelerated Learning Program, you scored in the upper 5 percent on I.Q. tests and achievement tests, a category generally referred to as "gifted." How do you feel about this label? What impact, if any, has this label had on you?*
- *Are you happy?*
- *What would you change, if anything, if you had to live your life over again?*

FIG. 1. The Survey of Gifted Women

Career development studies tell us that general career interests for average students change from junior high to senior high to college, but become more stable after about age sixteen. Gifted students show less stability in their interest patterns, and this can be attributed to their multipotentiality—their ability to select and develop any number of career goals (Kerr, 1991; Sanborn et al., 1976). Confronted with an abundance of options, gifted students may vacillate and dabble, fearing to commit themselves to one career. I suspected that the career development of gifted girls might be even more complex, reflecting indecision and abrupt change uncharacteristic of their male peers.

Hoping not to "lead the witness" too much, I asked, "How has your marriage history affected your career goals?" and "How has the birth of children affected your career goals?" Marriage and childbirth traditionally have a major impact on a woman's career development, far more than they do for men. How had their special education in a school for the gifted affected them? We asked straightforwardly, "What positive effects did the Accelerated Learning Program have on your life?" and "What negative effects?"

Surely their rigorous education had made a difference in the lives of these women, leading to lifestyles shaped by their intensive elementary and secondary education. Thus, noting that every student in the Accelerated Learning Program was required to score in the upper 5 percent on I.Q. and achievement tests, one question was "How do you feel about this 'gifted' label, and what impact, if any, has this label had on you?"

Finally, we asked about life satisfaction: "Are you happy?" "What would you change, if anything, if you had to live your life over again?"

In developing a survey for my women classmates, I had no intention of generalizing the results to all gifted women. I was only interested in this group of gifted women—women who had experienced a "model" education and who had graduated from high school at the beginning of the upsurge of feminism. I wanted to know why superb schooling in the late 1950s and the heightened awareness of women's potential in the late 1960s did not produce women of greater accomplishment. I mailed twenty-five surveys and received eighteen in return; four other classmates were briefly interviewed by phone, and partial information was gleaned from reunion booklets on two more. These replies, I felt, would explain the surprising career and life development of my classmates. I did not know what would later become evident: that the patterns displayed by my gifted friends appeared again and again in other studies of gifted women.

The content of the survey responses was fascinating, though at first I enjoyed reading simply for style and format. Half the women wrote long accompanying letters, and most interview responses were quite lengthy. Clearly our questions had stimulated significant reflection.

The responses were not only long, they were complex. Feelings were explored frankly; the answers made it plain that the survey itself was leading to new awarenesses. There were intuitive explanations of the motivations of self and others. My one-time classmates eloquently discussed value issues, constructing both sides of a particular conflict fairly and thoroughly before working through to some statement of resolution. All responses displayed extraordinary literacy and sharp, discerning wit. The style of the survey responses confirmed that the promise of youth was fulfilled, at least in the sense that this bright group of females had matured into articulate, psychologically sophisticated, knowledgeable members of society. The accompanying letters made delightful reading. As I read them over and over, I pictured the little girls I had known, now grown into thoughtful, fascinating women. Their responses typified the manner of expression of leaders and thinkers. The actual content of the surveys, therefore, was all the more surprising.

Basic Facts

Six of the twenty-four women who gave information about their education had not earned their bachelor's degrees by age twenty-nine. Twelve had received only bachelor's degrees; half of these were in education. Three had earned master's degrees (one in zoology, one in education, one in pre-dentistry). Among us were one medical degree and one law degree.

WOMEN			MEN		
HIGHEST DEGREE		CAREER STATUS	HIGHEST DEGREE		CAREER STATUS
J.D.	Law	Lawyer	J.D.		Attorney
M.D.	Medicine	Physician	Ph.D.		Ethnobotanist
M.S.	Zoology	Homemaker	Ph.D.		Chem. Engineer

16

WOMEN			MEN	
HIGHEST DEGREE	CAREER STATUS		HIGHEST DEGREE	CAREER STATUS
M.A.	Education	Schoolteacher	J.D.	Lawyer
M.A.	Dentistry	Grad. assistant	M.D.	Physician
M.A.	History	Teaching assistant	M.H.A.	Hospital administrator
B.S.	English	Homemaker	B.A.	News director
B.S.	Education	Schoolteacher	M.S. Eng.	Engineer manager
B.S.	Education	Homemaker	B.A.	Cellist
B.A.	Music	Homemaker	B.S.+B.A.	CPA
B.A.	Business	Account representative	B.A.	Personnel officer
B.A.	Education	Schoolteacher	B.S.	Actuary
B.A.		Insurance agent	B.B.A.	Manager
B.A.	Journalism	Homemaker	B.S.	Elect. engineer
B.S.	Education	Homemaker	B.B.A.	Business
B.A.	Education	Schoolteacher		
B.S.	Med Technology	Physician's assistant		
H.S.		Homemaker/clerk		
H.S.		Dental assistant		
H.S.		Craftsperson		
H.S.		Auditor		
H.S.	+ L.P.N.	Homemaker		
H.S.		Craftsperson		

FIG. 2. Educational and Career Attainments of Students in the Accelerated Learning Program

Basic information on fifteen of the twenty men who had graduated from the Accelerated Learning Program that year allowed us to compare educational attainment. All had received at least a bachelor's degree. In addition, these men held three master's degrees (two in business administration and one in anthropology), two Ph.D.s (botany and chemical engineering), two J.D.s, and one M.D. The educational attainment of these men was clearly superior to that of their female classmates.

The trend of less achievement for women became more pronounced as we examined information about current occupational status. The largest number of women were homemakers. Eight of the twenty-four women were at home, usually with children. Four were employed as nurses or medical technicians, and four as teachers. Two listed craftsperson and arts and crafts as their occupations. Two were graduate assistants. Representing the higher degrees, one woman was a practicing physician and one a lawyer, and two were businesswomen.

In contrast, all of the men were in professional or semiprofessional occupations. FIG. 2 shows six business/management personnel, three engineers, two lawyers, one doctor, one news director, one musician (cellist) and one ethnobotanist. None was unemployed.

Over half of the men and women had stayed fairly close to home or had returned to St. Louis. Fourteen of the twenty-four women were married at that time, eight were single, and two were divorced. Of the fifteen men, eleven were married, and the other four had never been married.

Denial of Giftedness

A particularly curious finding of our survey was that most of the women preferred to deny that they were gifted or special in any way. Though identified amid much publicity as gifted, and schooled for years in classes and tracks clearly labeled as being for the gifted, these women still repudiated the label.

"I have never really believed I was gifted," said Linda.
"I think it was all a mistake!"

The more scholarly response of a teacher with some advanced training in testing and measurement was, "It's a well-known fact that I.Q. tests are inappropriate measures of intelligence; they mean nothing." Another said, "I don't believe in treating intelligent children differently—neither did my parents." "I can't remember any big 'to do.'"

Several seemed simply to have ignored or forgotten: "I guess I've never thought much about it." "I forgot about the label." "I don't think I've ever known what 'gifted' meant, and so I didn't pay much attention."

One acknowledged a certain fear: "You know, I think I was so afraid of the idea of being gifted that as soon as I got away from that crowd by attending college, I felt very relieved, as if the pressure was off and I could just be normal."

The most ironic response came from a woman who said, "I

18

do not feel different; my life is, to my knowledge, materially and emotionally unaffected [by giftedness]." She went on, however, to lament that "[Gifted classes] enabled me to skip an introductory class or two in college. But I also skipped classical literature . . . somehow I never read Homer, a lack which I feel deeply." I wondered as I read this how many "average women" (as she claimed to be) deeply regret not studying Homer.

What caused this cheerful insistence on normality that I kept seeing? Is it truly forbidden in polite society to speak of one's own intelligence? Is giftedness so taboo in such a society that the same woman who boasts of running five miles a day would not dream of disclosing how many books she has read, how fluent she might be in a foreign language, or how extensive is her knowledge of genetics? Our survey, however, was private and confidential, and no public disclosures were to be feared; besides, the fact of our education was no secret among us. Of what use was it to prove to me that it had all been a mistake? As a psychologist, I was familiar with the clinical defenses of rationalization—"Gifted people accomplish great things. I've accomplished very little. Therefore, I must not be gifted after all!"—and of denial—"I don't feel anything! I'm not angry about this! I'm happy!" But I was not dealing with a group of neurotics. For the most part, these were psychologically healthy women, and these kinds of defenses seemed incongruous with their otherwise penetrating and comprehensive self-analyses.

A Conspiracy of Silence

One clue to the denial of these women emerged in the responses to the question about what their parents had told them. It appears that parents either told their little girls nothing at all about their giftedness, or felt a strong need to put their girls in their places. Most of the answers were similar:

"Nothing."

"Funny, I can't remember them saying anything."

"Absolutely nothing."

"They told me not to get a big head."

"They reminded me that I was just lucky and that this was nothing to brag about."

19

"I think they were worried I would become conceited, and the fact that my brother had not been identified as gifted made it hard to talk at home about my special school."

The last of these responses suddenly made me aware of the conflict of feelings parents must have felt: first, pride that their child was somehow special, a child of superior intelligence; then, puzzlement: What did this mean? What were Mom and Dad supposed to do about it? Did this mean special treatment—in a family where all the kids till now had received equal treatment? Certainly not! What if she came to expect special opportunities? What if parents couldn't provide them? She would just have to learn that she's not so special. That she'd better not "get a big head," and so on. At first, I imagined that this part was the same for gifted girls and gifted boys, but eventually the differences become clear. Perhaps the little girls had acquiesced in the parental judgement of what it meant, and the boys hadn't. Whatever the reason, the girls had come to agree with their parents and to share in the denial of special talents. All this may be related to the long-recognized observation that girls are more obedient and more compliant with parental attitudes throughout childhood and adolescence than are boys. The girls perceived quickly that an attitude of humility, or at least indifference to "special treatment," was the best means of securing parental approval, that most powerful reward of childhood. Whatever the reason, the adult women had largely come to agree with Mom and Dad that being gifted was definitely not OK.

Lowered Sights

The process that began in childhood of "learning one's place" continued, as could be seen by the lowering of aspirations over time. The average elementary school girl has already experienced the sex role stereotypes of her society. When asked what she wants to be when she grows up, she typically replies "nurse," "teacher," or "mother." This was not true, even in 1960, for these gifted girls. According to their memories of what they had wanted to be, the eighth grade girls of the Accelerated Learning Program included in their number an aspiring paleontologist, a lawyer, a doctor, a "traveler," and a writer, two would-be scientists, and only a sprinkling (three) of the traditional nurses and teachers.

By twelfth grade, four girls had firmed and narrowed their

ideas. One scientist saw herself as an electrical engineer. The other scientist now wanted to be a physician. A nurse had changed her career goal to "vocal performance." Another's aspiration had changed from "start a career in international relations and help the revolution!" to "get a boyfriend!" All the rest, except the one who had maintained an interest in teaching, had become "don't know" by high school graduation. Most respondents were emphatic about their confusion at the time they graduated from high school: "I really had no idea what to do with my life." "Now I was an adult! What was I supposed to do?" "I was very uncertain."

Five years after high school graduation, what were the goals of these gifted women? In fact, they hardly held career goals. Curiously, those who did displayed only vague, compromised goals that lacked direction.

"I had fallen into accounting . . ."

"Teaching, but maybe marriage . . ."

"To help others or to serve God."

"My husband I were completely uprooted. My school goals were confused and undefined."

"Just to be happy."

". . . seemingly stuck in a no-win situation—always having to work at whatever job I was qualified for (with one year of college credits, to earn the most money I could get to survive)."

"Get over a traumatic love affair so I could finish my thesis."

By this time, five years after graduation from high school, half of the college graduates planned to teach, usually wherever their husbands might be located. A few were on their way to well-paid, high-status professions: one had entered medical school, one an engineering graduate program, and one a law school.

Ten years after high school graduation, four were teaching, four were nurses and technicians, and eight were not employed outside the home.

The trend was clear: career goals were juggled, lost, confused, compromised, downgraded, and only rarely pursued in a determined, progressive way.

21

Adjustment to "Reality"

One would think that individuals who had found it necessary to change aspirations radically and compromise goals dramatically would feel at least some dissatisfaction. The following sad, self-aware comment would, I thought, be typical:

". . . My main gripe was that I was 'special' then; but becoming a mediocrity in the real world was a disappointment. It's taken me this long to come out of the rock bottom pits from that reunion. I knew many of my friends and acquaintances would be doing great things with their lives (I never have). I can't be too hard on the [Accelerated Learning] program. The lack of career counseling really left me wanting. I was armed with lots of knowledge, good grades, recommendations, and prestige, yet my parents' example of 'life is' (that is, that life is something to be grudgingly endured if you're not sleeping or escaping) overpowered the option of doing something constructive with this real opportunity to change the impending fate. It also sealed my failure complex since I didn't become anything near a physicist or a senator."

This response, however, was one of only two ambivalent replies to the questions about happiness. It was accompanied by a wry and poignant letter, describing the struggle to learn and to understand the nature and meaning of the writer's failure to live up to expectations from self and others. It had the ring of truth, and I heard it. It was from Big Mary.

The other ambivalent response was from Gina:

"Am I happy? This is tough. I think I have much more fury and anger than happiness in my life . . . This last broken engagement wracked me so that I find it difficult to write about. I want to get a hold of my life, you know, take charge and go to find what I want . . . Somehow, those classes never taught me failure or how to accept being second or how to gracefully admit defeat . . ."

Gina, too, was struggling with the conflicts between her goals and the expectations of others—especially of men.

The disappointment and bewilderment in Mary's and Gina's

letters were understandable responses to events in their lives. Schooled to believe that great accomplishment was inevitable, they found after graduation that the real expectations were for a success-ful marriage and acceptance of the kind of career goals that would not interfere with a timely wedding. Caught between their earlier dreams and the pressure of finding a man, they had ended up, at least for a while, dissatisfied with both their achievements and their relationships.

In other women's responses to questions about happiness, the disappointment was muted. Apparently, most of them were very happy with their life patterns. At first, I was puzzled. If the majority of these gifted women were unemployed or underemployed, ac-cording to normal standard for men, why were they so happy? Why were the complaints of lost dreams and unrealized potential so few and so muted?

The answer lies in the crucial, elementary fact about gifted individuals that has emerged from research on them: gifted people are generally well-adjusted (Terman and Oden, 1935). As children they are happier, healthier, and more socially adept than are other children. As adolescents they are more fun-loving, more popular, and more athletic than others are. As adults they are content, integrated, and easy to please. It would seem logical to conclude that the gifted woman's tendency to be well-adjusted makes her cheerful despite underemployment; that she is free of resentments toward people who openly or unwittingly discourage or fail to encourage her to achieve full potential; and that she endures personal disappointment with a smile or a shrug. She has a long history of being a "good girl." Most gifted girls are well-behaved in class and helpful at home, and they are praised for this. Gifted young women in high school are usually congratulated for being sensible but "sweet."

They continue to be rewarded for their sociability and good humor long after peers, parents, and even professors have lost interest in their academic achievement. Being well-adjusted in a society in which women are expected to achieve less than men demands calm adjustment, and the gifted woman complies. Also, she is psychologically hardier than her "average" peers, the gifted woman may deal creatively with conflicts between her original goals and societal expectations and is, therefore, less likely to complain about her lifestyle than is the average woman. Only those gifted women whose coping skills have not been adequate, or who have encountered extraordinary barriers and humiliations—like Mary and Gina—will cry out in anger that something is wrong. The others generally will continue, at least through young adulthood, to adjust to life as it is.

Patterns of Adjustment

Although the group of gifted women I had surveyed and interviewed was small, four distinct patterns of adjusting to giftedness emerged as I repeatedly read their statements. With some hesitation, I labeled these patterns, recognizing their superficiality, but feeling nonetheless that insights into behaviors that shape lifestyles emerged from the categorizations. Originally, I had labelled the groups Happy Homemaker, Disposable-Career Woman, Lone Achiever, and Dual-Career Coupler. Upon reading these titles in the first book, some women felt the terms were derogatory, particularly the first two. But the Happy Homemaker was meant to describe the satisfied, cheerful homemaker, and the Disposable-Career Woman was meant to describe the woman whose career was *not* the result of a long-term goal, but instead a career of convenience that could be set aside if wifely or motherly duties so dictated. Nevertheless, I am now trying some new titles: The Satisfied Homemaker and the Traditional Career Women.

The Satisfied Homemaker

At twenty-nine, she was married and had two children. She stayed at home and liked it. She resented those who said that homemaking wasn't work, because she had made a full-time job of it. She knew her skills as a homemaker were crucial to her husband's success. She understood his career and what he needed to do to rise higher on the professional ladder. She helped him with reports and presentations, revising, typing, and even rehearsing with him. She entertained his associates and got to know their spouses because she understood the importance of the informal social network to his future.

Her children were the best-dressed and best-behaved children in the neighborhood. Their Halloween costumes were the most original and the most carefully sewn; their Valentines were handmade and charming. She read child development books to help her plan appropriate experiences for her children. She took their education seriously, helping with their homework and planning activities to reinforce their learning.

She was a gourmet cook and a brilliant decorator. She created in her home a beautiful and lively environment. She was proud of what she had accomplished and knew that her money sense and planning had made it possible for her and her family to have all this.

Sometimes she worried about a life without her husband, or how she would adjust when her children were grown. She had given so much to others that she wasn't very good at giving to herself. She sometimes thought she could have done more, and she was aware that she was not realizing her full intellectual potential. She knew that life is full of compromises, however, and that she had chosen this life—and so she decided to be happy.

The Traditional-Career Woman

At twenty-nine years of age she had just dropped out of, was about to drop out of, or had just returned to her job as teacher, nurse, or office worker. Problems of identity were nagging her (just who was she, anyway—ex-teacher, homemaker, ex-homemaker?), but she thought she had found a lifestyle that allowed her to have a limited career, yet accompany her husband and leave her job when he and the children required it. She could stay home with the children, at least until they began school, and would excel as a mother and homemaker if the family could afford it. Her husband's career was more important than her own—inasmuch as his education was completed first, or they moved to his first job site.

When she was working, she took her job very seriously. As a teacher she was superb, planning her curricula and trying out techniques she had read about in education literature. She may have been bored with mediocre colleagues, but she hid the boredom. As a nurse or medical technician, she disliked being under a doctor's or dentist's authoritarian thumb, but she was proud of her work and aware of its importance to medicine, and she worked hard to improve her position and the status of her profession. As an office worker, she was ambitious, even a perfectionist, rising quickly to leadership positions such as office manager or executive secretary. She was often bored with other office workers but maintained pleasant relations nonetheless, enlivening a dull environment with her creativity. She was not sure what the future held for her because she was undecided about having more children and in the dark about how any job changes for her husband might affect her.

The Lone Achiever

Approaching thirty, she was about 90 percent sure that she wanted to remain single and commit herself to her profession. She had her first professional job or was nearing it, and she loved being at last in the work for which she had trained so long. She never found a man she could love, one as intelligent as she, and she couldn't imagine loving a man less intelligent. Perhaps she had tried a relationship with someone less intelligent or less ambitious and it just didn't work out. She was beginning to be pessimistic about relationships with men, because even casual liaisons seemed to lead to one or both partners feeling threatened by the other. On the other hand, she had established a warm and loving community of friends who cared about her as a person and respected her as a professional. If she could maintain these close friendships, she would have the support system to carry her through life. She was a dedicated professional who believed that medicine, law, research, or business management is a twenty-four-hour-a-day, seven-day-a-week commitment.

The Dual-Career Coupler

She was twenty-nine years old and exhausted but happy most of the time. She and her husband were both professionals who took their careers seriously. They may have been colleagues in the same profession, in which case no clear line divided their relationship at work from their relationship at home, or they may have been in different professions but knew quite a bit about what the other did, since work furnished a major topic of conversation. They were tired most of time, not only because they were workaholics but also because they were trying to share all the household tasks. If they didn't have children, they wondered how they would survive when they did. If they did have children, they had learned quickly to employ competent household help and to make loving, enriched child care their top budget priority. Their schedules were so tight and planned so far in advance that an unexpected work-related trip or a child's illness could throw their lives into temporary chaos.

Because of tenure-track obligations or her patients' or clients' needs, she took minimal time off to have a baby, a few weeks perhaps, leaving her even more tired than she had been before. And if she breast-fed her baby, she rued biology's temporarily making equal division of parental responsibilities impossible. Because she wanted to be the best mother possible as well as a successful professional, some thought she was trying to do too much, but she felt compelled to do all that she was capable of.

In figures three through six are quotations that seemed to fit my classmates in each of the four categories. Some are clichés, but some are novel insights. All display a diversity of values and opinions that characterized gifted women of 1980. Yet while these four patterns occurred frequently and quite unmistakably, at least two other known patterns were entirely missing.

27

FIG. 3 The Satisfied Homemaker

- I am happy being a homemaker because:

    *I can put my gifts to use
    being the best wife and mother possible.*

    I am going to raise gifted children!

    I am not really gifted.

    *Scripture tells me I belong in
    the home, serving my husband.*

    It's more fun!

    *My husband is gifted and needs
    a talented wife to support him.*

    *My children's need for a mother at home is more
    important than my selfish need for a career.*

    *I can accomplish just as much
    through volunteer work.*

    *I could never get a job up
    to my abilities in this economy anyway.*

The first invariably draws notice: it is a married lifestyle in which the woman is the primary breadwinner and/or has the stronger career orientation, while the husband stays in the home caring for the children. None of the gifted women in my survey was engaged in this lifestyle.

FIG. 4. The Traditional-Career Woman

> • **I want to be a (teacher, nurse, office worker) because:**
>
> *I can go wherever my husband goes.*
>
> *Our society needs gifted teachers now more than ever.*
>
> *I don't have to invest a lot of time and money in an education.*
>
> *I can quit anytime I want to.*
>
> *I don't mind not being in the spotlight as long as I can make a contribution.*
>
> *I want a career, but I don't want to compete with my husband.*
>
> *I don't think I have what it takes to get a higher degree.*
>
> *I can go back to (teaching, nursing, office work) after my children are grown.*

A second pattern, even more unusual, involves a "self-actualized" lifestyle. First described by Abraham Maslow (1967), it represents the person whose career has fully blossomed, often in a unique or self-created way. Self-actualized people care little for external evaluation—that is, other people's opinions of their worth as workers or human beings. They are totally absorbed in the process of living, in creating meaning in their lives through their work and involvement with humanity.

Intellectually gifted people would seem to be the most apt candidates for self-actualization. However, although some of my classmates may have been on the way to self-actualization, none appeared to have achieved it in 1980.

FIG. 5. The Lone Achiever

- **I'm happy being single and career-oriented because:**

Even though I get lonely,
I'm doing something meaningful.

I never considered not becoming a doctor

I haven't found a man
who could deal with my success.

I had two "maiden aunts," who were
models for me of achievement and self-sufficiency.

I've decided that my friends provide all
the support I need for my lifestyle.

My career requires that
I commit myself to it full time.

They did not have the autonomy, intensity, or creativity of the self-actualized person. Yet I believed that all of my classmates, men and women, had the potential for this full flowering of talents. Many of the women in this group had learned to deny their gifts in the same way others in their lives had denied them: they had learned to lower their sights and to adjust to "reality." Guidance for these women had been inferior or nonexistent. In most cases, no adult had affirmed their gifts, raised their aspirations, or challenged them to pursue self-actualization. In fact, in 1980 there was little concern for the failure of gifted women to achieve their potential. Few scholars found the issue of interest. A faculty colleague of mine expressed this "Why care?" attitude quite succinctly: "Barb is spending all her time trying to figure out why two percent of girls don't become nuclear physicists, when her time would be better spent on the ten percent of boys who can't read."

FIG. 6 The Dual Career Coupler

- **I want to be a (teacher, nurse, office worker) because:**

I can go wherever my husband goes.

*Our society needs gifted teachers
now more than ever.*

*I don't have to invest a lot of time
and money in an education.*

I can quit anytime I want to.

*I don't mind not being in
the spotlight as long as
I can make a contribution.*

*I want a career, but I don't
want to compete with my husband.*

*I don't think I have what it takes
to get a higher degree.*

*I can go back to (teaching, nursing,
officer work) after my children are grown.*

References

Kerr, B.A. *A Handbook for Counseling Gifted and Talented.* Alexandria, VA: American Counseling Association, 1991.

Maslow, A. H. *Motivation and Personality.* New York: Harper, 1954.

Sanborn, M. P.; Engels, D. W.; Pfleger, L. R.; and Rodenstein, J. M. "Career Education of Gifted and Talented Boys and Girls." Madison, WI: Research and Guidance Laboratory, University of Wisconsin (ERIC Document Reproduction Service No. ED 148 077), 1976.

Terman, L. M. and Oden, M. H. "The Promise of Youth." In *Genetic Studies of Genius*, Vol. 3. Stanford, CA: Stanford University Press, 1935.

Chapter 3

Twenty Years After

I didn't make it to my twenty-year high school reunion. I was eight months pregnant with my second child and involved in a big job decision . . . but I'd been a little apprehensive, anyway. Thomas Wolfe gave us that phrase, "You can't go home again," and I happened to concur with his perception. Some of the women I had studied were angry with me; the teachers (like teachers everywhere) were annoyed if not angered by the label "Disposable-Career Woman." The homemakers, particularly one very traditional Christian one, had come down on me pretty hard. I had received one letter telling me that with my values, I probably wasn't fit to be a mother myself. One of the feminists thought I hadn't discussed the political aspects of gifted women's experiences enough. Even though the majority of women in my class had agreed completely with my portrayal of us, I wasn't sure I wanted to face the inevitable feedback from those who hadn't.

But I heard a lot about it from friends who had gone. They all agreed that at 39, people seemed more comfortable with themselves and their chosen lifestyles. I found out that most of the women wanted me to continue the study. Most encouraging was a letter from Big Mary, whose support for the project had been extensive. In fact, she would show up at national conventions where I was speaking, stand up, and announce, "I'm Big Mary, and everything she wrote about me is true."

I appreciated their encouragement to continue my work, but I perceived a major problem with a twenty-year follow-up study: it would be even less scientific than the first one. Why? Because these women had already been studied, they knew they had been studied, and for the most part they had read the resulting book. Hence they were "contaminated" as research participants. Their responses to a follow-up questionnaire would be affected by what they had read about themselves in the previous book. In addition, there is some evidence from other follow-ups, such as the Terman study, that being the subjects of research may change the way people make choices about their lives, and so my subjects might now be atypical of gifted women in general.

However, I believed the resulting information might be helpful if it were combined with other studies, and if the stories of gifted women's lives could be used to illustrate general principles about bright women's career development. And so I proceeded.

The Questionnaire

In the second follow-up study, I sent a questionnaire to 25 gifted women whose addresses were still available to the reunion committee. Twenty-three women gave information about their educational degree, career, and marital and family status. Seventeen returned information about career goals, critical events, and satisfactions.

The second questionnaire was designed to focus on the developmental changes in the gifted women's lives as well as on the critical events which had affected their choices. The career development of gifted and creative poeple has often been conceptualized in terms of critical life events (Piirto, 1992.) Therefore, one item read, "What critical events in the last ten years have affected your career goals?" This made it possible for women to describe marital, career, health or any other kind of life change which may have led to a crossroads.

In the first survey, I had asked how the women felt about their giftedness; now I asked, "At your current age and in your present role, how does giftedness affect your life?" They had clearly denied or diminished the importance of their giftedness in the earlier study. Had they changed their attitudes in the ensuing years? Did being labeled "gifted" in the book have an impact on those who read about themselves?

In order to determine the women's point of view on the realization of their potential, I asked, "To what degree do you believe you are fulfilling your intellectual potential?" I was afraid that some might feel defensive about answering this, but I didn't know any other way of asking.

Ever since I had attended the psychologist Mihalyi Csikszent-mihalyi's presentation (1990) of his theory of creativity, I had been very interested in the continuum of boredom-challenge-frustration as experienced by gifted people. Csikszentmihalyi believes that any particular environment or situation can be described as creating a state of boredom, of challenge, or of frustration, depending on the degree to which an individual's talents and resources match the demands of the situation. I wanted to know how the gifted women's current environments were affecting their experience of these states.

For the second time in ten years, I asked the group of women, "Are you happy and satisfied with your life?" These few items, I hoped, would give some insight into the current state of the women's lives.

The Responses

The responses took longer to arrive than the last time. Seventeen of the 25 completed their questionnaires, and I had partial information on another six women. As before, the questionnaire was often accompanied by a friendly and informative letter, amplifying the responses to the survey.

After my first reading of the responses, I was struck by the fact that this time, I could make no generalizations about the women. Instead, the separate paths they had chosen made it necessary to draw conclusions based only on subgroups rather than on the group as a whole.

The demographic section illustrated the great diversity in the women's experiences. Table 1 shows educational, career, and marital status, and the number of children for gifted women at both the ten-year and twenty-year follow-up.

Five of the 23 women had advanced from B.A. to M.A.s. All of the other participants who had held a bachelor's degree in 1980 remained at that level. For some who had not changed their degree status, it was simply because they did not need further schooling. Some, however, had hoped to return for further education but had not been able to because of financial or time pressures. The four women who had not completed college in 1980 had not done so yet. For all of these, the prospect of returning to college had become more and more distant, and in one case, more irrelevant: "I always thought I would eventually go back to college. But it always seemed like there was something else that needed to be paid for besides college classes. Now the degree isn't relevant because as the owner of my own business, I don't need it."

Thirteen of the women had changed their occupational title. Some had advanced in terms of salary and status; they had made changes such as from homemaker to teacher or businesswoman, or from student to professional. Three had changed from paid positions to unpaid homemaking. For those who had advanced in salary and status, their motivation often was self-actualization and the pursuit of a valued way of life rather than the desire for more money: "I never thought about how hard it would be. I only thought of how great it would feel to finally be doing what I can do best." However, all of those who had changed from homemaker to another occupation had done so at least partly for economic reasons. For all three who had become homemakers, the change was based on deeply held values concerning family life: two identified themselves as Christians, and one wrote that she had changed her vocation to being an active mother and volunteer. One of the homemakers wrote, "I wish that you could have had the same experience as a mother that I have had. Perhaps with your second child you will be able to see that your child's precious first years are more important than your career advancement." A chemical engineer who was now a full-time mother proudly sent me clippings of her work as a volunteer teaching science at her child's school.

The interesting thing about the occupational status of the gifted women is that overall, it is somewhat different from women in general. The major trend in women's lives in the last decade has been the return to the workplace. Although the media have described career women returning to the home, the labor statistics show otherwise: the trend is overwhelmingly the other direction (Faludi, 1992).

All but three of the women in the study were married. Two had divorced, and three single women had married. The rest had maintained the same status. Again, these women differ somewhat from the general population: their divorce rate was lower than that of the rest of the population, and like Terman's gifted women, they tended to have more stable marriages.

Nine had had one child or more since the last follow-up, and eight of these women had gone from none to one or two children. It was definitely a child-raising decade for the gifted women in all occupational categories.

TABLE 1. Comparison of Ten- and Twenty-Year Follow-Ups of Women Graduates, The Accelerated Learning Program

1980	**1990**
# 1 B.S. Biology M.S. Zoology 2 Children Homemaker	B.S. Biology M.S. Zoology Married 3 Children Teacher
# 2 B.S. Education Married 2 Children Teacher	M.A. Education Married 2 Children Teacher
# 3 B.A. French/Education Married 1 Child Homemaker	M.A. Education Married 1 Child Teacher 1/2 day
# 4 No degree Married 1 Child Warehouse/Homemaker	No degree Single 1 Child Activist
# 5 B.A. Education, M.Ed. Education Married No Children Homemaker	B.A. Education, M. Ed. Education Married 3 Children Mom/Ass't. to Golfer
# 6 B.A. Married No Children Dental Assistant	B.A. Married 2 Children Homemaker/Volunteer

TABLE 1. Comparison of Ten- and Twenty-Year Follow-Ups of Women Graduates, The Accelerated Learning Program

1980	**1990**
# 7 B.S. Education Married 2 Children Homemaker	B.S. Education Married 4 Children Homemaker/Teacher Volunteer
# 8 B.A. Music Education Married Teacher	Information not available
# 9 No Degree Single No Children Accountant/Artist	No Degree Married 2 Children Bookkeeper
#10 B.A. Journalism Married No Children Homemaker	B.A. Journalism Married No Children Golf Pro Shop Manager
#11 B.S. Education Married No Children Nurse	B.S. Nursing Married 3 Children Physical Therapist/Nurse
#12 No Degree Married 2 Children Homemaker	No Degree Married 3 Children Owner Decorating Business
#13 B.A. Biology/Education Married No Children Teacher/Dental Student	M.A. Biology D.D.M. Married 2 Children Dentist/Oral Pathologist Assistant Professor

TABLE 1. Comparison of Ten- and Twenty-Year Follow-Ups of Women Graduates, The Accelerated Learning Program

1980	1990
#14 No Degree Married No Children Auditor/Navy	No Degree Married No Children Training Instructor
#15 M.D. Single No Children Physician (ObGyn)	M.D. Married 1 Child Physician (Perinatalist)
#16 M.A. History Single No Children Teaching Assistant (Graduate Student)	M.A.—Did not complete Ph.D. Married No Children Supervisor/Cost Analyst
#17 B.A. Elementary Education Single No Children Teacher	Information not available
#18 No Degree Married No Children Student Fashion Design/Homemaker	No Degree Married 1 Child Model & Cosmetics Business
#19 B.J. Journalism Married 2 Children Homemaker	Information not available
#20 B.S. Elementary Education Married 2 Children Homemaker	B.S. Elementary Education Married 2 Children Substitute Teacher

TABLE 1. Comparison of Ten- and Twenty-Year Follow-Ups of Women Graduates, The Accelerated Learning Program

1980	1990
#21 B.S. Med Tech Single No Children Physician's Assistant	M.S. Allied Health Med. Single No Children Assistant Professor/ Real Estate
#22 B.F.A. Interior Design Divorced Designer/Vocalist	B.F.A. Interior Design Married Opera Singer
#23 B.S. Chemical Engineering Married No Children Engineer	B.S. Chemical Engineering Married 2 Children Homemaker/Teacher/ Volunteer

Critical Events

All of the seventeen women who answered the critical events question listed family happenings as the crucial moments in their lives. Even major occupational or professional changes were usually in response to a family situation. Family events such as the birth of a child, marriage, and divorce were the pivotal situations in these women's lives. For example, one's divorce freed her to develop her career as an opera singer; another's husband's illness caused her to give up her career goal.

Fulfillment of Intellectual Potential

Most of the women, except for three who were highly accomplished in business, arts, and medicine, were unsure if they were fulfilling their intellectual potential. "I'm not sure I know what that means anymore, because I don't really know what my intellectual potential is. Could I be working any harder that I am? No! Could I be using my talents more fully? Maybe." They wondered if other choices might have led to actualized gifts and if their current jobs used their talents effectively. Two in homemaking roles dismissed the question as irrelevant, for fulfilling their intellectual potential was not a valued goal. Three sadly admitted that self-actualization was no longer a possibility. "I am currently working four part-time jobs to support my husband, who is disabled, and our children. I am too exhausted to think about my intellectual potential."

Challenge—Frustration—Boredom

The questionnaires displayed the full range of responses in this category. Of the seventeen women responding to this question, three felt bored and unchallenged; three felt overly challenged, that is, frustrated; four felt challenged and stimulated. The rest were unsure, claiming either to change often from one state to another or to be unable to identify the most frequent state.

The Role of Giftedness

At this point in the women's development, they were much less likely to deny their giftedness than they had been ten years before: only two continued to dismiss the concept of giftedness as being descriptive of them. However, even though the others did not deny their giftedness, they were for the most part ambivalent about the role of giftedness in their current lives. Only three believed their giftedness had had an impact on their careers. Most believed that giftedness had affected the way they led their lives, naming such behaviors as reading faster and with more comprehension than others, solving problems quickly, and being well-read enough to "talk to anybody about anything."

Several commented on what they perceived to be negative aspects of giftedness: being critical of others, feeling cynical about current events, and having difficulty with irrational people. "This last decade has been tough on me politically. How can people celebrate stupidity?"

Happiness

A smaller proportion of the group were happy and satisfied with their lives twenty years after high school. Five of seventeen who had become less satisfied gave several related reasons. First, they

41

were overworked. Most of them had more than they could do, every single day. At 39 years old, they felt rushed and harried at every turn. Some had several jobs at work, plus family responsibilities, and on top of that, roles in their community, all of which drew upon their energies. "No matter how much I do, people expect more of me. My friends say I don't know how to say 'no.' But that's not true! I say 'no' all the time. On the phone, to my students, to my family. That's part of what keeps me so busy, finding all the nice ways to say 'No, I can't do that for you.'" Finally, a number were dissatisfied because they saw their personal goals receding, and some were convinced they could not attain even such modest personal goals as traveling or completing the few academic courses needed for a degree.

A New Set of Categories

The categories devised for the earlier study were clearly no longer appropriate. Such titles as happy homemakers, disposable-career women, lone achievers, and dual-career women did not adequately captured the quality of these women's lives, so I searched again for some way of conceptualizing their experiences. I tried out several sets of clusters in presentations to my classes of teachers, counselors, and psychologists. I applied new theories of women's development, basing the categories less on occupational attainments and more on holistic considerations of women's lifestyles. After many tries, I came up with the clusters presented here.

As before, I categorized responses in a highly subjective manner. Another researcher might go about this clustering completely differently. I am no doubt affected by my own biases: because I believe the realization of women's intellectual potential *is* important, and because I *am* concerned about women attaining their personal goals, I interpret the information given to me in the following terms.

Committed Traditionals

At 39 years old, she is a teacher or homemaker who has seriously committed herself to her occupation as a vocation. If she is a teacher, she has an intense sense of mission, believing that teaching provides for the fulfillment of her intellectual potential as well as her values for service to others and the love of learning. If she is a homemaker, she may be less sure that she is fulfilling her intellectual potential, but she is deeply committed to her role and strong in her concern for the development of her children and the management of her household. She is in her role by choice, not necessity.

FIG. 7. The Committed Traditional

- **I am commited to a traditional role because:**

I love teaching. I can't imagine any other work.

I am now the head of my department at the hospital: I worked hard for this.

I have managed my husband's career (in professional sports) for many years now, and I know we've been a success together.

I've never wanted to work outside the home, and I am fortunate in that I will never have to. My work with my family and Christian youth groups fulfills me.

Although physical therapy is not where I started, I really enjoy this career, because I run my own practice.

The Transforming Woman

With few resources and limited education, this woman has transformed her life. She has created her own business which, in the course of the decade, has become extremely successful. (For example, one of my respondents had a cosmetics business, and one a decorating business.) She has used her natural abilities and her excellent elementary and secondary school education as a basis for teaching herself the kind of skills that usually belong only to those with M.B.A. degrees. Perhaps she has transformed a beloved avocation into a vocation. She has made major changes in her family or personal life to accommodate her transformation. (For example, one transforming woman divorced her businessman husband to pursue both a new life as an opera singer and a new relationship with a fellow musician. This transforming woman surprised herself with her own success, making her Carnegie Hall debut and singing with the San Francisco Opera Company.)

FIG. 8. The Transforming Woman

- **I have transformed my life and:**

  I don't really know how I did it
  but I'm where I want to be.
  I had <u>nothing</u> going for me but my abilities.

  Doing well in my business is partly brains
  and partly being at the right place
  at the right time.

  I made a decision to change my life and I did:
  I turned it upside down, and I'm better for it.

  My new husband and I committed ourselves to
  putting our careers first; we support each
  other's goals.

  My success surprised a lot of people, especially me.

The Continuing Professional

In this second decade the continuing professional completed her education and made progress in her profession. Among the handful of women who have entered the world of dentistry, medicine, or the military, she is now poised for making changes in those professions. She is satisfied, even fulfilled, in her work, and the combination of family and career works for her. She still has a tendency to work too hard and to forget her own needs.

FIG. 9. The Continuing Professional

- **I have continued as a professional because:**

We have advanced a long way together
professionally, my husband and I.

I am no longer a "pioneer" in my field;
now there are many women.

We have had to move several times
to find work in the same city.

I don't regret that I haven't married;
my work involves extensive overseas travel,
and a family wouldn't fit my schedule.

My work is satisfying and very challenging.

The Overwhelmed Woman

Once a homemaker or "disposable-career" woman, she is now a homemaker and a wage-earner in a low-paying job. She has no degree, or perhaps has a B.A., but she has not been able to complete her educational goals. She is terribly overworked. In this category is the woman who works four part-time jobs in bookkeeping; another cares for two elderly, ill parents while raising her children. The overwhelmed woman struggles to make ends meet as mental and physical health problems, marital problems, or poor employment conditions bar her from meeting her personal goals. She is fatigued and frustrated. She worries that depression will get the best of her.

FIG. 10. The Overwhelmed Woman

- **I am overwhelmed because:**

I am too exhausted to think about my own goals.

I am caring for two teenagers and two elderly parents, and I have no time to myself.

I may never be able to complete my college education.

Being labeled gifted only reminds me that I have many regrets and disappointments.

I have gained too much weight and used more pills and alchohol than I should.

I've been struggling to keep up an unrealistic standard of living. With my husband unemployed, it's impossible to go on living as we have.

Conclusion

In the second decade of the study, many changes which had affected women in the larger society had also affected this group. Some gifted women had entered the workforce, either out of necessity or in fulfillment of personal goals; a few had left the workforce. Most had growing families. Unlike the general population, they had a low rate of divorce. Their patterns of psychological and vocational development had changed. The traditional women seemed much more committed to and confident in their roles than they had previously. Even those who had originally chosen their occupations out of convenience were now thoroughly identified with their chosen work. Some women had blossomed unexpectedly into leadership roles, despite economic and educational limitations. An alarming finding was that some gifted women were overwhelmed by multiple roles and financial and health problems; this group saw little hope of change or of fulfilling their potential.

One conclusion that can be drawn from this follow-up study is that the choices made in late adolescence create clear limits on adult attainments. Those who did not complete a bachelor's degree by 1980 had not done so in 1990. Those who had created businesses without advanced training were limited to traditionally feminine fields such as cosmetics and design. Early marriage and childbirth delayed or derailed many women's career goals; later marriage and childbirth had less of an impact. In fact, women who had continued training, married later, and delayed having children came closest to achieving their goals during this decade.

Another conclusion that can be drawn is that the impact of giftedness on these women's lives is complex and ambiguous. Giftedness seemed to make it possible for most of them to achieve the highest status possible within the limits they or their society had created. Many said giftedness gave them a special perspective and an ability to conceptualize and articulate goals on a daily basis. On the other hand, having been labeled gifted was for some a source of regret and even annoyance, a perpetual reminder of external expectations which did not meet personal reality.

Once this second study was completed, I kept wanting to look at the material again, to re-conceptualize it. As before, my categories were highly subjective; another researcher might have clustered the responses in a completely different way. My strong bias concerning the importance of women realizing their intellectual potential has certainly affected my interpretation of the information my classmates gave me. What I hope emerges from all of this is an understanding of the ways in which gifted women work so diligently for excellence in their vocations and family life; the ways they transform their lives with whatever resources they have at hand; and the ways, when overwhelmed, they struggle bravely against exhaustion and hopelessness.

References

Faludi, S. *Backlash: The Undeclared War Against American Women.* NY, NY: Crown Publishers, 1992.

Csikszentmihalyi, M. *Flow: The Psychology of Optimal Experience.* New York: Harper Collins, 1990.

Piirto, J. *Understanding Those Who Create.* Scottsdale, AZ: Gifted Psychology Press, 1992.

Chapter 4

Eminent Women

Despite countless barriers that have kept many gifted women from persisting on the path to their goals, some do not stumble and fall. Why? Why is it that a few gifted women do accomplish extraordinary feats? And how does a gifted woman become an eminent woman?

To learn about the background, characteristics, and experiences of gifted women who reached their goals, I used the approach available to me: that of case or biographical study. In a truly empirical study, data would be gathered by objectively testing a random sample of eminent women on a variety of measures, then questioning them by means of standardized interviews. Not only is such research outside the scope of my endeavors, but it also is not the only way to learn how women succeed. A study of eminent Canadian women (Yewchuk, 1990) which used a questionnaire about lifestyles does provide a model for my work. Indeed, case studies are a rich resource for understanding what makes achieving women extraordinary and how they overcome barriers.

I examined the biographies of thirty-three eminent women whose lives spanned the middle nineteenth century to the present and who represent the wide varieties of lifestyles chosen by gifted, eminent women. To read their stories is to be amazed by the unique power of brilliant women to create new directions in art, science, literature, politics, and music. Of these thirty-three biographies, the nine selected to be excerpted here capture common themes and powerful, substantive tenets. A complete list of all the biographies appears at the end of the chapter.

The Women

Marie Curie: Scientist

The youngest of five children, Marya Sklodovska was born in 1867 in Warsaw, Poland, to two hard-working, loving school teachers who, along with friends and family members, were suffering under and resisting the tyranny of Russia. Marie's well-educated parents recognized their daughter's precocity and in fact were frightened by it: Marie could read—and read well—at four, having learned her alphabet from playing with her older sister, and she had an extraordinary memory. Events that had happened several years before were clearly remembered by the four-year-old, who furthermore was fascinated by her father's physics apparatuses.

In her childhood, Marie faced pain and difficulty. Her mother was slowly dying of tuberculosis, and her father's economic status declined steadily because he refused to be subservient to Russian authorities and because he became involved in a naive and unfortunate financial speculation. Marie's closest, oldest sister died of typhoid when she was nine. But Marie, with her gift for total concentration, performed remarkably at school throughout these dark days. When she read, she was oblivious to everything else.

After her mother died in 1878, Marie's father took over the care of the children as best he could. All four were brilliant; the family's life centered on intellectual activity, with every member teaching or attending school. It seemed natural to this family to want to know everything about chemistry and physics, to speak five languages, and to read Greek and Latin. Reading aloud was the main family entertainment.

Marie believed as a girl of seventeen that service to Poland was more important than marriage or personal ambition, and that the best way to serve her people was to educate the poor so that they could not be easily tyrannized. She joined the Floating University, an underground community of Polish scholars dedicated to educating individuals beyond high school so that they could go on to teach others. She carried on her work quietly and remained independent, despite the strong ideologies of her companions. When she became dissatisfied with the intellectual progress she and her siblings were fashioning in their makeshift academic environment, she made a deal with her older sister: Marie would get a permanent job as a governess to put Bronya through medical school, and then they would reverse roles.

Marie was miserable in her first job, working for a selfish, bourgeois family who rejected her when she and the elder son fell in love. The family refused to allow them to marry, and forced Marie into humiliation. Marie felt buried alive in this household, but nonetheless continued to read and study voraciously—physics, philosophy, literature and anything else she could find. She wrote often to her family and longed for home in Warsaw.

After three years her exile was over, and she returned to her father and the Floating University. Through a friend, she obtained a tiny laboratory where, working in her free time, she reproduced the great experiments in chemistry and physics. She was once again disappointed by the timidity of her boyfriend who, although he still loved her, was afraid to marry against his parents' wishes. She broke with him and decided to pursue the university education that her sister, now a doctor in Paris, wished to help her with.

At the Sorbonne, Marie nearly starved to death for the love of learning. Money that might have bought food instead paid rent for a quiet room that the studious Marie preferred over her sister's noisy house. With her constant studying, she also simply forgot to eat. Often fainting from weakness, she had to be revived by friends and family, who tried in vain to get her to take better care of herself. Ultimately, however, Marie's extraordinary academic performance— and encouragement from a friend—led to a scholarship that rescued her from further starving for the sake of her studies.

Marie had determined never to marry after her first disappointment. However, when she met physicist Pierre Curie at a friend's house, she knew that this man could fulfill her great intellectual and emotional needs. They fell very much in love and were nearly inseparable during their years together. Pierre Curie was a renowned scientist in the area of crystallography, but when Marie proposed for her doctoral research to investigate the newly discovered phenomenon of emissions from certain minerals (later to be named radiation by Marie and Pierre), he threw himself wholeheartedly into helping her.

Over their years of collaboration, they discovered polonium and radium, revolutionizing the whole periodic chart; they revealed the effects of radium on cancer; and they changed the direction of science through their theoretical and experimental work in atomic physics and chemistry. The couple received the highest awards of the scientific community, including the Nobel Prize.

They had two children whom they adored. From all reports, it is evident that Marie Curie had found a way to be an excellent, devoted mother while continuing her established level of intensity in her work. She hired nurses and helpers who lightened many tasks while freeing her to nurture the children's emotional and intellectual growth. Pierre shared in child care as he shared in Marie's scientific work.

Pierre's sudden death in a traffic accident in 1906 changed Marie's personality forever, for Marie lost not only her husband but also her companion in the intense intellectual quests she thrived on. Disconsolate and distraught, she became withdrawn and almost unreachable to any but her dearest friends and family. Ironically, Marie achieved worldwide fame during this tragic time and was plagued with callers, letters, and demands. Her shyness and sadness made public appearances grievously painful, but she consented to a speaking tour of America in exchange for a gram of radium, then the most expensive material in existence. Weakened physically and spiritually by this trip, she gradually sank into ill health, although she continued her work as a professor at the Sorbonne. She also devoted herself wholeheartedly to mentoring her daughter, Irene Curie, and her son-in-law, Frederic Joliot, teaching them virtually everything she knew about radioactivity and x-rays. In 1934, the three created the first artificial radioactive material; Marie died that same year. At the time of her death, she was attempting to complete an experiment, and in 1935 Irene and Frederic earned the Nobel Prize for their work in radioactivity.

Gertrude Stein: Writer

Also the youngest of five children, Gertrude Stein was born in 1874 to Amelia Stein, a homemaker, and Daniel Stein, who owned a wholesale wool business with his brother. After quarreling with his brother, Daniel took his wife and children from the United States to

Vienna. However, he soon returned to the U.S., leaving behind his family, who moved to Paris. Gertrude, attending kindergarten there, learned to speak French at age four. In time, Daniel brought his family back to America, and they all lived briefly in Baltimore with Amelia's Orthodox Jewish parents before relocating to San Francisco, where Daniel had obtained a high-paying job with the cable car company, thus enabling his family to live in a large house with servants. Gertrude had governesses and special lessons.

By first grade, Gertrude was more interested in reading and nature than in school. After their mother became stricken with cancer, Gertrude and her beloved brother Leo spent most of their free time in the library, then walking and talking about what they had read. Their father, who had always been nervous and unsettled, became even more difficult to live with because he was now forced to run the household, so Gertrude and Leo spent a great deal of time away from home. After Amelia's death, when Gertrude was fourteen, Daniel became tyrannical and disorganized. His death three years later was not greatly upsetting to Gertrude.

The older brother Michael, who was doing well in business, took over the support of his younger brothers and sisters. He also supported Gertrude's and Leo's love of literature and theater and sent them to Radcliffe and Harvard, respectively. At Radcliffe, Gertrude arrayed her short figure in odd, dark clothes and a funny hat and immersed herself in a world of ideas at neighboring Harvard. She studied with the great philosophers George Santayana and Josiah Royce and was considered the best student of early psychologist Hugo Munsterberg. Psychology was especially appealing to Gertrude because through it she was able to study thought, consciousness, and language. She was fascinated by automatic writing and experimented with herself, her close friend Leon Solomon, and then hundreds of subjects. William James, pragmatic philosopher and psychologist, stimulated her intellectually as no other scholar before, and with him she studied language and what is now called "altered states of consciousness" and engaged in many heated discussions. By ordinary standards, she was a careless writer, her thoughts and emotions rushing ahead of structure in most of her work.

In college, Gertrude had an active social life, for with her wit and infectious laughter, she made friends easily. She loved art galleries, opera, theater, boat rides and picnics. Upon graduation this gregarious, lively woman knew she wanted to be famous, but she didn't know how she would get there.

She tried medical school at Johns Hopkins, satisfying her

affinity for science and responding to the challenge of being among the first women medical students. She lost interest quickly, however, in this technical field and performed poorly. To her, boredom was worse than anything, and she left medical school to go to Europe with Leo, returning only briefly to do brain research, and then going back to Italy and England. Always during her travels she would visit museums and read in all the great libraries of the world.

Back in New York, she decided that she would be a writer. She began her first novel, working on it for a year in New York and then moving to Paris, to 27 rue de Fleuris, an address she would make famous. Her new home was in the heart of the artists' and writers' district, where a renaissance of creativity was taking place. In this city where she had always been comfortable, she began her career as author and arbiter of taste in the arts. She finished her novel, but did not wish to publish it; she had proved to herself that she could write, and that was enough.

She and Leo began to collect art for their apartment from among the works of new, extraordinarily talented painters. They understood the impact of Cezanne's talent long before anyone else did, and they helped the penniless Matisse by paying him the price he deserved for his works. In 1905, Gertrude met Pablo Picasso and began a lifelong friendship; she championed the cause of his movement, Cubism, and advertised his genius to all who would listen. His remarkable portrait of her was created over a three-month period during which she posed for him.

After finishing her novel, Gertrude translated several of Flaubert's works and wrote three short stories, seeking to accomplish in writing what the modern painters were doing in art: the creation of a new form, with rhythms mirroring real life and with each element as important as the others. While some friends were enthusiastic, publishers were not; in fact, they didn't understand at all what she was trying to do. Even the vanity press that agreed to publish her works for a fee had great misgivings about her unusual phrasing and odd use of punctuation.

She began an extraordinary novel, *The Making of Americans,* a history of one American family presented as the prototype of all families, written in her uniquely repetitious, rhythmic style. During this time she met Alice B. Toklas at a party. Alice was immediately struck by Gertrude's genius and was greatly attracted to her. Howard Greenfield, one of Gertrude Stein's biographers, writes that "Gertrude needed someone to believe in her, and Alice needed someone in whom to believe." They became constant companions. Alice moved in with Gertrude and Leo, where she typed Gertrude's manuscript, helped arrange her schedule, and ran the household; Gertrude and Alice came to love each other deeply and lived as lifelong partners. In 1925 Gertrude completed *The Making of Americans* and some brilliant portraits in writing, then traveled in Spain and Italy. She wrote a portrait of Mabel Dodge, a wealthy patron of the arts, while visiting her in Italy. Mabel had it printed and sent it to people who generally responded that they thought Gertrude was crazy. Her brother Leo simply thought she had no talent; he had also apparently grown indifferent to her in general, and she no longer needed his closeness now that she had Alice. He moved out and they divided their great art collection amicably.

Gertrude's fame grew, even though she had not yet been officially published. Her salon was always filled with the great artists, writers, and thinkers of the day. Mabel Dodge promoted her, and John Lane agreed to publish her *Three Lives*, the short stories she had written about three women.

During World War I, Gertrude and Alice worked for the war effort, driving supplies and opening supply depots. American servicemen loved her yet had no idea she was the famous friend to artists. After the war, the homeless and disaffected writers that Gertrude labeled "The Lost Generation" found hospitality and appreciation in her. She encouraged Sherwood Anderson, who in turn praised her as a great, original American woman. She helped Ernest Hemingway, reading his manuscripts and offering critiques. They became intimate friends as he shared his deepest concerns with her; Gertrude and Alice were godmothers for his son. Eventually, however, a quarrel ended their close relationship and began a widely-publicized feud that was to last throughout their lifetimes. Hemingway seemed unable to accept Gertrude and Alice's lesbianism. F. Scott Fitzgerald, however, whom Hemingway had introduced to Gertrude, became her great friend and also benefited from her criticism and encouragement. During this period, Gertrude published in small magazines and lectured; for a long time, however, she did not receive the fame for her work that her proteges did.

In 1929, she wrote her first book that could be easily read by the public, and it received fairly wide distribution. Her humorous account of her personal life with Alice, *The Autobiography of Alice B. Toklas*, was serialized in the *Atlantic Monthly* and was a huge success. Her obscurity was over.

She wrote the libretto for an opera called *Four Saints in Three Acts*, which opened in combination with a Picasso show and was so popular that extra cars had to be added to the train to Hartford where it played. Lecturing across America, she charmed reporters and was entertained at the White House. People everywhere were surprised that the avant-garde writer was a warm, witty woman who could explain perfectly well how she had composed her book.

She and Alice now had a large country house in Belignin, France, as well as a new apartment in the city. During World War II and the German occupation, they lived in the country house, oblivious to the danger they were in as American Jews. Their French neighbors protected them, however, and even the German soldiers quartered in her house did not know who she was. When the American Army invaded France, she returned overjoyed to Paris to open her home to American soldiers. She lectured at American bases in Belgium and Germany, where she was always received warmly.

In 1936 Gertrude became ill with cancer. She died a short time later, with the first copy of her loving narrative of American soldiers, *Brewsie and Willie*, in her possession, and Alice at her side.

Eleanor Roosevelt: Human Rights Activist

Anna Eleanor Roosevelt was born in 1884 to an affluent New York family. From the first, she was considered an ugly duckling. Her mother subtly communicated to Eleanor her displeasure in having a child so little resembling the beauties of the family and concentrated her attention on her two younger brothers. However, Eleanor's father, Elliott, favored her, and she loved him deeply, as only a lonely, sensitive child can love. When he was at home, they were inseparable.

Eleanor's happy relationship with him was not to last, however. He had a severe drinking problem, and when she was about six, the family sent him away. When Eleanor was eight her mother and brother died of diphtheria. From then on, she lived with her grandmother, where her father could visit occasionally. She read and spent her time in a world of her own, without friends or a loving family. She was alone and frightened most of the time.

At ten, when she learned of her father's death, she was

desolate and unbelieving. Later, as an adolescent, she could not overcome her sadness and her feelings of not belonging. She had been educated inadequately yet expensively for much of her childhood, but was finally sent to a French school in England headed by a Mademoiselle Souvestre, a talented educator and enlightened, opinionated woman. Here at last in her late teens Eleanor was able to catch up on what had been a spotty education.

Back in New York after three years, she felt suffocated by the necessity of "coming out" in a New York society that terrified her. However, she did as she was expected to do, for she had been reared to be completely submissive to the rituals of society. She knew no other life than one in which one's material needs were completely tended to by others and in which a woman had no responsibilities other than to visit and be visited. She was kept completely ignorant of relationships or marriage.

After her coming out, she saw her distant cousin Franklin Roosevelt frequently; when he asked her to marry him, she agreed because it seemed the thing to do. He seemed to recognize the strength, honesty, and ability in her that she did not yet recognize in herself.

When they were married in 1905, President Theodore Roosevelt, her uncle, gave the bride away. After the honeymoon, they lived in homes prepared and arranged by Franklin's mother, upon whom Eleanor became completely dependent for all her decisions—and yet wondered why she was often unhappy. For the next ten years, usually either pregnant or recovering from giving birth to her five children, Eleanor also played the role of conventional society matron while her husband advanced from his law practice to political activities to government service. When he became assistant secretary of the Navy, Eleanor accepted the burden of social responsibilities, forcing herself to participate in the daily round of visits that seemed so necessary.

World War I changed her life, for suddenly all women were expected to be part of the war effort. Volunteering in a canteen in Washington, Eleanor learned that hard work agreed with her and that she could help alleviate suffering. Galvanized by a visit to the federal insane asylum, where confused, neglected men wandered about unattended, she worked hard for better conditions, persuading the Secretary of the Interior to work in Congress for appropriations and encouraging charitable organizations to fund improvements for the hospital.

This experience created a new woman of Eleanor Roosevelt. By the time the war was over, her life as a socialite was finished, and her life as an agent of social change had begun.

Franklin's sudden affliction with polio in 1921 also caused great change. Now that her husband was severely crippled, Eleanor was forced to become a well-organized and autonomous planner for the family. His mother wanted Franklin to retire and to live in her home as an invalid, but Eleanor fought against this, establishing her first independence from her mother-in-law. She herself became active in politics, partly to reinvigorate her husband, who through determination and effort regained use of his arms and learned to walk with crutches. She persuaded him to run for governor of New York, and he was elected in 1928. After the crash of the stock market and through the deepening depression, she and FDR increased their national political activity, believing that there was important work to do.

When he was inaugurated as president in 1933, Franklin provided political solutions to problems besetting the nation; Eleanor provided personal ones. She rode across the country to see poverty and despair with her own eyes and to bring hope. Whether she visited women garment workers, coal miners, or jobless veterans, she listened and talked to Americans about their concerns. She was tireless and ubiquitous.

Eleanor Roosevelt had lost all fear, it seemed. She dared to work for change in areas where even her husband held back, such as civil rights for blacks and freedom for interned Japanese-Americans. She was not afraid to be seen speaking with Communist youth groups, because she wanted to hear their views, and she wanted to give them hers.

When Hitler's power grew, she decided she needed a keen understanding of the crisis in Europe. Using her contacts, she became an astute observer, advising and supporting her husband with unique talent. Her understanding of political events was matched by her unique charisma. She used her powers to persuade the American people of the horrors of fascism and nazism. Dictators hated this honest and outspoken woman who, like Thomas Jefferson, despised "all tyranny over the minds of men," whether that tyranny was right wing or left wing, ally or non-ally.

During the war she traveled 25,000 miles in the Pacific theater, visiting soldiers at bases and hospitals. When her husband died before the end of the war, she imagined that her opportunity to be of service was finished; to the reporters after FDR's funeral she said, "The story is over."

But it was not over. For the next fifteen years, until the end of her life, she acted, says Archibald MacLeish, as "the conscience of the nation."

President Truman appointed Eleanor ambassador to the United Nations. To the surprise of many, herself included, she elevated this assignment into a crowning achievement. She fought avidly for the rights of refugees the world over. She insisted that the United States uphold the right of the state of Israel to exist. She chaired the United Nations Commission on Human Rights, developing and attaining passage of the Universal Declaration of Human Rights. This document has become the foundation for individual freedom around the world and has shamed tyrants everywhere.

She later said that the story of her life might show how much a woman "of no great talents" could achieve if she overcame timidity and fear.

Margaret Mead: Anthropologist

Margaret Mead was born in 1901 to a "very advanced mother" who was a sociologist working on her Ph.D. and a father who was a professor in the Wharton School of Finance and Commerce at the University of Pennsylvania. She grew up in an academic environment, playing in her father's office and listening to constant talk about university politics. Her mother interrupted her graduate work to raise Margaret, her brother, and her two sisters. Her mother's child-rearing was loving but by the book; lacking imagination, she simply provided the proper food, home, activities, and education and remained very involved in the many liberal causes that typified New England Unitarians like herself.

Margaret's father was somewhat of a rascal, although Margaret claimed she was always a match for him. He was interested in the concrete side of economics and liked to be involved in financial schemes and to watch economics in action. He was often short of funds and seldom honest about it. His minor eccentric rebellions irritated Margaret but drew out the best in her; she claims it was he who taught her how to think like a scholar. He was flippant about her major life decisions but ultimately supportive. He tried to keep her from college by saying she would only get married (the real reason he objected was his lack of money), but when she graduated, he was proud of her and the Phi Beta Kappa status she had achieved. He offered her a trip around the world if she would not marry her first husband, whom she married anyway. He still sent her around the world, and later to Samoa, where she was able to do her first great work.

Throughout her childhood, the family moved around, and Margaret learned that home was wherever one made it. As a child she was never dressed in a typically feminine way and was allowed to engage in far more adventurous play than was her frail brother. Her elementary education was mostly carried out by her paternal grandmother, a superbly intelligent woman who rose to be a teacher and principal in a time when few women worked outside the home. Margaret claimed that this self-assured, creative, independent woman was a decisive influence in her life. In fact, the two women she grew up with were both mothers and professionals, so she never learned that "brains" were unsuitable in women. Margaret was an independent scholar from childhood, reading and writing much of the time and easily passing achievement tests to enter high school. Although she felt different there, she made a strong and successful effort to adapt.

At De Pauw University in Indiana, however, the rigid sorority system excluded Margaret because of her several faults: she was a New Englander, an intellectual, not the Evangelical Christian that most other students were, and she did not wear the right clothes. Experiencing her first true rejection, she nonetheless benefitted from being an outcast: she learned first-hand about racism, religious hatred, and elitism. She fought back, taking the leadership positions she could and making the best of it until she transferred after a year to the more congenial Barnard.

Margaret also learned at De Pauw that she preferred a same-sex rather than coed education. Having seen the conflicts women face when competing with men, she expressed her thoughts in a straightforward manner: "This made me feel that coeducation was thoroughly unattractive. I neither wanted to do bad work in order to make myself attractive to boys, nor did I want them to dislike me for doing good work." At Barnard, Margaret found the intellectual opportunities she had hungered for and a gifted, warmly affectionate group of students. She exchanged poetry with friends, organized seminars on burning issues of the day, became interested in the social sciences and was fascinated by anthropology. Ruth Benedict, assistant to Professor Franz Boas (together they gave birth to the field of anthropology), offered her "the opportunity to do work that matters," and she chose anthropology as her life's work.

Throughout college, Margaret had been engaged to Luther Cressman, a friend since adolescence who was five years her senior and who intended to become a minister. Their marriage was truly egalitarian, and Margaret kept her own last name as a symbol of that balanced union. They went through graduate school together, she in anthropology and psychology and he in sociology.

When her dissertation was completed, she wanted to do her fieldwork immediately; Luther had graduate work to do in Europe. With Boas encouraging her to research adolescence, Margaret persuaded Luther to allow her to go to Samoa, at that time a far too distant and dangerous place for a lone woman, but Margaret insisted that she could manage.

And so she did, throwing herself into her investigation of how Samoans dealt with adolescence in the female. She was "adopted" by a chief and his family. She invented new techniques in the field and was stimulated by her findings.

On the boat home, she met New Zealand psychologist Reo Fortune. Margaret was as excited about her recent discoveries as Reo was with his; fascinated by each other's ideas and thrown together for dinner by the ship's steward, they fell in love. She returned to Luther, however, and thought over her relationships.

Margaret learned from her doctor that there was a strong possibility that she could not have children. Ironically, she had chosen her first husband because he would be a good father. Reo, on the other hand, would be a better colleague. Since, childless, she would be devoting her life to her work, she reasoned that it would be better to be married to Reo. This pragmatic decision seems to have sat well enough with Luther, and so they parted.

She and Reo married, Reo redirected his interest to anthropology, and they arranged their separate sources of scientific grants to allow them to do field work in New Guinea together. Meanwhile, Margaret's first work, *Coming of Age in Samoa*, was a popular and scholarly success, and she had been hired as curator for anthropology at the American Museum of National History in New York City, where between field trips, she enjoyed seeking new objects and rearranging collections. Her next book, *Growing up in New Guinea*, was also a success.

She and Reo went on to study sex roles in culture with the

61

Arapesh and Mundamagor; however, their work did not satisfy them because their major questions were not being answered. The marriage was also beginning to be strained by such problems as Reo's lack of sympathy for Margaret during the fevers that anthropologists in the tropics must endure. After she had spent a difficult time in the field, her meeting with anthropologist Gregory Bateson in the New Guinea village in which he was working was another turning point for Margaret. The ideas she and Gregory developed on sex and temperament furnished the theoretical bridge she had been seeking in understanding problems of similarities in behavioral patterns across cultures. Again, intellectual excitement led her to love. Divorced from Reo, Margaret and Gregory went to work in Bali. Here they performed comprehensive work using new technology that formed a basis for much current field work.

After her marriage to Gregory, Margaret reconsidered the possibility of having a child. She truly wanted one now, and what had changed her mind was the negative effect she had observed in cultures that rejected children. She was determined to have a baby in spite of the strong risk of miscarriage and impaired health, and at last she and Gregory were successful. Mary Catherine Bateson (who was to become famous herself as the author of *Composing A Life.*) was born in 1939.

Margaret had to fight for the right to give birth naturally, to breastfeed, and to be with her child more often than the rigid hospital schedule allowed, but her perseverance won out and undoubtedly paved the way for countless women to do the same in later generations. She was able to have her baby her way, and to rear her with the nurturing that Margaret knew would serve her daughter.

Margaret treasured her role as a mother and found little difficulty in continuing her work as well. For thirty more years, she continued to produce new anthropological findings from the field and to improve the collections of the American Museum of Natural History. Her name became a household word; she was much in demand for public appearances because she communicated so clearly the pleasure of understanding other cultures. Although her work was to come under attack by scholars who criticized her field methods and the nature of her findings, her works are classics. She popularized anthropology and created a deep awareness of the similarity of all human beings in development, temperament, and relationships.

Georgia O'Keeffe: Artist

The second of seven children, Georgia O'Keeffe was born in 1887 in Sun Prairie, Wisconsin, to a Hungarian mother and an Irish father. Her mother loved books and had wanted to be a doctor; her father farmed a large piece of land, ran a dairy, and raised livestock. Perhaps predictably, Georgia retained a visual memory of the first time she was taken outside. As a child, she had a great deal of freedom, enjoyed a make-believe house of her own invention, and wandered happily through the countryside. Her mother took a strong interest in her children's mental development, reading them the classics and arranging for private art lessons, but was otherwise somewhat aloof. Georgia herself seemed sometimes to draw back from others, preferring to play by herself. She liked being different and refused to dress or act like her sisters or other little girls. She loved to play with her father, who was more affectionate and lively than her mother.

Georgia, recognized as an intelligent and curious child, entered school early. She asked questions constantly and was always admonished for having "crazy notions." Later she would say, "I decided that the only thing I could do that was nobody else's business was to paint." She was completely confident that she could do anything she wanted and was not ashamed to be a female. As a child, she even insisted that she knew that God was a woman.

At fourteen she was sent for a year to an exclusive girls' school, Sacred Heart Academy, in Madison. Although very restrictive, it gave Georgia intellectual and cultural stimulation, and so she adjusted to her sudden lack of freedom, performing well—better in her other subjects than in art—and eventually excelling. From an art teacher there she learned that she could paint.

When her family moved to Virginia, she was content to go along. The Wisconsin family was not easily accepted, but Georgia did not seem to be bothered. She was enrolled in an excellent boarding school for girls featuring a modern education rather than "finishing." She was admired by the other students for the extraordinary plain suits and severe hairstyle that made her a striking figure. She was also known, even envied, for her artistic ability: other girls would watch her paint. Georgia accepted their admiration but remained an independent spirit. She responded to the influence of her teacher, Elizabeth May Willis, who discovered her great talent and encouraged her.

This teacher, strongly guiding Georgia's artistic development, was instrumental in getting Georgia to enroll in the prestigious Chicago Art Institute. Here she applied herself seriously and received high honors after the first year. An attack of typhoid fever, however, prevented her from returning. After a year at home, she went to the Art Students' League of New York, where Elizabeth Willis had gone. She studied under the famous William Merritt Chase, who taught her how to use the artists' materials in new ways.

In New York she met her future husband, Alfred Steiglitz, whose gallery was the most daring, avant-garde establishment of its kind. During Georgia's year at the Art Students' League, his controversial gallery featured a completely new concept in art in the sculptures of Auguste Rodin.

Upon returning home after summer school, Georgia learned that her father's business was failing: involved in a number of ill-fated business ventures, he had gradually lost the family savings, so Georgia looked for a job. She worked unhappily as an illustrator in Chicago, hating the city and the tedium of her tasks. After two years and a bout of measles, she returned to Virginia. Her mother was stricken with tuberculosis, and her parents' marriage, strained by illness and business failure, fell apart. Georgia's mother moved with her remaining children to Charlottesville where she operated a boarding house. Her father followed there and tried to start a creamery. These misfortunes seem to have affected Georgia's personality: she became even more reserved and introverted than before.

Georgia went to summer school at the University of Virginia, learning much about the aesthetics underlying art from Alan Bement. He helped her find a job teaching art in the public schools of Amarillo, Texas, a wild frontier town with shootouts and brawls, but also with a surrounding landscape that astounded Georgia. She took long walks alone in the desert, and she taught. Preferring modern techniques, as a teacher she resisted the Texas law requiring uniform, old-fashioned art textbooks. In the summers, she returned to the University of Virginia to teach summer school and study with Bement. After seven years of saving and planning, she was able to return to New York to continue her training at Columbia University Teachers' College.

Alfred Steiglitz's New York Armory Show in 1913 turned the art world on its head. Hundreds of avant-garde European and

American paintings were displayed, and the age of modern art had begun. Georgia O'Keeffe was open to this new world and excited about painting in colors. She received excellent grades in her painting courses—her teachers considered her one of the best students ever—but she paid little attention to her education courses. The influence of modern art in Steiglitz's gallery, Steiglitz's "laboratory of ideas," the gatherings where he challenged artists to paint what was in their minds, and the new aesthetic theories of Charles Dow at Columbia University were having a profound effect on Georgia O'Keeffe: she sensed that she had a career as a painter.

Yet for immediate economic reasons, she again took a teaching job, this time in the sleepy town of Columbia, South Carolina. This position provided the solitude and free time to encourage a great breakthrough. She decided to give up all the influences of others, to give up color, and to return to basic black lines on white paper, intending to express what was in her mind. Behind her locked door, she created her first great abstractions in charcoal. She worked with simple lines and shapes, always being true to her visions and, upon finishing a work, hoping it would appeal to Steiglitz, whose independent opinion she valued above all others. Elated, excited, completely herself, she was having a peak experience.

She sent a roll of her drawings to an artist who was so astonished by the originality that she took them to Steiglitz. At this momentous event, Steiglitz is said to have cried, "At last, a woman on paper!" Steiglitz believed these abstractions to be the first brilliant expressions of the feminine intellect in art, and he wanted to share his reactions with her in person.

A new offer to teach in Canyon, Texas, contingent on her taking more courses at Columbia University Teachers' College, gave Georgia the excuse to leave South Carolina for New York. There Steiglitz arranged a show for her abstractions which, as he had foreseen, caused a sensation. He firmly encouraged her to continue her new work, and she was buoyed by his encouragement and the great public response.

Her blossoming career and Steiglitz's encouragement helped her through the difficult time of her mother's death and the final splintering of her family. She also gave up on a romantic relationship at this time, believing that love would interfere with her creativity at this point in her life.

She moved to Canyon, Texas, to teach and to absorb the essence of landscapes she had come to love. The extraordinary changes of the canyons and sky drove her to her water colors, and she now painted abstractions that burst with desert colors. These striking images made up her first solo show.

Steiglitz was greatly attracted to Georgia O'Keeffe, as she was to him. Impulsively visiting New York, she modeled for him; the photographs were to become famous. Their attraction increased, and Georgia returned to New York to live with him. (He was unhappily married to a rich woman.) This was the beginning of a long, creative partnership of independent artists. Alfred Steiglitz and Georgia O'Keeffe seemed to have an intensifying effect on each other's work in those days; she painted increasingly daring, erotic, and colorful abstractions, and he photographed brilliant images of her austere beauty.

After Steiglitz's wife divorced him, he and Georgia married. She wanted children, but he persuaded her that children would diminish her work, and she decided that her art must receive her primary attention. For eleven years, spending winters in New York and summers at Lake George, Georgia created the paintings that were to make up the first period of her work as one of the greatest American artists.

However, Georgia felt stifled and miserable in the contained environment of Lake George and the urban environment of New York City. She longed for the open spaces and unusual beauty of the Southwest. After many struggles with Steiglitz, who was frightened by the idea of separation from her, she went to Taos, New Mexico, for the summer, where the great second phase of her work began. For the rest of O'Keeffe's and Steiglitz's lives together, Georgia lived "like Persephone:" winter in the cold north with her husband, and summer in the Southwest alone with her work. Her paintings of bones, skulls, and flowers became famous for their strange juxtapositions of life and death, color and absence of color. Along with Eleanor Roosevelt and other distinguished leaders, she was named one of the most outstanding women in America by Good Housekeeping magazine. Although much sought-after for her opinions and conversations, she remained independent, holding off all people but a few friends and known by her acquaintances for her sarcasm and "sharp edges."

After Steiglitz's death, she moved permanently to Abiqui, New Mexico, where she furnished her adobe home precisely and in exquisite simplicity. There she painted until her eyesight began to fail, at which time, encouraged by a young artist friend, Juan Hamilton, she took up sculpture. As in the Renaissance, when parts of works were assigned to apprentices, she hired artists who painted as she directed.

The last years of her life were marked by controversy. Her family and friends worried about Juan's influence over her, and the conflict over her estate would live on after her. She died at the age of 99, her legacy a new vision of American art.

Maya Angelou: Writer, Dancer, Political Activist

Marguerite Johnson was born in California in 1928, the beginning of the Great Depression. Her mother, Vivian Baxter, was separated from her father, Bailey Johnson, when Maya and her brother were three and four years old; at that time they were sent to live with their paternal grandmother in Stamps, Arkansas. Maya and her adored brother were to spend most of their childhood in this small, completely segregated town. Maya had very little contact with whites at all, although she remembers being infuriated that white children called her grandmother by her first name. Her grandmother kept a general store that, through strong determination and good direction, she managed to keep afloat during the depression and beyond.

Maya and Bailey were brought up strictly and piously, their lives centered on schooling and church. Maya loved to read, although her reading material also reflected her isolation from whites: she read almost exclusively African-American authors. She tried to pass off Shakespeare, whom she loved, as black. As Maya and Bailey played adventurous games, she dreamed of a more exciting life, and she chafed against the racial prejudice that told her she couldn't do as she pleased.

When she was eight, she went to St. Louis to live with her mother. She learned much in the large African-American community where her mother lived, but her stay ended in tragedy: she was raped by her mother's boyfriend, who was later murdered, possibly in revenge for this act. Maya survived by turning inward, closing out the world by not speaking—by silencing herself—for some years, even after her return, as a young girl, to Stamps.

Maya continued her education under the watchful tutelage of her grandmother; moreover, she was also sent off to a Mrs. Flowers for instruction in the finer points of being a young lady. Embodying Maya's idea of absolute elegance and poise, Mrs. Flowers was the black community's answer to rich white women. She wore lovely voile dresses, was always fragrant and cool, and spoke with such precision and beauty that Maya loved to listen to her. She gave Maya books to read and poems to recite and made Maya feel special: "I didn't question why Mrs. Flowers singled me out for attention . . . all I cared about was that she had made tea cookies for me and read to me from her favorite book." As a woman, Maya would always remember Mrs. Flowers when she needed reserves of grace and intelligence.

Maya's teen years were difficult and unsettled. She lived at various points with her father in California, her mother in San Francisco, and with nobody at all as a runaway in a junkyard. In San Francisco, she won a scholarship to the California Labor School, where she showed a great flair in the dance and drama courses she took in the evenings while she attended high school. She received high marks and loved school so much that she hid an unexpected pregnancy until her graduation, when her baby was almost full term. At sixteen, she was a mother with a child to support—and herself as well.

She tried work as a streetcar conductor, a cook, and a waitress. She says she got "cocky" and tried to manage a house of ill repute. Trapped by her desire for someone who would take care of her, she was seduced by an older man who persuaded her to work for him as a prostitute. Maya sank lower and lower into cynicism and degradation, but she stayed because she believed in her man's love for her. When he clearly showed himself to be a pimp and a hypocrite, she felt betrayed and alone. At this point, she might have lost forever the chance to realize the potential of her intelligence and strength: she considered using heroin. But she was saved by a hopeless addict who showed her the final, horrible consequences of being a user: out of concern for her, he took her to a hit joint where miserable people like himself showed her clearly where she was headed.

So she returned to work, trying also to learn all she could about dancing, singing, and acting. She sang with a number of bands and hoped to land a serious acting job; her break was a part in *Porgy and Bess* for the touring company scheduled to entertain in Europe for the U.S. State Department. "Just imagine how I felt," she said in an interview. "Me, a poor black girl, in Paris." From this point on, Maya's life became a series of challenges that she met with vigor and intelligence. Truly a citizen of the world, she taught dance in Rome and Tel Aviv. Then Maya decided to move to the likeliest place for success in her field: Hollywood, where she sang and danced in the top night clubs. She met Billie Holliday, who at the end of her career felt a melancholy, wistful attraction to the stable Maya. She spent much time in Maya's home.

Her next move was to New York, where as a member of the Writers Guild she sharpened her already considerable writing abilities under the discipline of the Guild's harsh but fiercely supportive criticism. She wanted to do something to support the efforts of the civil rights leaders and of her people, who were rising everywhere against racial injustice. Together with Godfrey Cambridge, she produced, directed and starred in *Cabaret for Freedom* at New York's Village Gate, a show that brought the most powerful African-American talents into national success. Maya was justifiably proud, never having had any experience in production or funding. She was just spreading her wings. Not long after, she starred as the White Queen in Jean Genet's *The Blacks*. This extraordinary play, which lashed out at the racism of blacks as well as whites, was a sensation. Most of the players were, or went on to become, leaders in theater and film.

These were not the only occasions she drew upon hitherto-untapped wells of creativity within herself. Her success as an organizer had been noted by New York leaders of the Southern Christian Leadership Conference (SCLC); as a result, at age thirty-two she was asked by the Rev. Martin Luther King to be the northern co-ordinator for the SCLC. Wanting more than anything to be successful in this position, she threw herself wholeheartedly into the work of the organization. Through this position she met Vusumzi Make, a South African freedom fighter seeking support in the United States for his political work on behalf of his people. Maya immediately fell in love with him, and their shared commitment was the foundation of an ardent relationship. Vus Make made it clear that one reason he had come to America was to find a strong wife, and he felt Maya was the right woman from the start. She married Vus and went with him to Africa, where she lived a new life as the wife of an important politician, diplomat, and warrior. Her friends were the wives of ambassadors and politicians, and she lived with her son and Vus in comparative splendor in this high-level political world.

However, not satisfied to be kept in this splendor, she found

work as associate editor for an English-language mideastern newspaper in Cairo. Vus objected strongly, but her desire to act on her
abilities prevailed, and, setting out to learn everything about journalism, she succeeded. The conflict with Vus over her work was to
become one of many: He wanted her to be a traditional African wife,
and he wanted for himself the privileges of African husbands, which
often included permission to seek multiple sexual relationships.
Maya could not tolerate his infidelity or the role prescribed for her.
They quarreled frequently, and after a six month trial, agreed upon
in a traditional African palover ceremony, they separated.

Maya went to Ghana, where her son could attend an excellent
university. There, among free black people, she felt a falling away
of the humiliation she had suffered in a racist society. She nursed
her son through a near-fatal accidental injury, and she worked for
a newspaper in Ghana, committing herself to her career as a writer.

Her autobiographical books written in the late sixties and early
seventies, beginning with *I Know Why the Caged Bird Sings*, along
with her poetry, built her reputation as a great writer. She now lives
in New York, where she continues her work for her people and her
art. Often called a Renaissance woman, she believes that she is
among the few fortunate enough to have their gifts released while
many others suffer in silence. The poem she was asked to compose
and read for the inauguration of President Clinton established her
as a voice for the aspirations of all Americans.

Katherine Hepburn: Actress and Activist

It's hard to imagine parents more likely to produce this nonconforming, talented, and eccentric character than Thomas and
Katherine Houghton Hepburn. Katherine Houghton was the free-
spirited heiress of Corning wealth who insisted on a Bryn Mawr
education and earned a master's degree in art from Radcliffe in
1900; Thomas Hepburn was an independent, Johns Hopkins-
trained physician. Together, they were activists and crusaders for
women's rights, birth control, and the prevention of venereal disease. In the prim society of Hartford, Connecticut, where the couple
had moved so Tom could set up his practice, they grew used to
being "well-snubbed."

Katherine, the second of their six children, was born on May 12, 1907. In describing her family, she said, "What luck to be born out of love and in an atmosphere of warmth and interest" (p. 20). As a child she was allowed to be free, climbing trees in the woods, reading whatever she wished, and learning from her father gymnastics and diving. She remembers absolute freedom and no rules—except those against actions which might harm another. The Hepburn house, always full of lively conversation, was visited frequently by the political activists of the day: Lydia Pankhurst, suffragette and women's rights advocate; Margaret Sanger, crusader for birth control; Emma Goldman, anarchist; and Sinclair Lewis, writer and critic of small town mores. Kate was happy to be with her family and especially enjoyed the company of her beloved brother Tom. Desiring few friends outside of the family, the six Hepburn children seemed completely self-sufficient socially, which was convenient, since the other children at the local school were discouraged from associating with the wild Hepburn kids.

Kate's idyllic childhood came to an abrupt end when she was twelve years old: her cherished brother Tom died mysteriously at fourteen while the two were visiting an aunt. Kate found him hanging in his bedroom and in horror tried to cut him down and find help. It was never determined whether he had hung himself in a sudden fit of depression or insanity, or if he had been attempting a prank he had seen a few days before in a movie and had already tried, pretending to hang using a slip knot. The death increased Katherine's isolation from other children. "This incident seemed to sort of separate me from the world as I had known it. I knew something the other girls did not know—tragedy." Assaulted by newspaper headlines and terrible gossip, Kate refused to attend school—she could not bear the whispers of the other girls. Her parents allowed her to continue her education throughout adolescence with a series of private tutors. During this time she also became an avid golfer, playing almost every day. In this way, she passed through adolescence.

When it was time for college, she wanted to follow in her mother's footsteps at Bryn Mawr. There, once again, she had the problem of other girls. She avoided the dining room, spending most of her time in her own room. However, in her second year she got in with a group of girls as lively and independent as she was. She could drive a car, giving the group freedom that was unthinkable to most women of the time. Also at this time she got bitten by the theater bug. Acting in several college plays so pleased her that she began to consider a career on the stage. She met a theater producer who mentioned that she might come see him when she finished college, and that is exactly what she did. She was promptly given a part in *The Czarina*, but she was criticized for her metallic voice and rapid pace and was advised to take voice lessons. She chose to study with one of the greatest coaches, Frances Robinson Duff, who became an important mentor.

Her career was not off to a brilliant start. She got a part in *The Big Pond* but was abruptly released because she spoke too fast. She had a part in *These Days*, which closed after the first few nights. She was an understudy—for two weeks—for a boyish, adventuresome actress whom she admired. Throughout her numerous failures and small successes, her family supported her, even though her father thought acting was "a bit cheesy" as a career for his daughter.

Kate's romantic life was as unconventional as her professional life. She had fallen in love with a poet who was much older than she, but that flame died down as she became more involved in her work. She then fell in love with Ludlow Ogden Smith, an inventor who adored her. They married, but the marriage lasted only a few weeks. She was simply too intent on her acting to stay with him; she had had an offer in Hollywood and needed to go. Luddy was her friend for the rest of his life, even staying frequently with the Hepburn family in their seaside cottage, much to the chagrin of Kate's other lovers, but Kate decided she just wasn't the marrying kind.

She was in love with acting. She read for parts constantly, hoping for a break. She was in a "coma of excitement." Her break did not come quickly or easily, yet while she was being turned down for many parts and released from others, she was absorbing much about acting and her own style, learning how to let her inner spark of liveliness shine through her acting. Her role as a boy-woman in *The Warrior's Husband* was her first real success. She got to work with the great John Barrymore in her first film, *A Bill of Divorcement,* which was a success. She then had a series of good parts. In 1933, she won an Academy Award—one of the first ever given—for her work in *Morning Glory. Little Women* and *Spitfire* followed.

She then had a run of bad movies and so returned to the New York theater, only to get in with a cruel director who ruined her confidence: her acting was poor in *The Lake*, and she was thoroughly roasted by the critics. As her vocal troubles worsened, she sought advise from an excellent coach, but despite this help, she believed the play and her acting in it were doomed. She actually paid the producer every cent she had to get out of the production.

Fortunately she had her family, her dear friend Laura Harding, and the support of a great movie director, George Cukor. Her reputation as poison at the box office finally began to wane as she landed some good parts in great movies: *Stage Door* and *Holiday*.

In her brief affair with Howard Hughes, the aviator, inventor, and multimillionaire, she predominantly had in common with him a wild desire for fame. The great love of her life entered in 1937 when she met Spencer Tracy on the set of *The Woman of the Year*, in which they co-starred. While she first felt only great admiration for his acting, she finally discovered, at thirty-three, what "I love you" meant. Tracy was married and separated, not divorced, and would always stay that way, and so he and Kate never considered marrying, but they lived and worked together for twenty-six years, making nine pictures together as one of America's favorite film couples.

In 1947, Katherine Hepburn, in defense of the many black-listed Hollywood actors and filmmakers, spoke before the fearfully dreaded and powerful Committee on UnAmerican Activities. Her topic, of course, was freedom of speech.

Some predicted this daring act would end her film career, but she was one of the fortunate ones.

In all, Katherine Hepburn made 43 movies and will always be known as one of the greatest actresses of the twentieth century. However, she may also be remembered for her activism for women. Beginning in 1981, she gave her support to Planned Parenthood, the organization her mother had so ardently endorsed. During the eighties, as the political tide turned against women's rights, she fought for reproductive freedom, speaking out as she had during the McCarthy era on unpopular topics. Her films, her activism, and finally, her best-selling autobiography, *Me*, should insure her place in history.

Beverly Sills: Singer and Impresario

Beverly Sills was born Belle Miriam Silverman in 1929 in an all- Jewish section of Brooklyn. Her mother, a homemaker, played opera records all day, and as a tiny child Beverly memorized them and sang along. Her mother believed that all little girls should be able to sing, dance, and play the piano, so Beverly was sent to at least three lessons every Saturday morning. Although her father, an insurance company executive, was not enthusiastic about Beverly's becoming a child performer, he allowed her to appear frequently on the weekly local radio program featuring talented children. She loved show business and her mother supported her, taking her to auditions without pushing her.

At seven, she was renamed Beverly Sills and was given a singing part in a Twentieth Century Fox movie during the child-star craze begun by Shirley Temple. The movie was not a great success, but Beverly's interest in singing was established. She could perform whole arias beautifully in imitation of the great stars. Her mother decided to take her to the best vocal coach known to her, Estelle Liebling, the Coach for the World's Greatest Voices. Miss Liebling had never taught children, but upon hearing Beverly (and knowing that Beverly and her mother had traveled three hours to get there), she agreed to give brief lessons at no cost.

Miss Liebling became a second mother to Beverly, taking her career in hand and training her extraordinary operatic talent in a careful, comprehensive way. She arranged for Beverly to audition to sing for a weekly radio program on CBS, where Beverly's success led to frequent appearances and national recognition. Her father continued to support her because of the total education she was receiving; he paid for her language lessons as well as her special music lessons.

Despite appearances in soap operas and theatrical productions, Beverly's great love was opera. All through her adolescence she attended opera frequently, learned a vast repertoire, and read voraciously the plots of operas and the literary backgrounds of the storylines.

Her father wanted her to have a traditional high school education, but when the impresario J.J. Shubert proposed sending Beverly on tour with a light-opera company, her father allowed her to complete high school in the Professional Children's School in Manhattan. And when she won a math scholarship to Farleigh Dickinson, he was overjoyed, but she refused it in order to begin her serious opera training and performance.

Ending her long, happy career in show business, she set about her lessons with Miss Liebling with energy and enthusiasm. Before long, she debuted with the Philadelphia Opera Company and toured with the Estelle Liebling singers.

When her father died of lung cancer, she was on her way back from a tour of South America. She and her mother moved to a small apartment where they lived when they were not touring. Her mother was a capable and loving companion, making Beverly's costumes throughout her career.

A tour with the Wagner Opera Company, where many opera greats got their start, was the beginning of her operatic career. She sang Violetta in forty *La Traviatas*, learning acting and personal management techniques that would make her a true professional. After many straight, serious, and unsuccessful tryouts for the New York Opera Company, Beverly did an amusing, half-angry audition demonstrating that she did indeed have personality. Hired by the company, she devoted herself happily to her roles.

While she was on tour in Cleveland, newspaper editor Peter Greenough became attracted to her and successfully attracted her to him. He was a married man in the midst of divorce, a father, and a non-Jew, and so he had a great deal to overcome with her mother. He courted them both, and after his divorce, Beverly's mother willingly agreed to their union. Their marriage was a happy one, with Peter strongly supporting her career and Beverly enjoying the role of wife and mother to Peter's two daughters when she was at home between tours.

She wanted children of her own and had a girl, Muffy, and a boy, Bucky, twenty-three months apart. She had taken a leave of absence from the City Opera for a period of childrearing and homemaking in a large house in Boston. However, soon after the birth of their second child, they learned that Muffy was profoundly deaf, and that Bucky was severely retarded. The parents began a search for the proper schooling and help that would allow the children the fullest development of their abilities.

Her friends Sarah Caldwell of the Boston Opera and Julius Rudel of City Opera encouraged her to continue her singing, especially her lessons, in spite of her family tragedies. She did return to the stage, and she since has said that her children's difficulties have brought her inner peace; if they were strong and brave despite their handicaps, she could not be any less.

She went on to become a great American opera singer in a time when Americans had to struggle to be perceived as equal in competence to Europeans. For years she was prevented from singing with the Metropolitan Opera mainly because the Met's director objected to American singers. One of her mentors, Edgar

Vincent, helped her to get a role at La Scala. She sang all over the world, going mad as Lucia di Lammermoor in hundreds of places. "Queens, mad women, country girls, army mascots—I sing 'em all," she said. She met heads of state and sang at the White House. Her charming, bubbly personality (which had led to her nickname "Bubbles" as a child) made her an approachable classical singer to many Americans who had never attended an opera, and she created many new opera-lovers.

When Beverly experienced personal difficulties, she worked harder, thus maintaining her great emotional strength and avoiding self-pity. As chairman for the Mothers' March on Birth Defects, she took her role seriously, finding it to be one of her most rewarding challenges.

After the retirement of the imperious director Rudolf Bing from the Met, Beverly at last made her debut there in 1975. She had proved that one could become an international opera star without the Met, yet now she had the Met, too. However, at the peak of her career in the late seventies, she decided to give up singing before her voice weakened (as voices normally do in older middle age) and devote her energies to directing the New York City Opera—a painful although eventually successful transition from singer to leader. Unknowingly taking on a bankrupt organization, for several years she struggled to find public and private organizations and many personal friends to prop up the ailing opera company. Her tireless fund-raising efforts were doomed to failure as one financial tragedy after another struck. However, she made several creative decisions—one was to provide supertitles in English for all productions, and another was to stage classic light operas—which changed the course of the New York City Opera. By 1986, they were again solvent—and Beverly Sills was recognized not only as a great singer, but a great impresario.

Rigoberta Menchu: Agricultural Worker and Activist for Indian Rights

The youngest of the eminent women discussed here, Rigoberta Menchu was born in 1959 into poverty that is incomprehensible to most Americans. In the hamlet of Chimel, in a northwestern province of Guatemala called El Quiche, she and her family, as Indians, were members of the oppressed majority. Her people were as rich in love as they were poor in material goods, living as close to the earth as human beings can live, sleeping together on the floor of tiny grass huts, often with no covering against the chill of the Altiplano. Rigoberta's parents were village leaders, virtually the mother and father of the whole community. Her mother acted as midwife and nurse, and her father was the spokesman and intermediary for the village. She had many brothers and sisters, two who died young and five with whom she was raised. For a few months of the year they lived happily together in their village, cultivating land which had never been farmed before. In the village, they observed all of the secret and treasured rituals of the Indian people as well as the feast days of Catholicism, a religion they had adopted alongside the native beliefs. Their traditional beliefs had taught them much: that their people, descended from the Mayans, had once had plenty to eat and had ruled themselves; that they had had great kings and great cities; and that white people had taken all power and prosperity away from them.

Rigoberta had no formal education, for school was not possible or desirable for Indian children: they spoke no Spanish and their customs were regarded as dirty and inhuman by the schools. She spent most of the year with her family, working eighteen hours a day on the *fincas*, the coffee and cotton plantations on the coast. As a little girl, she would harvest any beans or cotton growing close to the ground.

The goal of the Guatemalan government and the ruling Ladino minority group seemed to be simply to exploit the Indians to death. Indeed, death was a constant in her life: death by exhaustion in the *fincas*; death by poisoning from lethal agricultural chemicals, commonly sprayed directly on workers; death by starvation in the homes of wealthy Guatemalans who allowed a tortilla and a few beans for their workers; death by disease, because the cure would cost a year's wages; and finally, death by torture at the hands of the government's police for opposing any of these conditions. Rigoberta witnessed all of these. As a child, she watched her little brother die of starvation on the plantation where she was working with her mother. Her mother could not afford a burial, since the *finca* charged exorbitantly for this, as it did for everything else; others had to help so that the child could be laid to rest. Her best friend died of poisoning and suffocation when the crop dusters flew overhead, yet nothing would stop the owners from this practice.

Rigoberta's passionate anger at her people's oppressors made her determined to change their lives, and her father was her model for principled protest against injustice. Although he could not read and spoke only a little Spanish, he persistently fought for his village's right to keep the land which they had discovered, cultivated, and finally made to produce. When the organized-crime families who held most of the power in Guatemala attempted to take over her people's land, her father sought help from lawyers and unions. However, frequently lawyers themselves were in league with the corrupt rich and made peasants' lives even worse. Her father realized that only by villagers banding together with other peasant groups could any change be made. Thus he became a spokesman, not just for his village, but for peasants everywhere who were losing their land and being forced into near slave conditions. Rigoberta went along with her father as he spoke publicly; he often asked her to rise and speak as well.

Rigoberta, a catechist for the Roman Catholic Church, as a child had developed the skills of an organizer and teacher by instructing children and adults in her village in the gospel and the rituals of the Church. Deeply respected as she was for her knowledge of this religion, she still could not speak, read or write Spanish. She was determined to learn. The priest and the nuns taught her some, but she knew she needed far more in order to help her people.

At thirteen, Rigoberta left the life of the agricultural worker to go into service as a maid in the house of rich people in the city. She who had never worn shoes was required by her employer to buy them, and clothes too, at the cost of several month's wages. In this house, she did all of the domestic work yet was treated with less consideration than the family dog, who got much more food. She was called obscene names and made to sleep in a closet. She nearly starved, yet made little progress toward saving the money that she had hoped would help her family get out of the *finca*.

Upon quitting this job and returning home, she learned that her father was in jail for helping his village keep their land. Although Rigoberta, her family, and all of their friends worked to get him out, he was imprisoned for a year and two months. Finally released, he immediately resumed teaching villagers self-defense against the armed soldiers sent to take over the land. Accused of being a communist (most Indians didn't even know what a communist was) and of illegal activities against the government, he was imprisoned again. This time, he met a political prisoner who taught him much about organizing. Freed again through the efforts of international organizations monitoring human rights violations, he happily went to work, telling his family, "Children, look after yourselves, because if I don't come back, you will have to continue my work." From then on he was in hiding, traveling throughout the mountains to organize the Indians.

Rigoberta also began travelling, and she joined the Comite de Unidad Campesina (CUC) and a clandestine peasants' rights group. She was still impassioned about her peoples' suffering but was confused. She didn't understand all the forces at work. For it was not simply the Ladinos who were the enemy, nor simply all Spanish-speaking people, nor even the soldiers, who often were peasants themselves, conscripted and then coerced into torturing and killing their own people. Rigoberta came to understand that the enemy was the entire social structure which ignored the basic rights of the Indians, which forced the poor Ladinos as well as poor Indians to work to their deaths so that a few families could be extraordinarily wealthy.

Rigoberta entered a period of reflection in which she studied the Bible as a means of discovering a way to fight injustice. "As far as sins go, it seems to me that the concept of the Catholic religion is that . . . God loves the poor and has a wonderful paradise in Heaven for the poor, so the poor must accept the life they have on Earth. But as Christians, we have understood that being a Christian means refusing to accept all the injustices which are committed against our people, refusing to accept the discrimination committed against a humble people who barely know what eating meat is but who are treated worse than horses" (p.134).

The Bible, and words, became Rigoberta's weapons. An excellent speaker, she brought great fervor to her work for the CUC. She learned Spanish rapidly from a Ladino co-worker in the movement, as well as two other Indian languages so that she could communicate clearly with all of the people she represented. From 1977 to 1979, her whole family carried on the work of teaching villages self-defense and of negotiating with the government for changes in the laws which oppressed peasants.

In 1979, Rigoberta's sixteen-year-old brother, also a secret organizer, was captured by the army. He was tortured for two weeks, his fingernails removed, his fingers cut off, his skin flayed, his eyes put out; all the while he was interrogated about the whereabouts of priests and nuns who were helping the peasants. After two weeks, he was brought with a truckload of other prisoners back to his own village. And there, before Rigoberta's eyes, he was burned alive. The soldiers warned the villagers that if they got mixed up with communism, this would happen to them, too. After witnessing this, her father left immediately to go and fight; her mother, saying that once one has seen her own child tortured to death, there is no other path, also left to organize; and Rigoberta and the rest of the children made individual decisions and parted from one another, each to join in his or her own way the struggle for justice for their people.

In January, 1980, the first major demonstration against the government by the peasants occurred. Rigoberta's father, along with a group of Indian peasants, took over the Spanish Embassy as a public protest. The Guatemalan government responded by bombing the embassy. Rigoberta's father died in the fire, a martyr to his cause. However, international attention was at last focussed on human rights violations and the oppression of the Indians and poor Ladinos. The conflict escalated, with the government labelling the opposition communists and calling for aid, and the peasants increasing their militancy and their efforts at defense of their land and villages.

After her father's death, her mother felt compelled to return to her own village; all of the leaders in that area had been killed, and she believed she was needed. That decision was her doom, for after a few months she was kidnapped. The tortures she endured were even worse than those suffered by her son: she was raped, tortured until she fainted, revived, and tortured again. The army let it be known that she was still alive in an attempt to get the Menchu children to come out of hiding, but Rigoberta and her siblings knew that it was a trap. Her mother, bound and torn, was left to die. Her body was eaten by dogs.

Rigoberta said, "We know very well, we're quite clear about it, that if the time comes for our parents to die, they die knowing it's for our cause. And I always hoped to see them again. If only we could all be together one day. My mother used to say that through her life, through her living testimony, she tried to tell women that they too must participate, so that when repression comes and there's a lot of suffering, it's not only the men who suffer . . . my mother told them that any evolution, any change in which women had not participated, would not be a change, and there would be no victory" (p.196).

Rigoberta now began to speak to the international community about the horrors she had witnessed. After that, she became a hunted woman. With words as her weapons she was an impassioned, articulate speaker, rapidly improving in all the languages that she needed to communicate her message from her hiding place in the capital. Soon her life was so gravely endangered by her work that she was persuaded to go into exile in Europe, helped there by her friends and by human rights groups. While in Paris, she gave her testimony in a book published first in Spain and then in the United States. *I, Rigoberta Menchu, an Indian Woman in Guatemala* was so simple, honest, and powerful that at last millions of people understood the plight of her own and so many other villages. At its publication, she was only twenty-three years old.

Although in the decade that followed, change was slow, increasing pressure from the international community did lessen the savagery of the Guatemalan government toward its people. Rigoberta continued her work, organizing around the world as she had once organized in the mountains of the Altiplano.

In the midst of her toils she painfully decided to renounce marriage and motherhood as long as she was a leader because, she said, she never wanted to be a widow or a tortured mother. She had been in love with a companero but had chosen her cause over love. Only later, when her global notoriety made her somewhat safer, did she dare marry a partner in the struggle. One of her greatest dreams is to someday be able to have children who can grow up in a country where her people are fairly represented in the parliament.

In 1992, Rigoberta Menchu was awarded the Nobel Peace Prize for her work for human rights. This young woman, who had lived in the greatest poverty and obscurity that is possible in this world, had become the voice of all poor and oppressed people.

The Eminent Women: An Analysis

The women I studied truly transcended the barriers to achievement that defeat so many other gifted women. How did they manage to do so? Clearly, the routes these eminent women took to attain their successes are as varied as their personalities. Some themes that emerge are unexpected. One might speculate, for example, that an eminent woman must have been blessed with loving, intelligent parenting, but many had at least one ineffectual, irresponsible, absent or deceased parent. One might expect all to have shown their genius early, but the giftedness of several went unnoticed in their childhoods.

One might further predict that all these distinguished women benefited from an excellent education, and that they performed as well academically as gifted girls generally do. Yet the truth is that many received only intermittent schooling, and many performed brilliantly only in their areas of interest. Finally, one might assume that these women struggled against sexism and inner doubts throughout their lives. Somehow, however, virtually all of these women decided at some point to ignore the limitations of traditional sex roles and to refuse to acknowledge that a problem existed for them simply because of their gender. Instead, they charged ahead. It seems then that several factors set these eminent women apart, not only from women in general but also from thousands of gifted women who do not achieve eminence.

Time Alone

As girls, all of these gifted women had time alone. Whether the solo time was by choice or by necessity hardly matters. Georgia O'Keeffe seemed to prefer aloneness, and her parents allowed her to explore the world by herself. Eleanor Roosevelt was isolated by circumstances that left her in the homes of relatives who knew little about providing for the social needs of a child. Marie Curie's intellectual hunger was so insatiable that it drove her to withdraw into private concentration even in the midst of a busy family. Maya Angelou was isolated by violence done to her. Rigoberta Menchu worked sixteen-hour days by herself, picking coffee beans.

This time alone can yield much fruit. First, it can encourage one to read or think and to nourish the intellect. Second, it allows one to experience the fulfillment of solitary work, of setting one's goals, then evaluating progress and rewarding efforts. Many adults may never create art, music, literature, or any work of enduring value, simply because they are unable to be alone. For most of us, productivity requires freedom from the distractions of others coupled with actual contentment in the work and in solitude. The eminent women's childhood time alone, if it taught them to highly value contentedness in self and work, may have helped them ignore the negative stereotypes of achievement so prevalent in adolescent peer groups.

Voracious Reading

Most of these talented women spent much time absorbing information, opinions, and new experiences through reading. All except Rigoberta Menchu were prolific readers in childhood—and Menchu became one as soon as she learned how to read. Eleanor Roosevelt described how her childhood reading took her into unusual worlds that were often unpopular with disapproving adults; she even found that if she asked questions about some controversial point in a book, the volume quickly disappeared. She said her copy of Dickens' *Bleak House* was missing for weeks! Some of the women, for instance, Eleanor Roosevelt and Margaret Mead, read widely in many subjects. Others, such as Georgia O'Keeffe and Beverly Sills, enjoyed reading intensively within their interest areas, even if it meant neglecting other responsibilities. Reading differed in pattern and also in function, providing for some immersion in a loved subject, for others an escape from tense family situations. Regardless of the primary motivation for reading, the result was that these women grew up under the influence of great thinkers, expressive advocates, and articulate story-tellers.

It is easy to forget that a child, especially a gifted one, may be as affected by the voices of authors as by those of family and friends. Genius sometimes seemingly emerges out of nowhere, and parents of distinguished people are often quite ordinary. For many gifted children, books take over information and guidance roles that might otherwise be played by family and school, and authors of favorite books become counselors, teachers, and sometimes even parents. Hence early reading may explain how some of these eminent women overcame a lack of parental guidance or nurturing.

Being Different or Special

All eminent women felt different or special, in both positive and negative ways. For those whose gifts were apparent early, adults could not help but communicate their admiration—or occasionally irritation—at the little girls' precociousness. Marie Curie was aware of her intellectual giftedness from an early age; her schoolmates amused themselves by testing her extraordinary memory. Beverly

Sills was a prodigy at seven, starring on a nationally broadcast radio show.

Some of the gifted women were aware early on that they differed because they belonged to an unusual family. Margaret Mead, embarrassed by her mother's progressiveness and her father's eccentricities, sometimes wished she could have a normal family. Katherine Hepburn also suffered the distinction of being from an "odd" family, a difference accentuated by her brother's death. Gertrude Stein set herself apart from her unhappy, explosive family, while Eleanor Roosevelt mourned not having a family at all.

For some of the eminent women, feeling different was heightened by their appearance: Eleanor Roosevelt was quite plain, Gertrude Stein stout, and Georgia O'Keeffe striking with her sharp features, all differences that set them apart from more traditionally pretty girls. There is and always has been an ideal physical model of a woman, although that ideal changes from era to era or magazine to magazine. At one time it was a flat-chested, bobbed-hair flapper; at another, a snub-nosed, long-legged athlete. But whatever "the look" may be, noted women often come nowhere near it, and so they learn to value their talents rather than their appearance. Even the beautiful Katherine Hepburn was made to feel that she was too boyish looking by her peers.

Individualized Instruction

Eminent women received individualized instruction as children, often in their areas of future fame. Language lessons, art lessons, music lessons, at-home scientific experiments, and home schooling were methods of individualizing education for the gifted girls who became accomplished women. This kind of training for girls was once more common than it is today, but the distinguished women described here had an especially large part of their education individualized. By allowing them to proceed at their own faster pace, individualized instruction probably kept boredom at a minimum while at the same time advancing their knowledge and skills. In addition, such tutoring was often provided by someone who also functioned as a mentor or model and who communicated clear attitudes and expectations about learning and achievement.

Same-Sex Education

It should be pointed out that for many eminent women, individualized instruction was given within the context of a supportive, same-sex educational environment. Many of the eminent women went to all-girl schools and/or all-women colleges, or benefitted from girls' activities. Same-sex education gave the girls and women the attention they deserved and provided many models of intellectual achievement. The affluent women, such as Eleanor Roosevelt and Katherine Hepburn, went to the best girls' schools and colleges. The poor ones found models and got a fair chance to stretch their talents in same-sex groups such as Rigoberta Menchu's catechist class.

Difficult Adolescence

Many of the eminent women studied experienced embarrassing social awkwardness in adolescence. Only one, Beverly Sills, was truly sociable and popular during her adolescence. Margaret Mead, treated cruelly by the sorority system, felt ignored and unpopular. Eleanor Roosevelt dreaded her coming out and was dismayed by her lack of social skills. Georgia O'Keeffe held companions at a distance much of the time, rejecting others to avoid risking rejection herself.

An awkward adolescence compounded other experiences for these women. First, it emphasized their sense of separateness, which often was rooted in a lonely childhood. Second, it left in them a lasting understanding of the costs and benefits of nonconformity. Third, it increased their time alone and encouraged them to focus inwardly on their dreams and intellectual achievements. Finally, for Margaret Mead, Rigoberta Menchu, and Eleanor Roosevelt, it stimulated compassion for and identification with the suffering of oppressed or unaccepted people.

Separateness and the Ability to Avoid Confluence

Many women view themselves entirely or primarily as a part of someone else. In a relationship some women may even experience confusion about their own interests and values and those "borrowed" from their partner. Some women seem incapable of saying *I*, but say instead *we*, as in "We feel happy" or "We like Tom's new job." Psychotherapists call this blending *confluence*, from Latin words meaning "to flow with." Confluent people confuse their own and others' feelings, and their sense of identity is not clearly their own but rather merges with the other. On the other hand, Carol Gilligan in *In a Different Voice* (1984) suggests that the search for connectedness which guides most women's decision-making is a healthy, normal aspect of women's development.

Somehow, most eminent women seem capable of connectedness in relationships without giving up their own identities and goals. It would appear that the women studied resolved the problem of confluence by the time they began their life's work. Many always felt separate from others; these women always had a clearly unique sense of self. Margaret Mead, Georgia O'Keeffe, and Gertrude Stein seem to have grown up with firmly established, even powerful, identities. Marie Curie struggled through a confluent, unhappy romantic attachment before she understood and appreciated her own identity. Eleanor Roosevelt's sense of separateness and identity emerged only after she accepted herself as having goals not necessarily tied to her husband's. When Eleanor visited the asylum and observed the misery of the patients, she knew her goal was to do something about the problem. From that moment, she devoted her energies to helping the poor, the disenfranchised, and those who lived in fear, not because these represented Franklin's political needs but because they represented her concerns. Husband and wife formed a creative partnership, with Franklin supporting Eleanor's interests. After Franklin died, she proved that her own commitment to human rights was lifelong.

Taking Responsibility for Oneself

One great decision altered the course of Eleanor Roosevelt's life: the decision to be guided by her own actions and beliefs. She determined that her own identity, convictions, and values were meaningful and worthwhile. Major single events and decisions similarly shaped the lives of many other distinguished women. Existential philosophers refer to this sort of decision or event as "taking responsibility for one's own existence." Each of the thirty-three women studied did just that. None was satisfied to identify herself in relationship to another person; each identified herself as a woman working on ideas or tasks.

Love Through Work

An early feminist of Georgia O'Keeffe's youth said, "First you must find your work; then you will find your love." This axiom held for most of these women. For many, their romantic lives were so entwined with their intellectual lives that the two were inseparable. Margaret Mead chose all three of her primary relationships because the partner fit her work at that period. Less pragmatic was the relationship of Georgia O'Keeffe and Alfred Steiglitz: their early relationship combined the ecstasy of romance with delight in the new images they were creating. The intensity of the relationship of Pierre and Marie Curie was that of mind touching mind as well as heart touching heart. And without her work, Gertrude Stein could not have attracted Alice B. Toklas, who exclaimed that "a bell rang" telling her that she was in the presence of genius when she met Gertrude, evoking intense feelings and making her want to stay by her side. The relationship of Katherine Hepburn and Spencer Tracy became a famous model of a man and woman working together and loving each other.

Refusal to Acknowledge Limitations of Gender

The distinguished women studied not only typically denied limitations of their gender, they often seemed to deny their limitations as human beings! Surely all knew the sex-role traditions of their society and the expected limitations on feminine accomplishment that those traditions imposed; however, they seemed to deliberately ignore any such limitations. Some, like Rigoberta Menchu, preserved a respect for the traditional role of women in her society, while consciously choosing another path because of the larger mission she saw for herself.

Just as Margaret Mead said she was always aware that brains were not unsuitable for women, most of these women characteristically assumed a stance of equality with men even when faced with strong resistance. Similarly, they denied any inferiority of their sex. Georgia O'Keeffe was furious when she was called "the greatest woman artist" because she did not see any reason for "woman" to be used as a qualifier.

Mentors

Most celebrated women have had mentors, men or women who nurtured their talents and provided them access to a profession. A mentor is not just a tutor or a coach, but rather is an individual who takes an abiding and intense interest in the person as well as in the talent. Mentors identify with their protegé's successes and support them through their failures. The close personal relationship of the mentor and protegé can become parental in nature, or may evolve into a romantic attachment. Mentors to eminent women always seemed to have access to the highest level of their profession. This does not mean that eminent women succeed only because "they know somebody." Rather, their talent is great enough to impress a member of the inner circle of a profession. A certain amount of luck may go into finding the mentor, but in the end, it is the giftedness of the woman that attracts the mentor. Beverly Sills's Estelle Liebling is an example of a maternal mentor to whom Beverly was "family." Franz Boas was a paternal mentor for Margaret Mead. Mentor Alfred Steiglitz developed a romantic relationship with his protegé.

It is possible, even likely, that without their mentors, many gifted women would not have achieved eminence. Historically excluded from the most elite professions, women more than men need mentors to gain entrance. Mentors open the network of power that guides professions and guilds. Even in areas relatively open to women, a mentor is often necessary to strengthen the chances of a superbly skilled but unaggressive woman to reach the top.

Thorns and Shells

Many of the gifted women needed to "grow thorns." Often, their predilection for excellence caused them to be impatient with and biased against the ordinary and mediocre. Their intensity expressed itself as intolerance, self-righteousness or arbitrary insistence, even with their peers. Gertrude Stein and Georgia O'Keeffe were sarcastic and sharp-tongued. Margaret Mead could be very brusque with those who disagreed with her.

Those who do not grow thorns seem to grow shells instead. Marie Curie never overcame her shyness; she was always uncomfortable except among a small group of friends and family; the stress of her public appearances certainly contributed to her ill health.

Eleanor Roosevelt, with substantial effort, did overcome her timidity in order to speak out for others, but she retained a personal modesty that made it difficult for others to know the private woman behind the public person. Maya Angelou gave up the shell she had taken on as a child but retained an assertive wit.

Again, Beverly Sills is the exception; her bubbly personality seems to need no protection, possibly because she always knew acceptance and admiration. Her life suggests that it is not female giftedness, per se, that produces thorns and shells, but rather others' reactions to this female giftedness.

Integration of Roles

Most of the illustrious women studied chose to integrate myriad tasks in their lives stemming from their roles as leaders in their field, as wives, as mothers, and as companions. Most of the mothers made use of nurses, governesses, and household help, as one would expect. Yet the evidence suggests that the eminent women who were also mothers were as committed to parenting as they were to their work. Marie Curie took her first baby everywhere with her—hiking, traveling, studying—happy to be sharing her life with her daughter. Margaret Mead fought to have natural childbirth and breastfeeding on demand at a time when social mores and hospital rules were strictly against these practices. Her work as an anthropologist gave her a knowledge of what was best for her baby, to which she held firmly despite pressure by the medical profession to bottlefeed on a strict schedule, to ignore the infant's cries, and to require the mother to be isolated from the child for the first few days. Fortunately, her friend, the famous pediatrician Dr. Benjamin Spock, supported her in her choices.

Beverly Sills found new strength through coping with her children's disabilities. She made sure not only that they felt her deep love but also that their future was secure, establishing financial trusts for the best care and education for her children. She extended her love to all children as chairperson of the Mother's March of Dimes.

As wives, these women frequently showed as much dedication in their relationships as they did in their careers, and often went "the extra mile." Eleanor Roosevelt nursed Franklin through the pain of his illness and planned his psychological rehabilitation with insight and determination. Marie Curie, even while contending with her loneliness and grief, finished the research her husband was working on at the time of his death and saw to it that the findings received the proper exposure.

89

None of these women were complaining "superwomen," either self-pitying or martyrs; instead they were strong women who decided calmly, if boldly, to live life to its fullest.

Ability to Fall in Love with an Idea

Of all of the capacities of eminent women, the most important was the ability to fall in love with an idea. This concept was first used by creativity researcher Paul Torrance to explain the process by which creative individuals choose their life's work. It is certainly related to the motive described by Nietzche as being stronger than love, hatred, or fear: the capacity to be interested. Falling in love with an idea is more than being able to identify an idea or subject that is personally exciting. It is a lasting, often intense, absorbing, life-long interest that ultimately leads to an expansion of that idea or subject.

All the eminent women described had that ability: Marie Curie nearly starved to death because she immersed herself so totally in the study of physics; Georgia O'Keeffe locked herself into a room with charcoal and paper; Gertrude Stein wrote a novel of hundreds of hours of work to prove to herself she could do it. Each of these is certainly an example of a woman in love with an idea. This ability, and the intensity involved, is almost certainly at the heart of the success of eminent women.

Conclusions

The characteristics of these eminent, gifted women reveal much about what it takes to accomplish one's dreams and goals. Time alone, a perception of being different, a sense of separateness, and even thorns and shells all seem to make it possible for a gifted woman to work, undistracted and unafraid. These conditions isolate and protect her from the daily barrage of stereotypic sex-role images and demands. They protect her from powerful peer pressures to conform, comply, and adjust to being a female. These conditions feed on each other: time alone leads to feeling different and separate, which leads to thorns and shells, which lead to time alone . . . and so on.

These conditions hurt sometimes. The difficulty of adolescence for gifted women seems to be compounded by aloneness, separateness, and difference at a time when most young people want nothing so much as to blend perfectly with their popular peers. Yet experiencing loneliness as a girl may lead to acceptance and even delight in solitude as a woman.

Voracious reading, individualized instruction, and mentoring nurture female genius. Clearly, a standard, unadorned public school education is not likely to be the means by which gifted young women attain their intellectual goals. Not that public school instruction is bad for gifted women: it is simply not enough for those with a chance for dazzling achievement in adulthood. Most schools do not provide equitable instruction for girls. Most schools allow little time for the intensive reading that gifted girls want; in fact, students are likely to get in trouble for reading outside material. The slow pacing and teaching to the lowest common denominator in the regular classroom essentially constitutes a waste of the precious learning time of gifted girls. Individualized instruction, especially concentrating in children's major fields of excellence, is imperative for nurturing intellect and talent in gifted girls. One-on-one instruction releases the student from pressures to conform to the group, to act dumb, or to await information passively. Same-sex education and guidance may provide the same freedom.

Mentoring is the crucial link between education and career for eminent women. A good mentor is a model, sharing trade secrets and protecting the bright woman from sex discrimination.

By meeting their significant other through work, successfully integrating roles, and refusing to accept gender limitations, many of the eminent women in our study got the support they needed for their rigorous lifestyles. It is evident that gifted women can be bold in pioneering new horizons in partnerships and mothering, just as they pioneer within their own intellectual domain, for with the three conditions listed above, gifted women may marry, become parents, and still contribute to the world of work.

Finally, assuming responsibility for oneself and the capacity to fall in love with an idea are distinctive properties of women who achieve their goals and overcome barriers to the fulfillment of their dreams. Eminent women are cheerfully obsessed with and adamantly committed to their ideas. These ideas make them free and fearless: they can face and enjoy aloneness; they have confidence in the paths they have chosen; they ignore opposition or meet it with firmness if not ferocity. Society has many ways of attacking and muzzling the gifted woman simply by ignoring her, but a gifted woman in love with an idea is well-armed against the apathy of others.

91

References

Andersen, Christopher. *Young Kate*. New York, NY: Dell.
This biography of Katherine Hepburn is somewhat more psychological than her own autobiography, searching for the roots of her extraordinary assertiveness and unique persona in her childhood among activists, suffragettes, and individualists.

Angelou, Maya. *I Know Why the Caged Bird Sings*. New York: Random House, 1969.

Gather Together in My Name. New York: Random House, 1974.

Singin' and Swingin' and Gettin' Merry Like Christmas. New York: Random House, 1978.

The Heart of a Woman. New York: Random House, 1981.

All God's Children Need Traveling Shoes. New York Random House, 1986.
These autobiographies, significant additions to American literature, reveal the milieu of many gifted black girls and women. Maya Angelou's struggle to realize her potential is compellingly and vividly described.

Curie, Eve. *Madame Curie*. New York: Doubleday (Pocketbooks), 1965.
A poignant and fascinating biography of a great scientist by her daughter, it describes the insatiable intellectual curiosity of the scientifically gifted girl as well as her struggles, similar to those encountered by many gifted women, in her search for knowledge. It is also the love story of a couple together by common work and mutual respect.

Greenfield, Howard. *Gertrude Stein: A Biography*. New York: Crown Publishers, 1973.
Probably the clearest, most objective biography of a woman who inspired much feeling, it describes well her unusual childhood and education as well as her gradual self-discovery as a writer and patron of the arts. The many photographs—especially those of Gertrude in her art-laden salon—are delightful.

Hepburn, Katherine. *Me: Stories of My Life*. New York, NY: Ballantine.
This energetic book is the result of Katherine Hepburn's fearless examination of her own life. In reviewing all the people and events that shaped her acting career, she saved the best stories for last.

MacLeish, Archibald. *The Eleanor Roosevelt Story*. Boston: Houghton Mifflin, 1965.
This great American poet's lyrical tribute became a film of the same name. With only a few pages of text and many photographs, his book captures the emotional response of a nation to one of its beloved citizens.

Mead, Margaret. *Blackberry Winter: My Earlier Years*. New York: Simon & Schuster (Touchstone Books), 1977.

A readable autobiography applying Margaret Mead's anthropological viewpoint and methods to the study of her own life. She shows how kinship, community, schooling, marriage, work, and childbirth shape intellectual and emotional life. Her story provides one example after another of the sense of autonomy and separateness needed by women in order to achieve.

Menchu, Rigoberta. *I, Rigoberta Menchu, An Indian woman in Guatemala*. New York, NY: Verso.

An emotionally difficult story full of Menchu's anguish in losing most of her family to torture and death, this biography of a woman whose fight for the freedom of her people is still not over is, in my opinion, the most important of this series. Like no other it shows the capacity of a gifted woman to endure unimaginable hardship and to embody extraordinary courage in service to her mission.

Roosevelt, Eleanor. *The Autobiography of Eleanor Roosevelt*. New York: Harper and Row Publishers, 1958.

Three volumes cover the time from her birth through her triumphs in the United Nations. The story of an underachieving, emotionally troubled gifted girl who blossomed into a far-sighted, active humanitarian when seized by the possibility of commitment to a cause, it is a modest but eloquent record of the thoughts of this great woman.

Sills, Beverly. *Bubbles: A Self Portrait*. New York: Bobbs-Merrill, 1976.

Sills, Beverly & Linderman, Lawrence. *Beverly: An autobiography*. New York: Bantam, 1987.

The indomitable soprano, with words and pictures, tells her story in such a way that this musically and dramatically gifted woman comes alive. The first book, realistically presenting her path from Brooklyn, N.Y., to the stage of the Met, would provide good career education for any vocally talented girl. The second includes the transition from opera star to impresario.

Stein, Gertrude. *Everybody's Autobiography*. New York: Random House (Vintage Books), 1977.

A stream-of-consciousness, chatty, hilarious ramble through the life experiences of the author, it is not for the reader who wants quick facts. Much of this book is incorporated in the one-woman Broadway play, *Gertrude Stein, Gertrude Stein, Gertrude Stein*. One of the most accessible of Gertrude Stein's books.

Supplemental References

Albert, R. S. *Genius and Eminence*. New York: Pergamon Press, 1985.

Barry, J. *Infamous Woman: The Life of George Sand*. New York: Doubleday and Company, 1977.

Bateson, M. C. (1984). *With a daughter's eye. A memoir of Margaret Mead and Gregory Bateson*. New York: Pocketbooks.

Bell, Q. *Virginia Woolf. A Biography*. New York: Harcourt, Brace, Jovanovich, 1982.

Blanchard, P. *Margaret Fuller: From Transcendentalism to Revolution*. New York: Delacorte, 1984 .

Bourke, White, M. *Portrait of Myself*. New York: Simon & Schuster, 1963.

Bradford, S. *Harriet Tubman: The Moses of Her People*. Gloucester, MA: Peter Smith, 1981.

Bullett, G. *George Eliot: Her Life and Books*. New Haven: Yale University Press, 1948.

Castiglia, J. *Margaret Mead*. Englewood Cliffs, NJ: Silver Burdet, 1992.

Cook, B. W. *Eleanor Roosevelt*. Vol. 1. New York: Viking, 1992.

Davis, A. *Angela Davis: An Autobiography*. New York: Random House, 1974.

DeBeauvoir, S. *Memoirs of a Dutiful Daughter*. New York: Harper & Row, 1958.

DeBeauvoir, S. (1962). *The Prime of Life*. New York: Harper & Row.

Douglas, E. I. *Margaret Sanger: Pioneer of the Future*. New York: Holt, Rinehart & Winston, 1970.

Gilligan, C. *In a Different Voice*. Cambridge, MA: Harvard, 1984.

Goldman, E. *Living My Life*. New York: Knopf, 1931.

Hale, N. *Mary Cassatt: A Biography of the Great American Painter*. New York: Doubleday, 1975.

Harns, T. F. *Pearl S. Buck: A Biography*. New York: John Day Company, 1969.

Hellman, L. *An Unfinished Woman*. New York: Little, Brown & Company, 1969.

Hogrefe, J. *O'Keeffe, The Life of an American Legend*. New York: Bantam Books.

Huxley, E. *Florence Nightingale*. New York: Putnam, 1975.

Johnson, T. H. *Emily Dickinson: An Interpretive Biography*. New York: Atheneum, 1980.

Kramer, R. *Maria Montessori*. New York: Putnam, 1976.

Lindbergh, A. M. *Bring Me a Unicorn*. New York: Harcourt, Brace, Jovanovich, 1972.

McDonagh, D. *Martha Graham*. New York: Praeger, 1973.

McFarland, D. T. *Simone Weil*. New York: Unger, 1983.

Meir, G. *My Life*. New York: Putnam, 1975.

Plath, S. *The Journals of Sylvia Plath*. Hughes, T., Ed. New York: Dial Press, 1983.

Reid, R. *Marie Curie*. New York: Dutton, 1974.

Robinson, P. C. *Willa: The Life of Willa Cather*. New York: Doubleday, 1983.

Schultz, G. *Jenny Lind, the Swedish Nightingale*. New York: Lippincott, 1962.

Sitwell, E. *Taken Care Of: The Autobiography of Edith Sitwell*. New York: Atheneum, 1965.

Tims, M. *Jane Addams of Hull House*. New York: Macmillan, 1961.

Wagenkencht, E. *Harriet Beecher Stowe: The Known and the Unknown*. New York: Oxford University Press, 1984.

Yewchuk, C., Chatlerton, S., & Jackson, J. "Survey of eminent Canadian Women: Demographic data." In J. L. Ellis and J. M. Willinsky, *Girls, Women, & Giftedness*. Toronto, ONT: Trillium, 1991.

Chapter 5

Major Works and What They Tell Us

When *Smart Girls, Gifted Women* was published, very little research had been done on the subject. Most of the information I had gathered was from decades-old studies and obscure microfiches. However, a few classic studies emerged which continue to have significance for today's gifted women. Terman's longitudinal study of gifted boys and girls, begun in 1921, was one of these, as was the Kaufmann study of Presidential Scholars and the Rodenstein and Glickhauf-Hughes study of gifted women who integrate career and family.

Now, several new works on gifted women add to our knowledge. A wonderful collection of research that has brought out most of the information about gifted women's lives through time has been recently published (Arnold, Noble, and Subotnik, 1996.) An ongoing study of high school valedictorians by Arnold (1994) shows great differences in achievement for gifted men and gifted women, and surprising differences in how gifted men and women perceive their own intelligence.

A 1969 study by Norma Jean Groth examining changes in gifted girls' needs for self-esteem and achievement acquired impressive support from a new nationwide study performed by the American Association for University Women (1991). These works are reviewed in the chapter on barriers to achievement.

Other new studies have great relevance to understanding gifted women. The 1992 study by Lyn Brown and Carol Gilligan assesses social and emotional development at a private school for girls. Holland and Eisenhart (1991) studied the "culture of romance" on college campuses.

Each of these studies, classic or new, will be described briefly, stressing only the most important points for gifted girls and women.

Gifted Women's Lives Through Time

Study I: Terman and Oden's Gifted Women

Psychologist Lewis Terman, often called "The Father of Gifted Education," believed that gifted children need to be identified and provided with a special education. He worked closely with psychologist Melita Oden to create studies which would initiate a new understanding of the gifted. In the early 1920s, using Terman's own recently-developed I.Q. tests, Terman and Oden first evaluated a group of eleven-year-olds. The subjects were subsequently reevaluated six times throughout their lives, either by Terman and Oden or by their successors (Terman, 1925; 1959; Terman & Oden, 1935; 1947). Now in their eighties, the subjects continue to be studied. The findings, which fill five volumes entitled *Genetic Studies of Genius*, destroy the myth that the brilliant youngster is peculiar, unhealthy, and doomed to insanity. In *Terman and the Gifted* (1975), May V. Seagoe tells the story of Terman's search for the factors that influence achievement and traits that characterize children of high I.Q.

The popular psychology of the early 1900s in America abounded in stereotypes of the intelligent. Many people believed in "early-ripe, early-rot: that the precocious child would surely wither by adolescence. Bright children were characterized as sickly and puny, nearsighted from reading too much, clumsy and incompetent at physical and athletic activities. Common belief held that intelligence went hand in hand with personal and social maladjustment. Little wonder, then, that a negative and disapproving concept of giftedness emerged. The more intelligent a child, the more physically, socially, and psychologically deficient he or she was expected to be.

In this climate, Lewis Terman and Melita Oden were determined to learn the truth about the nature, development, and life of the "genius." Working from a test devised by French psychologist Alfred Binet to separate mentally deficient children from average and above-average children, Terman developed an intelligence test that he believed would measure "the ability to acquire and manipulate concepts." The resulting Stanford-Binet (named for the original test and the university where Terman made his home) became the first and eventually the most widely-used individual intelligence test.

Terman and his four colleague-interviewers (women psychologists or graduate students who later became professionally eminent psychologists in their own right) set out to identify, on the basis of the Stanford-Binet, the top 1 percent of school children in the major California school districts. In 1921 and 1922 the interviewers asked hundreds of teachers to nominate their brightest students for testing. With a total of 1,528 children so identified, the amount of data gathered was astounding. Each child was administered an individual intelligence test, the Stanford achievement test, a general information test, seven "character tests" (measures of personal and social adjustment), and a test of interest in and knowledge of play. Besides all of this, thirty-four anthropometric measures (height, weight, etc.) were completed, along with medical exams, a home information blank, a school information blank, an interest blank, a two-month reading record, an assessment of socioeconomic status, and a case history. Rarely in history has any group of children received a more in-depth investigation.

Some surprising facts emerged. Although school achievement of these children was generally high, it was not as high as had been predicted. Then came the startling evidence that their social adjustment was not only better than had been predicted, but better than that of average children. Even physically, gifted boys and gifted girls were "superior": they were taller, stronger and more athletic than their peers. The myth and stereotype of the intelligent, awkward weakling had been put to rest. In addition, for the first time a portrait of the gifted girl emerged: she was found to be strong, healthy, confident and well-adjusted, with high aspirations and interests suitable for high achievement.

Study II: Women Presidential Scholars—What happened to them?

Dr. Felice Kaufmann, an educator of the gifted, produced a unique doctoral dissertation at the University of Georgia in the early eighties: she performed a follow-up study of the Presidential Scholars of 1964-1968 (Kaufmann, 1981). Her study differed distinctly from Terman's. First, the subjects were members of quite a different generation, the largest ever born: the Baby Boomers of the early 1950s, about two generations removed from Terman's gifted women. Second, far more than either Terman's subjects or mine, these Presidential Scholars inhabited a rarified intellectual realm, for with only two Presidential Scholars chosen from the top-ranking National Merit Scholars in each state, they had, literally, one-in-a-million minds. All were in the top one-tenth of 1 percent of the nation in academic achievement. While Terman's subjects were moderately gifted, the Presidential Scholars were highly or profoundly gifted, terms used to describe those who score 150 and above on I.Q. tests.

Kaufmann, wanting to know what had become of this extraordinarily intelligent group, assumed that regular contact had been maintained with the Presidential Scholars. After all, weren't they a rich national resource? The records of the Presidential Scholars were kept in the U.S. Office of Gifted and Talented, but that office became defunct during Reagan's term of office. Finally, she located the records in Washington and made a shocking discovery: no contact had been made with these scholars after they were first recognized at the White House!

What she had thought would be straightforward research became grueling detective work as Kaufmann made thousands of phone calls and visits, hounding families, friends and acquaintances of Scholars. She enlisted the aid of found scholars in locating her subjects, and within a year she had located 501 (83 percent) of the Presidential Scholars and had sent each a forty-one item questionnaire.

Since the 322 subjects who responded were representative of the entire group of Presidential Scholars, the data seemed accurate and valid. The results were intriguing: the career development of the Presidential Scholars reflected the turbulence of American society during the late sixties and early seventies, with many gifted individuals in nontraditional careers. Most had participated in the counterculture, yet even so, the educational and professional attainment of the group was extremely high. The marriage and childbirth rates for the gifted women in the group were low compared to that of the general population; they had achieved more than the women in the Terman study but still were poorly paid, compared to gifted men. Felice Kaufmann added another follow-up study (1986) that focused on the impact of mentoring. Her findings had educational, economic, and political significance: she found that women who had had mentors earned salaries equal to those of men. Only the women Presidential Scholars who had failed to find a mentor were in low-salary occupations. Kaufmann's findings document how a group of highly gifted women born five decades after Terman's women have fared in their career and personal development, and how the critical variable of mentoring changed the course of gifted women's lives.

Study III: The Illinois Valedictorian Project

In 1981, Dr. Terry Denny, Professor at the University of Illinois at Champaign-Urbana, attended graduation ceremonies at high schools all over the state of Illinois. His goal was to enlist the valedictorians of as many high schools as possible in his study of the development of academically-talented students. The eighty-one top achievers who agreed to participate have been followed up ever since with surveys and interviews. After Denny's retirement, Dr. Karen Arnold, who had begun to work with Denny as a graduate student, took over the project. A former valedictorian herself, Arnold had a special interest in the development of the women students.

The Illinois valedictorian project (Arnold, 1994) is important in several ways. First, it is among the few studies in existence which measure giftedness by performance; these students had proven their intellectual ability by a near-perfect performance in high school coursework. Second, the study used an excellent combination of survey and interview material to present a truly vivid picture of these students. Third, Arnold's special concern for women seems to have insured that the questions asked by the study illuminated women's lives, making it a penetrating look at gifted young women who came of age in the 1980s.

The subjects had grown up in a conservative region during a conservative era of diminished expectations and pragmatism, yet they also were the first generation of whom it was expected that women would work for at least part of their young adulthood. Despite this expectation, the realization of early promise was far more difficult and complex for women than it was for men, according to Arnold and Denny's findings. Beginning in the sophomore year of college, there was a steady attrition of academically achieving women, coupled with a severe lowering of intellectual self-esteem that continued throughout young adulthood.

Although women and men participants had received equally high college entrance examination scores and had subsequently earned equal college grade point averages, women lowered their estimates of their intelligence over their college years. The women, but not the men, showed a sharp drop in their view of their own intellectual abilities between the senior year of high school and the sophomore year of college. By the senior year of college the women had raised their self-assessments somewhat, but they never caught up with the men again in intellectual self-esteem. Not a single woman believed she was far above the average in intelligence, although a quarter of the men believed they were.

By the sophomore year of college, women were very concerned about combining career and family; in fact, they began to drop out of challenging academic programs, fearing that they couldn't fulfill both career and family goals. Apparently, men were not concerned about combining family and work, because they did not discuss this issue as a part of their career and life planning.

Furthermore, the study also found that most of the women planned to drop out of or to interrupt their careers for child-rearing, whereas none of the men intended to do so. The difference between women who pursued high-level careers and those who didn't was not ability; rather, it was values surrounding career and family combinations, along with willingness to interrupt career plans, that most determined the career status of gifted women ten years after graduation.

Three Studies of Gifted Young Women's Passages

The conflict between the need for achievement and the desire for connectedness in relationships seems to recur in studies of gifted women. Three research studies have focused on the critical periods in which this conflict becomes most intense.

Study IV: An Abrupt Change in Wishes

First, there was an unusual and interesting study by Norma Jean Groth on declining achievement in gifted women. This obscure work, now on a barely-readable microfiche, was presented at the national convention of counselors in 1969. Truly cross-sectional, it included subjects of widely varied age groups. It is *still* the only comprehensive study of gifted girls and women at each stage of life development. Gifted ten- to fourteen-year-olds were drawn from a summer institute for gifted; gifted men and women, from fifteen years to seventy, were drawn from the Los Angeles MENSA, an organization for the gifted.

Groth was interested in how her subjects compared on need levels as described by Maslow's hierarchy of needs. According to Maslow, when such basics as food and water are denied, those needs dominate behavior until they are filled. Then the needs of the next level emerge. Beginning with the physiological, the needs progress to safety, love and belonging, self-esteem, and finally, self-actualization. Therefore, an individual is not likely to be free for creative activities (self-actualization) until he or she has met all of the other needs. Only at the level of self-actualization are individuals able to utilize their full potential, Maslow believed. He encouraged people to fashion lives that met needs at each level until the need for self-actualization came into the forefront.

Groth assessed the level of needs simply and straightforwardly by having each individual list three wishes, for commonly people's fantasies reflect current needs. She then determined the highest level of need inherent in the wish. In this way, she was able to discover just how far gifted girls and women had progressed in meeting their needs and striving toward more complex goals.

Both gifted women and gifted men progressed and regressed considerably in level of needs throughout their lives. However, the pattern of progression and regression of females was especially interesting in light of the Terman and the Realization of Achievement Potential studies. Women were observed to have strong self-esteem or achievement interests until the age of fourteen. At that point, desires for love and affection became much stronger than desires for self-esteem and achievement. The intense need for love and affection continued in women until the age of forty, when self-esteem regained importance. Men, on the other hand, tended to

101

maintain strong interests in achievement throughout adolescence and adulthood, until retirement age. This study has important implications for gifted females at particular ages: there may be critical periods during which gifted females are more or less likely to experience needs for achievement. A review by Carolyn Callahan and Sally Reis (1996) comparing older and newer research on gifted girls and women uncovers continued evidence of these critical periods for intervention.

Study V: At the Crossroads

Dr. Carol Gilligan set out to study girls when nobody else was interested. In the early 1980s there was not enough material on girls to make up a chapter of a textbook of adolescent psychology. Gilligan had established herself as an authority on women's development: her book, *In a Different Voice* (1984), was both a scholarly and popular success. In it she argued that men's ways of making decisions, particularly moral decisions, were fundamentally different from women's. Hence women's moral development, she claimed, should not be measured by male standards. In the early eighties, she began a research project with Lyn Mikel Brown which aimed to expand our knowledge of the psychology of girls using the girls' own voices.

Brown and Gilligan (1992) worked with students at the Laurel School for Girls in Cleveland, Ohio. Although not labeled gifted, the subjects were certainly a select, bright group, and the results of the study have implications for a general understanding of gifted girls. Interviewers met with girls in the first, fourth, seventh and tenth grades at the start of the project in 1986; each year thereafter, follow-ups of each girl were conducted.

The girls were asked to describe a time when they had experienced a conflict. Clear differences emerged in the younger and older girls: early primary girls were outspoken and opinionated and worked hard to be heard, while older girls often doubted their opinions and decisions, had difficulty expressing themselves, and were not as concerned about being heard. Brown and Gilligan saw the girls change over time: the same ones who were confident and outspoken became unsure of themselves. The authors attributed much of the change to the increasing tendency as girls got older to pretend to have feelings they did not have. They also hid feelings and opinions which they considered possibly hurtful to others. By learning to be "nice," girls gradually lost touch with their own voices. One measure of growing uncertainty was the remarkable increase in the number of times adolescent girls said "I don't know" in the course of their conversations. Statements like these, as well as pauses, hesitations, and other qualifiers, were characteristic of adolescent girls' communication in a process which Gilligan and Brown call self-silencing.

Although most of the results of this study are disturbing, particularly for gifted girls, there was one hopeful result: girls involved in the study emerged in leadership positions in the school. Apparently, just having an adult take them seriously was all that was needed to help them find their voices.

The Culture of Romance

Anthropologists Dorothy Holland and Margaret Eisenhart were especially interested in young peoples' peer cultures and wanted to know how women respond to the university and to experiences of discrimination within the university. Holland and Eisenhart (1990) also wanted to know how women's everyday experiences in college, particularly their experiences with the peer group, affected their choice of a major and a career. Their study was ethnographic, meaning that interviews and subjective responses were emphasized rather than objective tests and measures.

Chosen for the study were twenty-three women from two schools, one a large southern university and the other a predominantly African-American university. The subjects had records of strong academic performance (B+ or better) and a serious commitment to pursuing a career. One-half of each group at both universities were math and science majors. This group of talented young women was closely watched for three semesters, contacted again at graduation, and studied again four years after graduation.

The interviewers were young women a few years older than the participants, to each of whom an interviewer was assigned for the length of the study. Many of the interviewer-student pairs became close. The interviewers recorded not only the answers to their questions about majors and careers, but also all of the commonplace conversations which took place among the participants and their friends in the residence halls and gathering places.

103

A first observation, backed up by a survey of the women's most common activities, was that very little time was spent in conversation about or activities focused on academics and careers. Less than 25% of their activities were directed toward schoolwork or career, and many did not know the majors or academic interests of their peers. More important, the dominant topic of conversations among the participants and their peers was relationships with men. Even talk about other women centered around those women's ties to men.

Holland and Eisenhart also confirmed the findings of earlier researchers of campus culture: all found that while men achieved status in the peer group through activities and accomplishments or through relationships, women attained status only through relationships with high-prestige men. The participants in their study seemed to understand this, and many did not like having to be in a relationship with a man to achieve status. Some women resolved this by quickly establishing a relationship so they could be off of the "auction block." The authors said, "To spend time and money to make oneself physically attractive, to hear from others about romantic endeavors, to plan for activities in which romantic possibilities can be exercised and even to give up one's own interests, activities, and plans, all make sense when viewed from the perspective of the model of romantic relationships and the route to prestige it prescribes for women" (p. 106).

Very few women in the study were oriented toward academic work which enhanced their career development. All were quite bright, but their attitudes toward scholarly life kept them from fulfilling their intellectual potential. Those whose academic goal was just getting by never committed to their majors. Some saw their goal as doing well, especially getting As, but when they discovered how hard it was in college to earn high grades, they often concluded they lacked the ability needed for those particular courses and sought less challenging ones. A third group, trying to "learn from the experts," became demoralized by the considerable expertise of their professors, thinking that such achievement was beyond them, but they did continue to work hard. Only this group had a sense of purposefulness and direction that carried them over disappointments with grades, teachers, and coursework. For most of the students, however, the culture of romance served as a distraction from any purposeful career development. The longterm result was that most women in the study changed to less challenging majors or let themselves drift away from career goals they had once held. By the end of the study, at the four-year follow-up, most were in what the authors termed "marginalized" jobs: lower-status jobs which afforded little opportunity for self-actualization or increasing development of talents. As women's career identities became more marginal, their romantic identities became more central. None of the women attempted to escape the demands of the culture of romance. It was simply a fact of life, one which greatly influenced women's attaining or not attaining their goals.

Study VI: Never Catching Up—The Realization of Potential Study

Josefina Card and her colleagues (Card, Steele, & Abeles, 1980), in studying bright people born after 1945, found that two major factors accounted for sex differences in achievement. The first, early socialization, had been recognized for some time. Other researchers had shown that girls are subtly taught to relate their failures, but not their successes, to ability. Boys, on the other hand, are taught that their successes are a reward for their abilities, while their failures reflect bad luck. Over the years, girls lose their confidence in their achievement ability; boys by contrast gain confidence. Such differences in early socialization by parents, teachers, and others have been shown to have striking impact on achievement, resulting in women failing to realize their potential.

However, Card and her colleagues at the American Institutes of Research in Palo Alto, California, believed that the differences in realization of potential for men and women were so great that some additional factors must surely be present. And so they focused their attention on another aspect: the difficulty of women in traditional roles in American society to devote time to the achievement-related world of school or work. From a human capital perspective, one has only so much time and energy to invest. Life patterns that lessen one's time for intellectual, physical, or social development reduce the likelihood of further achievements. For women, marriage and parenthood usually reduce drastically the time and energy available for investment in education and the workplace. By contrast, men traditionally have less conflict between family responsibilities and their investment in education or work.

Card and her colleagues studied this second factor through follow-up data on 4,035 Project Talent high school students. They expected to find sex differences in realization of potential in all socioeconomic levels, and that whether rich or poor, a woman who had homemaking and childrearing responsibilities would have decreased achievement. They further suspected that the difference in achievement for men and women would increase with age, with women becoming progressively less able to participate in careers. Third, they believed that the futures of women with high potential would be the most affected by family life, since they had the potential to go further in a career.

To measure realization of potential, one must first estimate that potential. Card and her colleagues developed an achievement potential composite, which scored each subject on five existing measures of actual achievement, including academic aptitude, as measured by ninth-grade achievement scores; high school grades; how the student reacted to parents' expectations; how the student viewed the expectations of friends for his or her education, ranging from "will quit high school" to "will complete professional or graduate school;" and the student's own expectations, ranging from "definitely will not go to college" to "definitely will go to college." Actual achievement was measured six to ten years later by combining educational attainment, annual income, and job prestige. By comparing predicted with actual achievement, the authors obtained a Realization of Achievement Potential (RAP) score for each person.

As predicted, the average man showed a positive realization of potential, and the average RAP score for the women was negative. Sex differences in average educational attainment and average salary were striking. Average prestige differed, but only moderately because more men were in very low- or very high-prestige jobs, while most women were in average-prestige jobs.

The prediction that poor and rich women alike would be underachievers turned out to be true. Socioeconomic status had little influence on realization of potential, even though the poor subjects began with less potential.

Subjects in the highest 25 percent of achievement potential produced the most impressive findings. As the author notes, "These were individuals who showed early signs of being able to succeed in obtaining a good education and a prestigious, well paying job. Failure on the part of these talented individuals might result in keen losses to society" (p.19).

In the group of the highest achievement potential, women fell furthest behind men. Women with average potential achieved less than men with average potential, while high potential women achieved far less than high potential men. Strikingly clear also were the hindering effects of marriage and childbirth on achievement, particularly for those women with the highest potential. The more children gifted women bore, the more difficult it was for them to realize their potential in career attainment. The importance of the Card study lies not only in its description of women who under-achieve, but also in its clarification of the economic and environmental reasons for their underachievement.

A particularly telling aspect of this 1979 study is that it has stood the test of time. Research today continues to affirm its findings. A study presented at the American Economics Association (Loprest, 1992) showed similar results: women's salary growth did not keep pace with men's, with women's tendencies to move to part-time positions keeping them from catching up with male peers.

Study VII: The False Choice— Career vs. Family

In an early study of gifted women's career paths, Judith Rodenstein and Cheryl Glickhauf-Hughes (1979) at the Guidance Institute for Talented Students in Madison, Wisconsin, noticed that gifted girls in particular were reinforced for their abilities, but simultaneously taught that the acceptable female role was a supportive one. Paradoxically, increasing numbers of women in the 1970s and 1980s successfully combined career and family. Since many were gifted women who had participated in the Guidance Institute as high school students, the authors decided to follow up former participants in the Institute since 1957 in order to understand how "integrators" (women who combined family and career) differed from single career women and homemakers. The 201 gifted women located, born in the 1950s, were between 24 and 35 years of age at the time of the study. This was the first study which compared three possible lifestyles for gifted women.

Rodenstein and Glickhauf-Hughes carefully defined the terms career-focused, homemaker, and *integrator* and categorized their subjects accordingly. They then found important differences among the groups: career-focused women had had more scientific interests; homemakers more social interests. Integrators fell between the two. As girls, all had had parental support for their choices, but surprisingly, the career-focused ones as girls apparently ignored both positive and negative feedback from parents. The most important finding, however, was that integrators were as satisfied with their careers as career-focused women and as satisfed with their roles as wives and mothers as integrators. The study results clearly disproved the myth that career and homemaking could not be successfully combined, and the data shed light on upbringing, education, interests, and traits that foster the integrator's lifestyle. This study, too, has stood the test of time, for recent research on dual career couples shows high levels of adjustment and well-being for women combining career and family. Because the vast majority of gifted girls who are now entering adolescence will have careers as well as families, the choice of career *or* family is now obsolete.

These findings continue to be supported not only by the research, but also by the actual lives of gifted women. Subotnik and Noble (1994) in *Beyond Terman* and Arnold, Subotnik and Noble in *Remarkable Women* describe numerous examples of ways in which gifted women have integrated career, marriage and children.

References

Arnold, K. *Academically Talented Women in the 1980s: The Illinois Valedictorian Project.* In K. D. Hulbert & D. T. Schuster (Eds.) *Women's Lives Through Time: Educated Women in the Twentieth Century.* San Francisco, CA: Jossey-Bass, 1994.

Arnold, K., Noble, K.D. and Subotnik, R.F. Remarkable Women: Prespectives on Female Talent Development. Cresskill, N.J.: Hampton Press, 1996.

Brown, L., and Gilligan, C. *At the Crossroads.* Cambridge, MA: Harvard University Press, 1992.

Card, J. J.; Steele, L.; and Abeles, R. P. "Sex Differences in Realization of Individual Potential for Achievement." In *Journal of Vocational Behavior* 17, 1-20, 1980.

Greenberg Lake Analysis and American Association for University Women. *Shortchanging Girls, Shortchanging America.* Washington, D.C.: AAUW, 1991.

Groth, N. J. "Vocational Development for Gifted Girls." ERIC Document Reproduction Service No. ED931747, 1969.

Holland, D.C. and Eisenhart, M.A.(1990) *Educated in Romance: Women, Achievement, and College Culture* Chicago, IL: University of Chicago

Kaufmann, F. "The 1964-1968 Presidential Scholars: A Follow-up Study." In *Exceptional Children*, 48, 2, 1981.

Kaufmann, F., Harrel, G., Milam, C. P., Woolvertoon, N. and Miller, J., "The Nature, Role and Influence of Mentors in the Lives of Gifted Adults." In *Journal of Counseling and Development*, 64, 9, 1986.

Loprest, P. J. "Gender Differences in Wage Growth & Job Mobility." In *American Economic Association Papers and Proceedings*, 82, 2, 526-532, 1992.

Rodenstein, J. M., and Glickhauf-Hughes, C. "Career and Lifestyle Determinants of Gifted Women." In *New Voices in Counseling the Gifted*, N. Colangelo & R. T. Zaffran (eds.) Dubuque, Iowa: Kendall/Hunt, 1979.

Seagoe, M. *Terman and the Gifted* Los Altos, CA: Kauffman, 1975.

Sears, P. S. and Barbee, A. H. "Career and Life Satisfaction Among Terman's Gifted Women." In *The Gifted and Creative: A Fifty Year Perspective*, J. Stanley; W. C. George; and C. H. Solano (eds.). Baltimore: Johns Hopkins University Press, 1977.

Subotnik, R. and Noble, K. *Beyond Terman: Contemporary Longitudinal Studies of Giftedness and Talent.* Norwood, N.J.: Ablex, 1994.

Terman, L. M. "Mental and Physical Traits of a Thousand Gifted Children" In *Genetic Studies of Genius*, Vols. 1 & 2. Stanford: Stanford University Press, 1925.

Terman, L. M. "The Gifted Group at Mid-Life" In *Genetic Studies of Genius*, Vol. 5. Stanford: Stanford University Press, 1959.

Terman, L. M. and Oden, M. "The Promise of Youth" In *Genetic Studies of Genius*, Vol.3 Stanford: Stanford University Press, 1935.

Terman L. M. and Oden, M. "The Gifted Child Grows Up" In *Genetic Studies of Genius*, Vol.4. Stanford: Stanford University Press, 1947.

Chapter 6

Bright Beginnings:
The Gifted Girl

Katie's lavender skirt and T-shirt are as soiled as if they've been worn all day, although it's only 9:00 a.m. Since seven this morning, when her mother brought her to the daycare center, the four-year-old has rolled on the floor like a tank, piled up milk crates with Timmy and Josh and tumbled down from the top, and bitten Ben on the chin when he fell on her, starting a free-for-all.

Miriam, a second-grader, likes her Brownie troop, shopping at the mall, and making cookies with her mom. But nothing compares to reading horse stories and galloping around the house on her stick horse, Grits, imagining that she is a famous horsebreaker, renowned for her ability to tame the wildest stallion.

Ten-year-old Jennifer has been told that she has an I.Q. of 165, but she doesn't want any special recognition. She hopes her test score will let her get out of a few boring classes at school so she can read in the school library. She thinks being a librarian must be heaven.

These are three gifted girls, definitely child-like, recognizably female, but somehow different from most other girls. Like birds in the spring, they are in their most colorful phase. Later on, they will blend in, perhaps so much that their gifts will never be spotted. But for this brief time of childhood, gifted girls are enthusiasts, scholars, clowns, dreamers.

Few educators or psychologists have studied the gifted female in this bright and florid phase, from preschool to junior high. Most of the available knowledge about the gifted girl comes from Terman's long-range study, where the girls, like the boys, were healthier, taller, and stronger than were average youngsters. They were as happy and well-adjusted (or more so) than average child, and they had more "social knowledge" than did average children, meaning that they knew how to read subtle cues in interpersonal situations and understood group dynamics at an early age. In short, they understood people, and they knew what people wanted of them. Time after time, studies comparing gifted girls to gifted boys, average girls, and average boys have shown gifted girls to have less depression, fewer conduct disorders, and fewer social/peer relationship problems than any other group. This Terman finding has stood the test of time.

Gifted girls in Terman's study displayed more leadership ability, rising naturally to dominant positions in children's groups. They were more achieving—but not extraordinarily more—than other girls in school. Their families were somewhat higher in socioeconomic status and often had more education than did those of average children, but many gifted girls were born to working-class families with low education levels.

What about differences in identifying boys and girls as gifted? More boys than girls were identified by Terman—116 for every 100—even though the Stanford-Binet had been constructed with fairness to gender in mind. Boys' and girls' scores were combined in the original standardization group; therefore, it is likely that the disproportionate number of boys was a statistical fluke. In all studies of the Stanford-Binet I.Q. test, no evidence of sex differences in scores has been found. In the revisions and restandardizations of this test, care continues to be taken so that the test will select an even number of girls and boys (Lutey & Copeland, 1982).

At first testing, psychological sex differences appeared to be less apparent within this gifted group than across the population as a whole. Gifted girls tended to like the same school subjects and play activities as gifted boys. They were more like gifted boys than they were like average girls in many interests and activities, the tests showed. This explains why so many eminent women, as children, enjoyed the company of brothers and other boys; their biographies burst with images of active, exciting, outdoor play. As a girl, author Willa Cather rode her pony over the prairie all day long, and Margaret Mead built villages in her back yard. Again, current studies have confirmed Terman's finding, and the characteristic now called androgyny is common among gifted girls.

Gifted boys and girls did show differences in preferences and activities. Boys preferred adventure stories; girls, straight fiction. Amazing Stories, an early science fiction magazine, was a favorite of the boys, while the girls read Good Housekeeping. Boys enjoyed science and math in school; girls loved English. Girls liked dramatics; boys liked leadership activities. Girls were more easily influenced by disappointments than boys, or at least they had a greater tendency to admit such influence. Girls mentioned their mothers as a major influence in their lives six times more often than boys did.

Although gifted girls were more like gifted boys in many ways, they nonetheless maintained attitudes, values, and social behaviors expected of girls, perhaps to keep themselves from seeming markedly different from the norm. Being a well-adjusted gifted girl meant being similar enough to the average to avoid notice and gain approval. The highly gifted girls sometimes did not seem to be as adjusted or as concerned about approval.

Gifted girls today have even higher career goals than did the girls in Terman and Oden's studies. Now, gifted girls' childhood goals are almost indistinguishable from those of boys, except for a bias toward "people" careers.

Like their male peers, highly gifted girls were sometimes loners without much need for recognition, as Felice Kaufmann's study documented. This may explain why eminent women, as girls, spent so much time alone. Some of the comparisons and contrasts of males and females in Kaufmann's study yielded unexpected results. A high percentage of the girls were second-born females in their respective families. Most of the female Presidential Scholars were from suburbs and small cities rather than from rural or urban areas. Perhaps urban and rural gifted girls are blocked from high academic achievement by the scarcity of educational resources characteristic of many rural and inner-city schools. Rural schools may also add pressures to conform, preventing gifted girls from displaying their scholarly abilities. As girls, the female Presidential Scholars generally did not have remarkably high career goals. Even so, they maintained

113

outstanding academic achievement—the highest possible throughout school. They seemed to love learning for its own sake, a trait that may have been for them, as it was for the eminent women studied, the beginning of developing a sense of mission or vocation.

A commonly held belief is that the relationship among parental influences, career, and lifestyle choice is a simple one: that is, many believe that more encouragement and modeling will automatically produce a stronger career orientation in girls. However, many a parent who is eager to support her gifted daughter's achievement is surprised by how unresponsive the daughter is to parental encouragement. But equally ignored are the many parents who actively discourage and deny their daughters' talents; fortuitously, Gertrude Stein and Margaret Mead tuned out the tactics of their discouraging fathers. As the Rodenstein and Glickhauf-Hughes study showed, most of the parents of the gifted girls were supportive, but the actual occupations of the parents did not influence whether the gifted girls become career-focused women, homemakers, or integrators. Not much relationship existed between the parents' support for accomplishments and the lifestyle that was chosen, and the amount of encouragement given to pursue education or career plans seemed to make little difference. Interestingly, the career-focused gifted women *rarely paid attention to parental support for a career choice*. These results can be better understood in the light of my findings about parental ambivalence toward girls' giftedness. Parents may have been encouraging, but the encouragement may have been so minimal or ambivalent that the women who became career-focused were only those able to ignore the mixed signals they were getting. The career-focused may have had very strong inner direction and sense of purpose.

Finally, Norma Jean Groth's study of the wishes and needs of young, gifted girls seems to agree with Terman's psychological profile of such girls. She interviewed a large sample of ten-year-old gifted girls to determine at what level of need they were functioning. Clearly, the basic needs of food and shelter were met for these girls and, most likely, the need for basic security was, too. What interested Groth was how gifted girls would respond to the higher order needs, which range in complexity from affection to self-esteem to self-actualization.

When asked to tell stories about wishes they had, the girls most frequently told stories or described wishes related to achievement. At age ten, they were actively attempting to fulfill needs for self-esteem and were intensely interested in school or club successes that could contribute to their self-esteem. Relationship issues, such as the desire for girlfriends or boyfriends, were clearly not as important to gifted girls as achievement issues. Many teachers and parents of younger gifted girls can be reassured by these results—particularly that gifted girls at this age may survive quite well with many books but few friends.

Carol Gilligan's interviews with bright girls of this age at the Emma Willard school also portrayed these girls as confident in their opinions, strong in their preferences, and willing to tell anyone what they thought.

Summary

The major studies cited are the sources of most of what is known about preteen gifted girls. They afford only glimpses of the girls' lives, but because these studies are based on well-designed research, these are probably accurate glimpses. The subjects of these studies ranged in ability from bright girls in the upper 25 percent of achievement potential to highly gifted girls in the top one-tenth of one percent on standardized achievement tests. From this research emerge some key dimensions, as well as answers to some basic questions about the experiences of younger gifted girls.

Key Points:

- Many gifted girls are superior physically, have more social knowledge, and are better adjusted than are average girls.
- In their interests, gifted girls are more like gifted boys than they are like average girls. Even so, they usually maintain enough behaviors of other girls so as not to seem too "different."
- Gifted girls have high career goals.
- Gifted girls are more strongly influenced by their mothers than are gifted boys.
- More highly gifted girls are not as likely to seem well-adjusted.
- Highly gifted girls are often loners without much need for recognition.

- Highly gifted girls are often second-born females.
- Suburbs and small cities produce more female Presidential Scholars than do rural or urban areas.
- Highly gifted girls aspire to careers having moderate rather than high status.
- Highly gifted girls have high academic achievement.
- Actual occupations of parents do not affect gifted girls' eventual choice of a career.
- Career-focused gifted women may have had, as girls, to be indifferent to all pressures or encouragements in order to pursue their interests straightforwardly.
- Gifted girls at age ten express wishes and needs for self-esteem.
- Gifted girls are interested in fulfilling needs for self-esteem through school and club achievements.
- Gifted girls are confident in their opinions and willing to argue for their point of view.

Questions and Answers

- *Do gifted girls have common early childhood experiences?*

Sex differences in young gifted girls and boys are less apparent than they are in the population as a whole. This means that young gifted girls are likely to enjoy the type of play that boys like. The gifted girl may not necessarily be a tomboy, but she is likely to be more active than other girls are, to be a little more interested in adventurous play, and to prefer the company of boys. She may like dinosaurs and science fiction, "Dungeons and Dragons," and computer games more than most girls do. She has vivid, dramatic career goals.

She may be more sensitive than other girls are and more sensitive than gifted boys, especially to disappointments. Her sensitivity may show in irrational or frequent worries and fears, upsetting nightmares, or easily-hurt feelings.

Despite these sensitivities, gifted girls are likely to have excellent social knowledge and therefore are able to be "well adjusted"— if they so choose!

In other words, gifted girls usually know what they need to do in order to fit in. Commonly, this means that they will read girls' magazines, participate in feminine play activities such as playing house and playing school, and behave as average girls do most of the time. Gifted girls will readily participate in traditionally feminine activities, even if they aren't crazy about them, simply because they are usually cheerful, friendly and compliant little people. They want to please, and they accurately read that society will be most pleased with them if they are not too different from other little girls.

There is some evidence that the brighter the girl, the more likely that she may not choose to please. Some highly gifted girls may choose social isolation over conformity if none of their true interests coincide with those of their peers. Some gifted girls observe the results of a lifetime of attempting to please, and decide to do differently.

Are there typical family patterns of gifted girls? It seems that gifted girls can happen in almost any family! There is no evidence that girls of working or professional mothers are more likely to be gifted than girls whose mothers stay home, or vice versa. Birth order may be related to giftedness in girls, but the findings are unclear and complex. Terman's gifted were more often first born; Kaufmann's highly gifted were more often second born.

- **Do gifted girls have any academic experiences in common?**

One of the most common findings of the major studies was the superior academic performance of gifted girls. They not only outperform average girls and boys, they consistently outperform gifted boys in grade school and high school. They receive higher grades than gifted boys do, at least until just after high school graduation; highly gifted young women continue to get better grades than their male peers in undergraduate years. Like average and lower-performing girls, gifted girls prefer English and humanities to the sciences. Unlike average girls, quite a few gifted girls excel in and enjoy math. Gifted girls tend to participate in many school activities, although there is some tendency to prefer dramatics to the leadership activities preferred by gifted boys. Gifted girls are interested in school achievement and seem to meet their need for self-esteem through their achievements. As a result of their behaviors and attitudes, the typical teacher seems to like gifted girls and vice versa. This generally leads to contentment in the school environment. Gifted girls, in elementary school, are off to a bright start.

References

Brown, L. & Gilligan, C. *At the Crossroads*. Cambridge, MA: Harvard University Press, 1992.

Card, J. J.; Steele, L.; and Abeles, R. P. "Sex Differences in Realization of Individual Potential for Achievement." *Journal of Vocational Behavior*, 17, 1-20, 1980.

Groth, N. J. "Vocational Development for Gifted Girls." ERIC Document Reproduction Service No. ED931747, 1969.

Kaufmann, F. "The 1964-1968 Presidential Scholars: A Follow-up Study." In *Exceptional Children*, 48, 1981.

Lutey, C. and Copeland, E. P. "Cognitive Assessments of the School-aged Child." In *The Handbook of School Psychology*, C. Reynolds and T. Gutkin (Eds.). New York: Wiley, 1982.

Rodenstein, J. M. and Glickhauf-Hughes, C. "Career and Lifestyle Determinants of Gifted Women." In *New Voices in Counseling the Gifted*, N. Colangelo & R.T. Zaffran (eds.). Dubuque, Iowa: Kendall/Hunt, 1979.

Seagoe, M. *Terman and the Gifted*. Los Altos, Calif.: Kauffman, 1975.

Sears, P. S. and Barbee, A. H. "Career and Life Satisfaction Among Terman's Gifted Women." In *The Gifted and Creative: A Fifty Year Perspective*, J. Stanley, W. C. George, and C. H. Solano (eds.). Baltimore: Johns Hopkins University Press, 1977.

Terman, L. M. "Mental and Physical Traits of a Thousand Gifted Children." In *Genetic Studies of Genius*, Vols. 1 & 2. Stanford: Stanford University Press, 1925.

Terman, L. M. "The Gifted Group at Mid-Life." In *Genetic Studies of Genius*, Vol. 5. Stanford: Stanford University Press, 1959.

Terman, L. M. and Oden, M. H. "The Promise of Youth." In *Genetic Studies of Genius*, Vol. 3. Stanford: Stanford University Press, 1935.

Terman, L. M. and Oden, M. H. "The Gifted Child Grows Up." In *Genetic Studies of Genius*, Vol. 4. Stanford: Stanford University Press, 1947.

Chapter 7

The Adolescence of the Gifted Girl

For the first time in her life, Stacey is not worrying about getting straight As. She is becoming increasingly popular among her seventh grade peers, and her best friend says that Sean Davis, the most popular boy, wants to go out with her. Stacey can't think about much else.

Tonya, one of the highest-scoring students in the Talent Search in mathematics in her state, has attended special summer institutes for the gifted for the last two years. She loves the summer institutes, where she has made some good friends, and hates coming back to her high school, where she is unpopular and considered weird. She wants to get out of high school as soon as possible, enter college early, and study medicine.

Jodie has received a National Merit Scholarship and has applied to and been accepted by Bryn Mawr and by Stephens College. She has decided to attend her state university instead, however, because she thinks she wouldn't like a women's college and because she'd like to stay closer to home. Also, at the state university she's being rushed by the sorority her best friend is in,

119

which is her boyfriend's little-sister house. Going away to college with strangers just seems too scary.

The major research studies paint an interesting portrait of the gifted girl's adolescence. She is still achieving academically, but she is also beginning to have different needs and to respond to those needs. Or she's become so concerned with conformity and the right clothes that she daydreams while her career goals slide.

In 1927 and 1928, the gifted boys and girls of Terman's study were followed for the first time by his associate, Melita Oden, who had taken over the study. The gifted group members had maintained their superiority; most had entered college and were succeeding academically. Their social lives seemed normal, and they were active in extracurricular pursuits. Some unusual findings emerged, however, and some clear differences between gifted girls and boys appeared on I.Q. tests as well as in other areas. As a group, the gifted adolescents dropped an average of nine points on their individual scores, but the decline in scores was five times larger for the girls than for the boys. Girls scored thirteen points lower than they had at the time of the original testing, while boys scored fewer than three points lower. This striking difference makes it highly improbable that the gender difference was due to chance. In fact, the group I.Q. test and the achievement tests yielded similar results.

Paradoxically, Oden noted, parents failed to see a decline. Parents of gifted girls believed their daughters had maintained the same level of ability as the gifted boys had. Their beliefs were likely based on school marks, because the girls had continued to receive high grades.

Terman and Oden were not sure of the cause of these sex differences in I.Q. in gifted adolescents. In *Genetic Studies of Genius* (1935), they speculated that the disparity in scores could reflect male superiority or some aspect of the tests.

What was happening? It seems unlikely that inherited "male superiority" could explain differences at seventeen and eighteen years of age when these differences had not existed six years previously; only some traumatic change could alter some hypothetical genetic potential. Terman and Oden suggested that the I.Q. tests emphasized training more often received by boys than girls. For example, Sadker and Sadker (1994) wrote that girls received far less challenging and stimulating educational experiences than do boys. Yet another possibility, not suggested by Terman or Oden, is that the girls had decided not to try on the I.Q. test. Though the girls may have felt it socially acceptable to continue to receive high marks in school and to achieve in extracurricular activities, they may have found the label of gifted unacceptable, knowing this would be the price to pay for a high score on an I.Q. test. Since gifted girls are good adjusters, they adjusted—and may have begun to hide their giftedness.

Terman's gifted young women did continue to perform admirably in school. More women than men earned the fifteen high school recommending units (*As* or *Bs*) required for admission to top-ranking colleges and universities. More women than men held honor society membership. Even though a year younger than their peers of average intelligence, more than a quarter of the women held important elective offices in high school. And fifty years after Terman's study, gifted girls continue to outperform gifted boys throughout high school in their grade point average (AAUW, 1991).

The beginnings of underachievement are too subtle to be detected in grade point average, and gifted adolescent girls' underachievement may first appear in their selection of courses. In high school, more bright girls than bright boys opt for less challenging courses. Not only do they often reject the "hard sciences" like physics and the advanced math courses; they also avoid the more rigorous social studies courses such as European history. As a result, gifted boys achieve higher scores on achievements tests in the areas of math, science, and social studies, as Nick Colangelo and I found in our studies of high scorers on the ACT (Kerr & Colangelo, 1987).

After high school, 87 percent of the men and 84 percent of the women in Terman's study entered college, a remarkable proportion considering that only 30 percent of the general population graduated from high school during this period. These young women continued their high achievement in college, with more women than men achieving a *B* average or better. As had been true in their younger years, the gifted women's interests were closer to men's than they were to those of average women. Few gifted women chose education as a major, even though one-fourth of college women overall chose teaching. Gifted women more typically chose social science and "letters" majors than did college women in general.

The issue of conformity versus achievement was highlighted by the Kaufmann study of highly gifted girls, from which a composite picture of adolescent Presidential Scholars emerged. The study showed them to be loners and nonjoiners, high achievers without much regard for recognition. The picture seemed to match that of other studies of the highly gifted, who are never quite as "normal" socially as are the moderately gifted; they seem to be more concerned with self-actualization—being all they can be—than with adjustment.

In the study, school interests reflected an increasing difference between teenage gifted boys and girls and, apparently, in how they came to view themselves. Boys preferred careers in physical sciences; girls, the humanities, although many with humanities leanings were also interested in math. Occupational goals differed markedly. The boys aspired to high status careers as doctors, lawyers, professors; the girls, to moderate status careers in business and secondary education. Significantly, more men attended highly-selective top universities and colleges, although an abundance of scholarships would have made it equally possible for the women to attend these institutions. As a result, more men went on to prestigious graduate schools. It is clear that many of the highly gifted women of this study, despite their abilities and others' recognition and encouragement, had lower aspirations than men by their senior year in high school.

The bright girls in the Realization of Potential Study, like those in Terman's, maintained higher grades in high school than their male counterparts. As a result, they started out with slightly better achievement potentials. They also were more advantaged than the boys in other ways: they had college-educated parents more often, and in high school rated themselves higher on positive personality traits than did average girls. Their advantage did not last, however, because of a critical shift in adolescence from achievement needs to relationship needs, a change highlighted in both Groth's (1969) and Brown's and Gilligan's (1992) studies. Fourteen-year-old girls, when asked about their wishes, told stories vastly different from ten-year-olds'. At fourteen, girls' wishes centered on friendships and romantic attachments—finding the perfect boyfriend. (This may explain why younger gifted girls talk so excitedly about challenging careers—paleontology, space exploration—at least until age thirteen.) With the great emphasis on love needs at fourteen, however, girls' "maturity valence" suddenly dropped and continued to decline until they were forty, when it began to rise again. The major shifts in psychological needs of gifted girls probably account for the conflicts felt by so many eminent women as adolescents. It is likely that society's emphasis on the impossibility of combining love and achievement forces many gifted girls to become preoccupied with their relationships rather than with personal achievement.

During the period when the girls studied were most concerned with relationships, the boys were more interested in careers. From fifteen to twenty years of age, males revealed a strong need for self-esteem, an interest in accomplishment that continued, according to studies of older males. The young men, "self-esteem-motivated" to pursue careers, received much encouragement for this focus. The inner lives of gifted teenage girls and boys are indeed very different.

More striking support for Groth's conclusions came recently from the American Association of University Women's study (1991) of the self-esteem of adolescent girls: a plunge in self-esteem between eleven and seventeen was found, paralleling Groth's results. Brown and Gilligan also found a tremendous decline in the confidence with which girls asserted their opinions.

What influences the roles gifted girls eventually choose? Rodenstein and Glickhauf-Hughes (1979) were able to extract background elements from the women's adolescence that helped account for their chosen lifestyles. The career-focused women, the homemakers, and the integrators of their study were different in important ways as adolescents.

The career-focused group, early on, were often unaware of or indifferent to parental attitudes toward their career goals, which these women had defined during high school and had continuously strived toward. This single-minded pursuit is similar to the commitment of eminent women to their vocations. Unlike those in the other two groups, the career-focused women were interested in scientific professions (e.g., physician, dentist, physicist) as well as social occupations (e.g., teacher, nurse). They maintained this clarity and interest, from the time of their first career choice through high school and college and the attainment of their goals, despite any desire in their parents for them to pursue social occupations.

From their earliest career choice through high school graduation, the homemakers' main interests were social occupations such as elementary education and librarian, occupations that have traditionally been woman-dominated. They had little interest in the more traditionally male-dominated occupations (e.g., physician, engineer, physicist).

Homemakers had the support of their parents, who also

123

tended to choose a limited range of occupations for their daughters.

In their career development, the integrators, like the home-makers, chose social occupations most often, but they were similar to the career-focused women in their frequent choice of scientific occupations. The integrators had overwhelming approval from their parents for their career choices. Although many of their parents chose social occupations for their daughters, some proportion also chose scientific careers.

It seems, then, that the degree to which gifted girls embrace social needs and goals may have a strong effect on their eventual lifestyles. As parents of adolescents have ruefully noted, their influence on teenagers' interests is minimal. With gifted career-focused girls, their effect may be even more limited.

Summary

By early adolescence, many gifted girls have already marked out the path they will take in adulthood. In choosing traditional, feminine social activities, some have become virtually indistinguishable in mannner and style from girls of average intellect. Others, by continuing not only to perform well in intellectual pursuits but also to enjoy them, have learned they can survive being different. Sadly, some have become confused about who they are and what they want, a disorientation that may be long-lasting. The key points that emerge from the studies about gifted adolescents are these:

- Gifted girls' I.Q. scores drop in adolescence, per-haps as girls begin to perceive that giftedness in females is undesirable.

- Gifted girls are likely to continue to have higher academic achievement as measured by grade point average.

- Gifted girls take less rigorous courses than gifted boys in high school.

- Gifted girls maintain a high involvement in extracur-ricular and social activities during adolescence.

- Highly gifted girls often do not receive recognition for their achievements.

- Highly gifted girls do very well academically in high school.

- Highly gifted girls attend less prestigious colleges than highly gifted boys, a choice that leads to lower-status careers.

- Girls in the Realization of Potential study had higher grades than did their male counterparts.

- Girls in the Realization of Potential study rated themselves higher on positive personality traits than average girls did.

- The age from twelve to fourteen years, when a strong shift of values occurs, is a critical time for gifted girls.

- The change in values at this point is related to strong needs for love and belonging.

- Adolescence may also bring a steep decline in self-esteem and confidence in opinions.

- Gifted adolescent girls who became career-focused were interested in scientific, idea-oriented careers.

- Gifted adolescent girls who later became home-makers were interested in social, people-oriented careers.

- Gifted adolescent girls who became integrators of career and homemaking chose social careers most often, but were also interested in scientific careers.

- Gifted girls fear having to choose between career and marriage, yet this "either/or" dilemma is not in fact a reality for many gifted women.

Questions and Answers

- *Are there common experiences among gifted girls in puberty and adolescence?*

Yes. Adolescence seems to be a time of crisis for gifted girls, and the year immediately preceding puberty is a time of peak interest in activities enhancing self-esteem. This is a time when gifted girls might be very interested in achieving and exploring careers; at this stage, Terman's gifted girls were still attaining high I.Q. scores.

Soon after the onset of puberty (girls reached puberty around thirteen at the time of Groth's study, but now do so around eleven) gifted girls seem to undergo great change, a restructuring of personality that is far more extreme than the change occurring in average girls. Interest in careers recedes, replaced by intense needs for love and belonging. The gifted girl who recently spent most of her time reading about astronomy and rock hunting now plays records with her new best girl friend, talks about boys, and prepares for parties. She may still earn high grades in school, especially if they come easily, but her social intrigues are complex. After a few years, a retest on an I.Q. test may show a drop-off, as happened in the Terman study. Few sixteen-year-old girls want to be labeled gifted. Likewise, on personality tests, gifted adolescent girls show a drop in self-esteem.

- *What happens? What starts the decline in academic performance and self-esteem?*

Blaming it on the physiological changes of adolescence was once popular: Groth quotes research on the "systolic changes" that supposedly lead to less energy for intellectual pursuits, a pretty silly idea by present-day standards—yet the blindness to the effect of social pressures that once produced such theories is still distressingly prevalent among scholars.

The more likely cause of the abrupt change in a gifted girl's interests is the abrupt change in society's attitudes toward her. Until puberty, she has usually been rewarded and encouraged for her intellectual achievement, with parents proud of her astounding marks, friends admiring her abilities, and teachers professing interest in her. However, with adolescence, her attractiveness to boys and the impact of her giftedness upon her "likeability" begins to worry her parents, who after all want only her happiness, and social happiness does not come to girls who are different. They praise her appearance more now, show greater interest in her social life, and perhaps unconsciously trivialize or gloss over her intellectual achievements. Her peers are caught up in symbols and rituals of adolescence in America: current clothes, hairstyles, music, heroes, beauty queens, cars, parties and proms, dating, going steady, sexual awareness, and experimentation with alcohol and drugs. In fact, her parents are right: her acceptance into this world, like anyone else's, requires knowledge of the symbols and gracefulness in the rituals. And the adolescent culture is a quickly-closed one; if she doesn't join in when she gets her chance, she may face ongoing social rejection.

Most gifted girls, eager to conform and to be indistinguishable from the rest of the crowd, learn to pose as average girls. Unfortunately, they may act the part so well that they become it, debasing their vocabularies, squelching their flow of ideas, and holding in when they have something to say. If the gifted girl dresses attractively, is interested in boys, and is asked out and invited to parties, her parents are relieved and probably show it in their enthusiasm for her social life. If she continues to participate energetically in the rituals of adolescence, her friends will disregard her embarrassingly excellent academic performance. If she is not extremely popular, she may have to tone down her academic pursuits so as not to further jeopardize her social standing. If she knows within herself that she is different, she hopes no one can tell.

A few gifted girls refuse to take the plunge into the crowd. Some are so bright and motivated that their intellect simply will not focus on social expectations or urges for intimacy. Their thirst for knowledge is so intense, their perception of the world so sophisticated, their need for creativity and productivity so strong, that they cannot or simply do not take time to be conforming teenagers. Of this group, some willingly accept isolation in exchange for mental aliveness, even when their choice embarrasses parents and wearies former friends. But others, dumbfounded by their lack of popularity, have no idea that the 3 a.m. poetry is precisely why they do not "get it" as a teen. They've decided to be fully alive mentally, yet cannot congratulate themselves for an admirable choice—mental growth over group acceptance—because they do not understand that voracious reading seriously inhibits their ability to talk like everyone else. Still others knowingly do not try the social scene because of a negative self-image: a gifted girl who thinks she's unattractive may conclude that putting time and energy into becoming popular is too steep a price, and it may not pay off anyway. She turns to her studies with extra energy, determined that high grades and academic reward will compensate her.

Many gifted women remember their adolescence as a time of betrayal. One of my fellow graduates remarked:

> *"Until I was in junior high, my dad was my best friend. We read together and played chess together. He was proud of my intelligence and he showed it. Then, when*

I entered junior high, he began to show ambivalence toward my achievements. He still said 'great' when I got good grades, but he began asking me about boyfriends and praising me for looking pretty. Somehow this made me feel bad, but I never could express it. I was just frustrated with him, and felt betrayed. He just wanted me to be like the other girls."

It's a shock for most gifted girls when the cheering for intellectual achievement is replaced by steady pressure to be feminine and popular. Most of them master their surprise and sense of betrayal, congenially adopting the expected values and behaviors. A few refuse and must find ways of coping with being alone.

- ### Do Gifted Girls Share Similarities in Their Career Development?

Gifted girls now are interested in careers in business, medicine, and law in equal proportions to gifted boys but still have much less interest in engineering and the hard sciences. Gifted girls differ from average girls in their career goals, with fewer interested in education, more interested in social sciences. A steady lowering of career aspirations beginning in adolescence is marked by choosing moderate rather than high prestige careers, attending less selective colleges, and dropping out of graduate and professional training more often than is characteristic of men.

Age at marriage is an important predictor of the achievement of young gifted women, for the younger they marry, the less likely they are to achieve their goals, and early birth of children further compounds the negative effects of early marriage. Most gifted women do not marry early; among highly gifted young women, marriage is later than average. If a gifted young woman is to establish and maintain a professional career, the timing of marriage and children is crucial. Even if her vocation is an unpaid one, she must plan just as seriously how she will fulfill her mission.

References

American Association for University Women. *Shortchanging Girls, Shortchanging America.* Washington, DC.: AAUW, 1991.

Arnold, K. *Academically Talented Women in the 1980s: The Illinois Valedictorian Project.* In K. D. Hulbert & D. T. Schuster (Eds.) *Women's Lives Through Time: Educated Women in the Twentieth Century.* San Francisco, CA: Jossey-Bass, 1994.

Brown, L., and Gilligan, C. *At the Crossroads.* Cambridge, MA: Harvard University Press, 1992.

Card, J. J.; Steele, L.; and Abeles, R. P. "Sex Differences in Realization of Individual Potential for Achievement." In *Journal of Vocational Behavior,* 17, 1-20, 1980.

Groth, N. J. "Vocational Development for Gifted Girls." ERIC Document Reproduction Service No. ED931747, 1969.

Kaufmann, F. "The 1964-1968 Presidential Scholars: A Follow-up Study." *Exceptional Children,* 48, 2, 1981.

Rodenstein, J. M., and Glickhauf-Hughes, C. "Career and Lifestyle Determinants of Gifted Women." In *New Voices in Counseling the Gifted,* N. Colangelo & R. T. Zaffran (eds.). Dubuque, Iowa: Kendall/Hunt, 1979.

Sadker, M. and Sadker, D. *Failing at Fairness: How America's Schools Cheat Girls.* New York: Scribners Sons, 1994.

Terman, L. M. "Mental and Physical Traits of a Thousand Gifted Children." In *Genetic Studies of Genius,* Vols. 1 & 2. Stanford: Stanford University Press, 1925.

Terman, L. M. "The Gifted Group at Mid-Life." In *Genetic Studies of Genius,* Vol. 5. Stanford: Stanford University Press, 1959.

Terman, L. M. and Oden, M. H. "The Promise of Youth." *Genetic Studies of Genius,* Vol. 3. Stanford: Stanford University Press, 1935.

Chapter 8

Gifted College Women

As a high school student, Sarah couldn't wait to get to college. Everybody said she'd finally get the intellectual challenge that she had always needed. But somehow, now that she's finally here, it isn't coming true. No deep discussions in the student union with professors and classmates. No long conversations about religion or philosophy late into the night with friends. Only constant talk in the hallway about guys, clothes, hair, and dating.

Ennia is very serious about becoming a microbiologist, studying very hard and doing all her lab work very carefully. But her professors seem indifferent to her, and she's losing confidence, especially since she got a C on her first calculus test. She wonders if she has what it takes.

Bronwyn has never had so much fun in her life. She parties all night and sleeps most of the day. She has arranged her schedule so she doesn't start class until noon. Everyone said college was supposed to be hard, but she's getting straight As without even trying. With only fifteen hours of classes and about two hours of study, what is she supposed to do with the rest of the week? College is just like summer camp, she writes her best friend, only you get to have sex.

131

The gifted young woman enters college with a puzzling combination of characteristics. She has higher high school grades than
gifted young men, but she is probably less prepared: her coursework, particularly in math, science, and social studies, has probably
been less rigorous than his. Her career goal is likely to be higher
than that of an average woman, as high in status as that of a gifted
man. She has high educational aspirations, expecting to do postgraduate work. Nevertheless, her self-esteem, declining since early
adolescence, is at the lowest point ever. She has lost confidence in
her opinions and tends not to disagree with others because she
wants to maintain friendly relations (Brown & Gilligan, 1992). She
is not likely to assert herself in class and is not likely to stand up well
to criticism.

With this precarious blend of high aspirations and low confidence, the gifted young woman enters an environment which is
indifferent, if not hostile, to her intellectual goals. There is increasing
evidence that the typical American coeducational college campus
is a chilly environment indeed for women. In class, professors will
call on men three times more often than women. Men will be chosen
more frequently for mentoring and for special assistantships. Despite gifted women's strong participation in campus groups, gifted
men are more likely to lead in these activities (Sandler, 1983).

The gifted college woman will receive little in the way of
guidance, encouragement, or support. Her parents live far away,
and the special teachers who mentored her in high school have a
new set of gifted students. The only career counseling available on
campus is likely to be a computerized career information service
and some perfunctory interest test interpretations.

Added to this indifference toward her goals is a relentless
pressure from her peers to groom herself for a relationship, find a
man, and establish a commitment. The "culture of romance"
focuses her attention on attractiveness rather than intelligence. She
learns quickly that high grades and leadership on campus gain little
recognition from her peer group; in fact, her friends may not even
know what her major is, or that she was a National Merit Scholar.
What counts among her peers is a relationship with a high-status
man, and she strives to attain this goal just as determinedly as she
as pursued her academic goals in the past (Holland & Eisenhart,
1990).

By her sophomore year, the gifted young woman has responded to all of these changes by adjusting to the new culture in

which she finds herself. She has begun to see herself differently. Her estimation of her intelligence is lower than it was when she graduated from high school. If she has received any low grades in the courses in her chosen major, she may be reconsidering and looking for less demanding fields of study.

By senior year, she may have lowered her career goals as well as her educational aspirations. She may be in a relationship she values and may be willing to subordinate her own goals in favor of her boyfriend's. All along she probably continued to receive good grades. She may not have noticed that the college campus was indifferent to her goals and dreams or that her own esteem, confidence, and aspirations slipped away.

The gifted women studied by Terman and Oden (Terman, 1947) fit this pattern, even though high aspirations were very unusual at that time, when very few women went to college. Gifted women in that study had higher grades in high school than gifted men, and more held honor society memberships. In high school, these gifted young women had also held more elective offices. Eighty-seven percent of gifted women entered college, compared to eighty-four percent of gifted men, and eighty-seven percent of this group earned at least a *B* average, compared to seventy-seven percent of the men. However, a smaller proportion of women than of men completed college (66.5% vs. 69.8%), and far fewer went on to graduate work.

The high school valedictorians studied by Arnold and Denny (Arnold, 1994) fit the pattern of declining confidence and aspirations, with women shifting career goals to less demanding college majors at the same time that they were lowering their estimations of their intelligence.

Two-thirds of the bright women in the Holland and Eisenhart (1990) study of the culture of romance on campus had changed their career goals in college, with most of them putting their boyfriends' goals first.

What about the lucky few, the women who don't lower their confidence or change their goals? What makes it possible for some gifted young women to survive the chilly climate of the American coeducational campus and to graduate with dreams intact? Several factors seem to help women keep their original plans. One is extreme giftedness.

In Kaufmann's study of Presidential Scholars (1981), the gifted women held high career goals upon entering college, and they kept

133

those goals. As many of the women as the men graduated with plans to become physicians, lawyers, and professors. It may be that these women were simply too intelligent to be able to blend into the culture of romance; they could not help but stand out among the crowd of college students. Their extreme giftedness may have ensured that they received the same recognition that men of more moderate abilities were routinely given by professors. It is also possible that the Presidential Scholar Award, one of the most prestigious awards for intellectual achievement at that time, may have provided enough encouragement and recognition to see the women through four years of college. In this case and others, it seems to be the extremely gifted women who persist and ultimately gain recognition for their abilities.

A second factor that distinguishes the women who carry out their dreams is a strong identification with a particular profession or area of interest. In the Holland and Eisenhart study, the valedictorian study, and several studies of women in math and science, the persistent gifted young women are those with a firmly-established identity in their field. The young woman who sees herself as an artist, scientist, or politician is more likely to stay with her chosen field than one who sees herself simply as a college student. This internalized career identity is comparable to "falling in love with an idea," a hallmark of the eminent women in my study.

A third factor seems to be leadership and maturity. In the Card, Steele, and Abeles study (1980), the women who realized their potential tended to be stronger in these areas. While leading campus organizations or participating in assertiveness workshops can give one basic leadership skills, activities which expand a bright woman's awareness of what she can do are most effective in building both leadership and maturity. For example, eminent women tended to participate in fringe campus groups, at the margin of collegiate culture, which had religious, political, or intellectual goals. The women Presidential Scholars were active in student political movements which opposed the Vietnam war and promoted the causes of the youth culture. On current college campuses it may be environmental groups, AIDS awareness organizations, or any group which encourages outspoken activism which can ignite a bright young woman's leadership and help her transcend her self-imposed limitations.

Another factor in strengthening women's resolve is the availability of mentors. In the Kaufmann (1986), only those women who were linked to mentors in their field achieved occupational status and salaries similar to those of the male Presidential Scholars. During the critical period of college, many of these mentorships began. Similarly, eminent women entered into mentor relationships during their young adult years. Mentors encourage, guide, and support; they also continually remind the gifted young woman of her own dreams and goals. When the mentor is a woman, she also serves as role model, exemplifying the fulfillment of potential.

The recognition of giftedness, identification with one's chosen field, leadership and maturity, and the presence of mentors all foster the achievement of gifted women in college. Yet these qualities and commodities are in short supply on the typical campus. There is one sort of place, however, where women's achievements are recognized, where women are encouraged to pursue their goals, where opportunities for leadership are readily available, and where mentoring is more likely: a women's college.

Women's colleges produce more women scholars and leaders than coeducational colleges, and have been doing so for a long time (Sadker and Sadker, 1994; Tidball, 1980). However, during the last two decades, enrollment in women's colleges declined dramatically. As young women were given more choice in their own future, they increasingly chose coeducational colleges, often under the mistaken notion that at women's colleges they would have no opportunities for social relationships with men, or that women's colleges would limit their choices of majors too much. Parents often believe that gifted young women must learn to "compete in a man's world" and that co-ed colleges will help them to adjust to this. The evidence is that co-ed colleges hasten the process of adjustment all too well, teaching gifted women a second-class role they may never transcend. It is also clear that women's colleges do not protect women from leadership and competition—in fact, the opposite is true. With more opportunities for assertiveness in the classroom and leadership in campus activities, women's colleges are a place where skills for future professional leadership are incubated. With less than three percent of young women even considering women's colleges, it is likely that only a lucky few will receive this special preparation for fulfilling their dreams.

Summary

The college years are a critical period in which most gifted young women will disengage from their original goals, having been caught up in a culture emphasizing romance over intellectual achievement. Only those who attain recognition of their giftedness, a chance to identify with their field, opportunities for leadership, and mentoring seem to survive with dreams intact.

Key Points

- Gifted young women enter college with higher grades but less rigorous course preparation than gifted men.

- Gifted young women's self-esteem is at a low point upon entrance to college.

- Valedictorians were found to lower their self-estimate of their intelligence by the sophomore year of college.

- The typical American coeducational campus is a chilly climate for women, with inequities in and out of the classroom.

- A powerful campus peer system supports a culture of romance, which rewards a woman's romantic "achievements" while disregarding her intellectual ones.

- Women's colleges provide the recognition for giftedness, identification with fields of study, chances for leadership, and the mentors which gifted women need to succeed; however, only a tiny fraction of gifted women choose these colleges.

Questions and Answers

- *My daughter insists on going to a coeducational college or university. How can we make the best of a bad situation?*

This question is a good argument for preparing gifted girls early for the idea of a women's college. If your daughter knows the facts—that she is likely to receive an inferior education and inequitable treatment—and yet she persists in wanting a coed campus, look first of all for a college or university with a high proportion of tenured women faculty; thirty per cent, a high proportion for American schools, is a sign that women are taken seriously. Second, find a campus with a strong women's studies program, a women's resource center, and specialized services for women. A campus daycare center and a women's health center are very good signs that the college is supporting women's goals. Third, try to find a campus where the culture of romance is not too virulent; any college or university known as a party school is a bad bet. Watch out also for poorly-supervised Greek systems or residence halls which provide little supportive programming for women and plenty of education in romance. Look for a strong student activities advisors and carefully planned campus programs.

- *How can a college woman find a mentor?*

Begin with the teacher of your favorite class. Offer to help with his or her research, as a volunteer or in return for individualized course credit. Remember that mentoring is a reciprocal, mutual process, and that productive professors are always looking for excellent students; be attentive and assertive in class, and make sure your potential mentor sees what your skills are.

- *I am in a relationship that I want to keep. I don't want to subordinate my career goals to his, but I don't know how to plan for the future.*

No couple should have to plan for their future without help. Dual career counseling is needed by couples who are committed to meeting two sets of goals. Perhaps someone at the college counseling center can help you two figure out how to meet your mutual and individual goals. Besides giving help with decision-making and problem-solving, the counselor may know innovative methods by which dual career professional couples create working families, such as commuter marriages, five-year plans where moves are re-negotiated so that each partner's careers alternate in primacy, and ad-hoc extended families where childcare and household responsibilities are shared.

References

Arnold, K. "Academically Talented Women in the 1980s: The Illinois Valedictorian Project. In K. D. Hulbert & D. T. Schuster (Eds.) *Women's Lives Through Time: Educated Women in the Twentieth Century*. San Francisco, CA: Jossey-Bass, 1994.

Brown, L., and Gilligan, C. *At the Crossroads*. Cambridge, MA: Harvard University Press, 1992.

Card, J. J.; Steele, L.; and Abeles, R. P. "Sex Differences in Realization of Individual Potential for Achievement." In *Journal of Vocational Behavior*, 17, 1-20, 1980.

Holland, D. C. and Eisenhart, M. A. (1990) *Educated in Romance: Women, Achievement, and College Culture*. Chicago, IL: University of Chicago.

Kaufmann, F. "The 1964-1968 Presidential Scholars: A Follow-up Study." In *Exceptional Children*, 48, 2, 1981.

Kaufmann, F., Harrel, G., Milam, C. P., Woolverton, N. and Miller, J. "The Nature, Role and Influence of Mentors in the Lives of Gifted Adults." In *Journal of Counseling and Development*, 64, 9, 1986.

Sadker, M. and Sadker, D. *Failing at Fairness: How America's Schools Cheat Girls*. New York: Scribners Sons, 1994.

Sandler, B. *The College Campus: A Chilly Climate for Women*. Washington, DC.: ACE, 1983.

Terman, L. M. and Oden, M. H. "The Gifted Child Grows Up." In *Genetic Studies of Genius*, Vol. 4. Stanford: Stanford University Press, 1947.

Tidball, M. E. "Women's Colleges and Women Achievers Revisited." In *Signs*, 5, 504 -517, 1980.

Chapter 9

The Gifted Woman

Esther once thought she was stuck forever in a marriage of misery, managing her husband's fast food establishments while he spent all the money. Now, because she has written a novel about a woman's spiritual exploration, she is free. She has money and friends among the thousands who have bought her book. She can't believe her sudden transformation.

Marie always thought she'd go to college, get married, have babies, maybe work a few years. But she's thirty-five, single, and on the fast track professionally. She loves her work as a human resources consultant, and her friends—and their children—provide her with all the family she needs. Nothing is as she had expected, and she senses her parents' vague disappointment in her, but she truly enjoys her life.

Carolyn, fifty-one, is an Air Force wife of thirty years who has lived all over the world. She's reared a large family and taught in six middle and high schools, yet she is intimidated as she plans to finish the master of arts degree she started twenty years earlier. Her advisor is patronizing; her fellow students are friendly but uninterested. She knows that she is more knowledgeable and at least as intelligent as her student colleagues, but she nonetheless doubts herself.

Sixty-three-year-old Helen is a professional volunteer, the wife of a retired bank executive. She has never had to work outside the home, but she has been a leader in the League of Women Voters, the Junior League, and many other political and service organizations. Looking back on her life, however, she is unable to point to any accomplishments that her career-oriented daughters might respect. She wishes she could do it all over again, using her leadership skills in a profession and being paid for her work, but times were different when she started out, and no one expected such achievement of her.

Research on gifted adults shows that women take different paths from men. Most gifted women in the past achieved less in the way of professional careers than gifted men their age, and those who were employed in high-level occupations were underpaid. Marriage and children had much greater impact on gifted women's career development than on gifted men's (Card, Steele, & Abeles, 1980). Gifted women can best be understood by examining the different phases of their adulthood, for the concerns of young gifted women differ from those at midlife, and those at midlife differ from those of the elderly.

Gifted women now graduating from college face completely different expectations than did the graduates of ten years ago. Most gifted young women are now expected to be successful in a career as well as in marriage, yet they have few models and little guidance from older women. The ten- and twenty-year follow-up of my classmates showed that at 29, the majority of women in traditional roles were satisfied and happy with their lives; at 39, these same women were ambivalent about roles and satisfactions, and many had transformed their lives and their attitudes toward work and relationships. On the other hand, a few women who had been very career oriented had gone the other direction—and had become ambivalent about their work. Little is known about older gifted women: Terman's study, the only one following women into their elderly years, found them resourceful in composing lives around the limitations imposed upon them by society and themselves.

Terman and Oden's (1947) information on the employment of the gifted at their twenty-year follow-up showed strong differences between gifted men and women. Only about 1 percent of gifted men were unemployed, a figure much smaller than that for men in general; however, the majority of gifted women were not employed, whether married and calling themselves housewives or single. Most women with advanced degrees were working, but even of this group, one Ph.D., one M.D., and one lawyer had relinquished their careers entirely.

Considerable underemployment existed among these gifted women. Only 10 percent had entered the higher professions (those requiring advanced graduate training) or university teaching. Most of the employed gifted women had chosen "disposable" careers: teaching below college level or working in official business occupations and as service providers such as social worker, nurse, and librarian. Childhood I.Q. scores did not predict level of employment for gifted women, for the childhood I.Q. score was about the same whether the woman was employed or not. Even when males and females held similar occupations, job status was lower for women. Salaries of gifted men and women in identical occupations showed marked disparity (see FIG. 11).

FIG. 11. Facts about the Terman Gifted

PERCENT OF GIFTED WOMEN	PERCENT OF GIFTED MEN	ACHIEVEMENTS
93.0	84.0	Earned "high-school recommending" units
55.0	38.0	Held honor society membership
27.0	20.0	Held important elective offices
87.0	84.0	Entered college
87.0	77.0	Achieved at least a B average in college
66.5	69.8	Graduated from college
39.8	47.6	Continued for graduate study
14.2	31.1	Earned advanced degrees (Ph.D.)
5.7	1.0	Unemployed in 1940
.5	7.5	Earned $5,000/year in 1940
11.0	86.0	Employed in professional or managerial careers in 1955

Five years later, in 1950, a repeat survey showed the percentage of employed women dropping again. Oden attributed this to more women marrying and having children. At this time, many women were returning to the home from temporary jobs held during the war. The pattern of low salary and career status remained.

In 1955, yet another Terman follow-up portrayed "The Gifted Group at Mid-Life." It described gifted people in their mid-forties with lifestyles and well-established patterns of social, intellectual, and emotional behavior. For at least half of the gifted women, vocational achievement and actualization of intellectual potential through traditional channels had apparently come to an end; they listed their occupations as homemakers. The authors struggled to characterize these women. Were they to consider women who dropped out as failures? That made no sense, but what could they do? Given their definition of success, they had to leave women out entirely. Oden wrote:

> *"The study has been limited to men because of the lack of a yardstick by which to estimate the success of women. By means of rating techniques, it is possible to identify fairly accurately outstanding chemists, astronomers, mathematicians, or psychologists, but no one has yet devised a method for identifying the best housewives and mothers, and this is what the vast majority of women aspire to be. The few women who go out for a professional career do so with one eye on the preferred alternative. Those who make no pretense of wanting a career are willing to accept any reasonably pleasant and respectable employment that will bridge the gap between school and marriage. For some the gap will never be bridged, and the result is that there are highly gifted women working as secretaries, filing clerks, elementary teachers, and telephone operators."* [1]

In 1955, one-half of Terman's gifted women were housewives with no employment outside the home. Marriage did indeed seem to be the major factor in determining employment or unemployment; among single women, only three independently wealthy women were not employed; of married gifted women, fewer than one-third were employed. Married women did not differ markedly in their educational preparation from single women; however, women with advanced degrees were predictably more likely to be employed than those with lower degrees.

What occupations did bright women choose? Most frequently, gifted women earned their salaries in elementary and secondary teaching; next most often, in office occupations. College faculty

---

1 NOTE: From L.M. Terman and M. Oden. "The Promise of Youth." In Genetic Studies of Genius, Vol. 3, Stanford University Press, 1935. Reprinted with permission.

positions and higher professions followed, with the remainder scattered among a number of occupations. The tendency of gifted women to be in traditional, woman-dominated occupations was still quite high. When compared to the group of gifted men, the gifted women had disappointing occupational histories, at least in terms of financial gain or occupational status. The gifted men were mostly in professional and managerial occupations, such as lawyer, college professor, and engineer. By 1955 the gifted men had steadily progressed to improved status and higher salary jobs, more often represented in lucrative professions than were male college graduates in general, and maintaining their financial gains.

Although many women had discontinued achievement in the world of work, some were pursuing outstanding individual careers. Apparently, among this gifted group, as among my classmates, there were transforming women. Oden describes those who achieved their dreams despite societal limitations as follows:

"Several scientists have made important contributions to research to the extent that seven women are listed in American Men of Science. Among the distinguished biological scientists is one who played an important part in the development of the vaccine for poliomyelitis and who is continuing to work in virus research. The social and behavioral sciences include several women who are outstanding in the fields of psychology, education, and social welfare.

"Only one woman is working as a high-level physical scientist. Since taking her Doctor of Science degree, she has worked in private industry where she has successfully competed with men for advancement and is now one of the most highly paid women in our group.

"But not all the conspicuous achievements have been in the sciences. One of our most distinguished women is a gifted poet whose work has received wide recognition and who is rated among the outstanding poets of our day. Others among the women writers are a feature article writer who contributes to leading magazines, two novelists, a member of the editorial staff and an executive editor of a nationally circulated magazine, and still another is the editor of a small literary magazine. Other writers include the author of

a successful Broadway play (also produced as a motion picture), several journalists including a reporter and feature writer for a metropolitan daily paper, and several technical writers. One of our women is a gifted painter whose work has appeared by invitation in many exhibits and who has won considerable recognition. Several women have been phenomenally successful in business; two of these are in the real estate business, another is an executive buyer in a large department store, and still another, herself a pharmacist, is the owner and operator of a prosperous pharmacy."

No comparison of vocational attainment is complete without comparing financial status—the pay for labor—for gifted men and gifted women, yet the income comparison was almost ludicrous. Terman and Oden did not even list an average for gifted men's salaries because it would have been so unbalanced: earnings of the men ranged from $50,000 to $400,000. Instead, they reported a median income ($9,640) for the total group of men and women. This overall median was almost twice that for employed gifted women ($4,875), with the highest belonging to a female physician making $24,000 and the lowest given as below $3,000.

Education seemed of little financial help to these gifted women, even though it had benefited average college women graduates; at that time, average women graduates typically could expect to earn 2 1/2 times as much as non-degree working women. Gifted women graduates, on the other hand, earned only about one-fourth more than did nondegreed gifted women. The authors cautioned repeatedly that salary should not be considered the most important measure of success.

One phenomenon gleaned from Oden is particularly revealing: upon reflection, many of these poorly-paid gifted women expressed ample satisfaction with their lives and careers. Pauline Sears, who inherited the Terman study, sent a questionnaire about career and life satisfactions to the Terman women in 1972, when the average age of the 430 gifted women who responded was sixty-two. Ninety-one percent were or had been married. Forty-three percent had worked for most of their adult lives; the rest were classified as homemakers. Seventy-five percent had at least one child; 25 percent were childless. Sears and Barbee had predicted that women who were married and who had children, income-producing work, and a lifestyle based on a higher-than-average income would report higher satisfaction than those who were unmarried (widowed, divorced or single), childless income-earners. But with survey results in, they found that "as with many naive theories, most of these predictions proved false." In this study, persons were labeled "satisfied with their life work" if they indicated that they would make the same choice if they had it to do over again (i.e., to be a homemaker, to have a career most of one's life, to have a career except when raising children, or to have simply worked for money). The results were complex and striking.

Many of the total sample were pleased with their lives. When divided into heads-of-household (women who were on their own, either single, divorced or widowed since 1960) and non-heads-of-household, the head-of-household group showed the largest number of especially satisfied women. When these two groups divided further into income worker or homemaker, the income workers overall had the largest proportion of extremely satisfied women— and a striking 92 percent of heads-of-household who were income workers were quite satisfied. When these four groups were broken down still further into "no children" or "children," the group with the largest number of highly satisfied women were the head-of-household income workers with no children. With childless gifted women almost across the board showing more satisfaction, Sears and Barbee (1972) wondered if mothers were becoming an endangered species! Clearly, single gifted career women had spent fulfilling lives, despite having grown up in an era when such women were often pitied and mocked. By contrast, many gifted women who were homemakers reported a feeling of having missed out on opportunities for challenge and self-development. Heads-of-household homemakers (divorced or widowed women who did not work outside the home), especially those without children, were the least satisfied women; they had missed the chance to define themselves either through careers or families.

Income had little to do with high satisfaction: many gifted women led satisfied lives despite being in the lowest income category. Whether most gifted women were generally satisfied depended on "an early ambition for excellence in work" and vocational advancement after age forty. The early qualities associated with later satisfaction were self-confidence, persistence, and minimal feelings of inferiority.

The Terman study has important implications for gifted women. By viewing the development of a large group of gifted

145

women over a forty-year span of the twentieth century, one gains a rare perspective and unprecedented insight into the brightest and most promising women of an earlier era and how their world evolved. The Terman study provides clear warnings, hopes, and encouragement for gifted women.

Kaufmann's study (1981) shows that extraordinarily able gifted women are unusual in several ways besides intellect. Her data showed them to be high achievers. Some were not very socially active. Their marriage rate was surprisingly low, their childbearing rate correspondingly lower. Despite extraordinary achievements, they did not receive much recognition.

Even though they married relatively late by usual standards, 30 percent of the women (as opposed to 19 percent of the men) were married by age twenty-one. While the scholars' average age at the time of the study was thirty-one, 39 percent of the women and 49 percent of the men had never married. Thirteen percent of the women and seven percent of the men were divorced by age thirty-one. The marital patterns of these highly gifted men and women probably resembled each other more than they resembled those of the population as a whole, yet differences remained: the women married more and divorced more, and almost half of the men were single.

Despite these trends, men and women earned an almost equal number of higher degrees (M.A.s, Ph.D.s, L.L.B.s, M.D.s), and high employment levels were typical. Even so, 11 percent of these highly gifted women were unemployed or homemakers, compared to 4 percent of the men.

Men's higher aspirations and more prestigious educational backgrounds seem to have carried them along to higher status careers. The average status of men's first jobs was superior to the average status of women's first jobs. By the time of the second job, the gap had widened from fifteen to twenty-two points on a prestige ladder devised by sociologists. However, in Kaufmann's survey in 1986, the gap in job status between men and women had narrowed noticeably.

Even in prestigious jobs, equal pay for women seemed unattainable. Kaufmann's women, like Terman's, were woefully underpaid, even when they pursued the same careers as the men, and men's average income was almost twice that of women. While some women may now be benefitting from equal-pay-for-equal-work legislation as well as comparable-pay legislation, most would not, because their professional jobs, unlike men's, were most likely to be temporary, part-time, or subject to availability of funds. A physician with only a half-time practice with a medical group, a public administrator hired through federal grant money, or an election-year paid campaign director may have high status work, but the talented women who fill them are paid less than those in permanent, full-time, "hard-money" positions of similar status.

Marriage and childraising have had drastic effects on the career development of gifted women who decided to "drop out." Card and her colleagues (1980) and Loprest (1992) showed women's difficulty in catching up after dropping out of careers: five years after high school, women with unusual potential were still ahead of high potential men, at least in terms of the prestige of the job they held and their job satisfaction. However, eleven years beyond high school, the picture changed dramatically, for greater job prestige and job satisfaction among gifted women had disappeared. Instead, men showed significantly higher levels of education, more men were working full time, and men had significantly higher incomes. Men's achievement grew while women's declined with age. The increased flexibility in the workplace in the nineties (at least in white-collar and professional occupations), required maternity leave, and other new laws to protect women may significantly help the new generation of gifted women planning families, but evidence suggests that women who drop out for periods as short as a year suffer professional setbacks.

The differences between the high potential men and women were consistently higher than the differences in the average groups; in other words, bright women, when compared to men of comparable intelligence and potential, underachieved to a much greater extent than did women of average abilities in relation to men of the same potential. Clearly, gender was more important in predicting achievement among gifted people than was affluence, background, or other factors.

What traits differentiated the high-achieving gifted women from low-achieving gifted women? Leadership and maturity were the most important factors, along with age at first marriage and the number of children born (Card et al., 1980). Leadership and maturity appeared to be quite important to female success; for male success, job experience carried them to prominence.

Women with high potential for achievement are particularly affected by problems of managing work and family, while high-po-

147

tential men are relatively unaffected. As women marry and families grow, their achievement becomes less, and it is also less likely that they will eventually realize their potential. Perhaps women will return to work as their children grow up, the authors (Card, Steele and Abelas) suggested. Even so, they warn: "Sex differences in achievement will not disappear with time. Men's prior investments, manifested in terms of greater seniority and experience on the job, should keep them ahead of women for the duration of the cohort's working lives." The most unfortunate aspect of the conflict between career and family is that the current American economic system does not allow talented women to easily "catch up" if they take time out to engage in homemaking or childrearing.

What inner needs of gifted women might impel them to change goals and lifestyles in adulthood? The decline in career orientation between fourteen and forty in the females Groth (1969) studied was due largely to their high needs for love and belonging. These needs alternated with needs for esteem throughout this period, but in the long run, needs for love and belonging prevailed. Fourteen and forty were found to be milestone years in gifted women: at fourteen, most gifted girls experienced a great surge of wishes centering on love and belonging, a trend which continued until forty, which marked the end of the childrearing phase for most gifted women. Having met their needs for love and belonging, these women now wanted self-esteem through careers and self-actualization through creative activities, desires that continued for the rest of their lives. This may explain the urge of many of the women in my study for self-actualization and transformation.

The conflict of career versus family has repeatedly emerged in studies of women's career development and popular literature, so much so that many believe career and family to be mutually exclusive. In *Backlash* (1991), Susan Faludi makes it abundantly clear that throughout the eighties and early nineties, the increasing flow of women into the professional job market was accompanied by an increasingly frenzied attempt by the media to create the myth of the Superwoman: the woman whose ambition to be successful impaired her feminity, friendships, looks, marriageability, marriage, childraising, and even health. Young women are still cautioned, "You can't have everything." Yet the Rodenstein and Glickhauf-Hughes (1979) study fifteen years ago showed that for gifted women the integration of career and family is both a possibility and an actuality, although it is not the only approach that provides satisfaction. Nevertheless, it is not classic studies such as these, and the research which supports their findings, that are picked up by the media. Faludi documents all of the recent studies which show that women can and do integrate relationships and careers; that children can and do thrive in homes where both parents are career-oriented; and that women who pursue their own goals are as healthy or healthier than their peers. She shows how many careful scientific studies are eclipsed by popular ideas and fragments of findings which are used to prove the dangers of trying to have it all.

The career-focused group in this study reported much satisfaction from work and from recognition for accomplishments. The single career woman is stereotyped as socially inept, isolated, dedicated solely to her work. Yet in reality these women report deriving much satisfaction from friendships and close personal relationships, from work, and from lifestyles that overall are consistent with those of the single eminent women presented earlier. Income was not a major source of satisfaction for them, nor were religion, community activities, or children. These self-starters who seldom wished to rely on others viewed personality and mental stability as critical to their success. Another element in the false stereotype of the career-focused woman is that once she makes her career choice, she will no longer want a homemaker or integrator role, but 38 percent of career women in the Rodenstein study did plan to have children at some point in their lives. Hence the choice to be career-focused did not preclude either of the other two lifestyles as far as these gifted women were concerned.

The homemakers got less satisfaction from their work than did integrators or career-focused women. Sixty percent of the homemakers reported satisfaction from their work as compared to 84 percent of the working (career and integrator) groups. Personal relationships, hobbies, and children were very important to the homemakers. Despite a common belief that housewives get work-related satisfaction from community activities, community service was not of significant interest to them. Lastly, the homemakers attributed their life accomplishments to significant others, good mental stability, and an adequate education, and they did not feel their personalities had affected their choices.

Integrators demonstrate that women can have both a family and career. The myth holds that both cannot exist simultaneously without each interfering with the others. The women in this group, however, reported satisfaction from their work (86 percent) and from recognition of their accomplishments (82 percent). Further, they reported much satisfaction from their personal relationships (97 percent), their children (96 percent), and their avocations (82 percent). They had both career and family and were highly satisfied with both.

This group showed characteristics of both the career-focused group and homemaker groups, a combination that is difficult to adapt to and which requires great balance. In fact, more than those in other groups, integrators thought that good mental stability was an important contributor to their life accomplishments. The women gained strength both from within and from outside themselves: family and friends were important, but so was their own strength in persisting toward a goal. Again, the description of this group fits that of many eminent women who integrated work and family. This study, done fifteen years ago, has still not been refuted by research on gifted women. Instead, the evidence continues to mount that the earlier a gifted woman begins to integrate her own goals with the goals of those she loves, the less likely she is too become an overwhelmed woman, and the more likely she is to compose a satisfying life.

Summary

Research findings suggest that although the combination of career and family may be difficult, gifted women can maintain both. Gifted women integrators are more satisfied with their careers than gifted single career women, and they are as satisfied with their families as gifted homemakers. A forced choice between career and family is not necessary for the gifted woman.

Key Points

- Gifted women's academic and vocational achievement, compared to that of gifted men, continues to decline, particularly during childbearing years.
- Gifted women's I.Q.s do not predict career achievement or employment.

- Only a small group of gifted women in the past entered the higher professions; despite indications that this is changing, a backlash exists against woman of high aspirations.

- Salaries of gifted women have been much lower than those of gifted men in occupations at the same level. In 1955, the gifted women's median salary at midlife was one-half that of gifted men. Today, gifted women's lower salaries seem to be directly related to the fact that they are in more temporary and part-time positions. However, income is not related to life satisfaction.

- Single, working, childless gifted women, looking back on their lives, are highly satisfied as a group.

- Gifted women engaged in income-producing work are more satisfied with their lives than are those who are not.

- Highly gifted women need time to catch up to men.

- Highly gifted men's income has averaged almost twice that of highly gifted women.

- Only a small proportion of highly gifted women were unemployed 15 years after high school graduation.

- Early remarriage and childbirth are closely related to low achievement of career goals.

- Marriage and childbirth affect the achievement of high-potential women much more than they do that of high-potential men.

- Women who drop out of careers to marry and raise children may not catch up with their male peers for the rest of their working lives.

- Age forty may mark another critical change in lifestyle values for gifted women, as a point in time when esteem needs become highly important and the urge for self-actualization may be great.

- The age of forty may mark a period of either transforming or being overwhelmed for women who have not been focussed on their vocational goals.

- Single career women derive great satisfaction from their work, and also enjoy their friends, hobbies, and community activities.

- Homemakers receive less satisfaction from their work than do single career women or integrators. In addition, many do not seem to derive satisfaction from community activities and hobbies.

- Integrators are more satisfied with their careers than are single career women and are as satisfied with their families as are homemakers.

Questions and Answers

- *How does the conflict between social expectation and personal potential affect gifted women?*

All of the women in the studies described felt the conflict between social expectations and personal potential. Much more than women of average ability, they were given two very different messages. On the one hand, they were encouraged to achieve their full potential: tested and identified as gifted, sometimes given special education, they received positive recognition and awards for their academic performance. On the other hand, they were encouraged to be feminine; they were discouraged from achieving too much, or from achieving in a manner that interfered with attracting marriage partners.

As is true for today's gifted women, many were given the unhappy choice of career or marriage by counselors who would never have considered giving that choice to men. Many gifted women are encouraged to take the path of least resistance when they learn that society does not punish for withdrawing from accomplishment. Even though society responds harshly to a gifted male who drops out of education or a professional career, a woman who drops out to marry or raise children, or even to seek a partner, is simply considered to be practical. Finally, many gifted women give up achievement when they learn that their efforts are never going to be rewarded as much as are those of men.

While gifted women are still in any kind of school, their hard work dependably leads to high marks, but after graduation, salary is the only "grading system" available. In all follow-up studies, gifted women were earning far less than men, usually one-half. They earned less not only in women's professions such as nursing and teaching, but also in the same professions as men, such as college teaching and law. The seeming hopelessness of this situation surely leads many gifted women to devalue their work just as it is devalued by society.

• *Are there characteristic ways by which adult women adjust to being gifted?*

The lifestyles and the accompanying patterns of adjustment that emerged from the research were very similar to those apparent in the gifted women in my follow-up survey.

It appears that Big Mary, Linda, and Gina, as well as the whole group of young adult gifted women who had been my classmates were not atypical of gifted women. They had experienced the same kind of childhood, full of promise and the excitement of being special, and like the majority of gifted women, they did not go on to become eminent. They had weathered the crises of adolescence: the change in parental and societal attitudes, the choices between the denial of gifts and social isolation. They had developed lifestyles that were attempts to cope with two powerful forces: society's inevitable, constant pressure to be feminine, to settle for less, and to live through others, on the one hand, and their own sense of responsibility for the actualization of their intellect on the other. The evidence from my most recent follow-up with my classmates shows that the urge for self actualization grows as women near forty, when, as the Groth study predicted, needs for self-esteem once again arise.

Gifted women today seem very much like gifted women throughout this century. In attempts to cope with socialization, career development, and lifestyle, gifted women do, indeed, adopt characteristic patterns of adjustment. Those described by Roden-stein and Glickhauf-Hughes are still evident: the career-focused, the homemaker, and the integrator. However, to these must be added the transforming woman, who changes roles in midlife, perhaps more than once. Each pattern has its own assets and liabilities; every woman must assess her personal gains and losses for adjustment choices. But only if she knows the factors influencing her can she make knowledgeable decisions.

References

Card, J.J.; Steele, L.; and Abeles, R.P. Sex Differences in Realization of Individual Potential for Achievement. *Journal of Vocational Behavior*, 17, 1-20, 1980.

Faludi, S. *Backlash: The Undeclared War Against American Women*. New York: Crown, 1991.

Groth, N.J. "Vocational Development for Gifted Girls." ERIC Document Reproduction Service No. ED931747, 1969.

Kaufmann, F. "The 1964-1968 Presidential Scholars: A Follow-up Study." *Exceptional Children*, 48, 2, 1981.

Kaufmann, F., Harrel, G., Milam, C.P., Woolvertoon, N. and Miller, J. The Nature, Role and Influence of Mentors in the Lives of Gifted Adults. *Journal of Counseling and Development*, 64, 9 , 1986.

Loprest, P.J. "Gender Differences in Wage Growth and Job Mobility." In *American Economic Association Papers and Proceedings*, 82, 2, 526-532, 1992.

Rodenstein, J.M., and Glickhauf-Hughes, C. "Career and Lifestyle Determinants of Gifted Women." *In New Voices in Counseling the Gifted*, N. Colangelo & R.T. Zaffran (eds.). Dubuque, Iowa: Kendall/Hunt, 1979.

Sears, P.S. and Barbee, A.H. "Career and Life Satisfaction Among Terman's Gifted Women." In *The Gifted and Creative: A Fifty Year Perspective*, J. Stanley; W.C. George; and C.H. Solano (eds.). Baltimore: Johns Hopkins University Press, 1977.

Terman, L.M. The Gifted Group at Mid-Life. *Genetic Studies of Genius*, Vol. 5. Stanford: Stanford University Press, 1959.

Terman, L.M. and Oden, M.H. The Promise of Youth. *Genetic Studies of Genius*, Vol. 3. Stanford: Stanford University Press, 1935.

Terman L.M. and Oden, M.H. The Gifted Child Grows Up. *Genetic Studies of Genius*, Vol. 4. Stanford: Stanford University Press, 1947.

Chapter 10

Barriers to Achievement

Until the last decade, there were no theories of women's career development. Vocational psychology and career counseling were created in a world where men worked and women stayed home. Although a few researchers attempted to understand women's unique patterns of career development (Farmer, 1976; Harmon, 1977; Fitzgerald & Betz, 1983), only recently have books devoted entirely to theories and practice of career development with women been written (Walsh & Osipow, 1993). Now, however, the full-time homemaker is rapidly becoming the exception rather than the rule. Data show that 45 percent of the labor force is now female; the odds of women working between the ages of eighteen and sixty-four is more than nine out of ten. More than half of all mothers of young children work outside the home. In addition, women's wages have become increasingly important to family income: a wife's earnings now constitute 50 percent of black family income, 40 percent of Hispanic family income, and 35 percent of white family income. The reality of the changed world of work has made old assumptions about woman's place archaic (AAUW, 1991).

Furthermore, the theories of career development that have helped in counseling men have proved disappointing for guiding

155

women. Work options for women have traditionally been limited to a small group of occupations, but now, few occupations are closed to women. Nevertheless, many women continue to be relegated to jobs that are low-level, low-status and low-pay. Career theories based on men cannot explain why this is so.

Many writers of popular and scholarly works agree that barriers to achievement for gifted women are both external and internal. External or societal barriers include training subtly geared to lower status for girls, discrimination and harassment in education and the workplace, and lack of resources. However, the picture has changed during the last twenty years because the women's movement has raised society's awareness of discriminatory practices against women and of cultural pressures they face.

Yet even when there is little discouragement or discrimination from our society, girls and women may be prone to internal or personal barriers. Once these were given "disease names"—"Horner Effect," "Cinderella Complex," "Imposter Phenomenon"—for it was assumed that women's own self-defeating "sick" attitudes toward success, independence, risk-taking, and brilliance were what kept them from success. However, recent research indicates that these dramatic internal barriers may not be what is keeping back the new generation of young women. Rather, it may continue to be the neglect of girls' ideas and goals in our families and schools that leads to a plunge in self-esteem during adolescence, as the AAUW Self-Esteem Study reveals. Ironically, however, psychological adjustment—not psychological disability—seems to be the greatest internal barrier for gifted girls.

All gifted women must find ways of coping with the "handicap" of being female. Such adjustment surprisingly parallels adjustment to disability, disaster, or even dying. There are several explanations of how and why.

External Barriers

Shaping for Femininity

The moment a baby is born, adults begin to shape its behavior toward the masculine or the feminine. Pink clothes and sex-typed nicknames come with girls, along with certain expectations of appropriate adult attention. It is almost impossible to find girls' clothes in any color besides pink and lavender, even for older girls, and surprisingly, children's clothes and toys are more sex-segregated now than ever. Once one shopped the aisles of Ben Franklin or Wooolworth's for unisex basics like balls, jump ropes, and board games, but now one enters huge warehouses divided into colorful boys' and blindingly pink girls' aisles. Girls' toys are determinedly sex-typed, offering little opportunity for exploration or problem-solving, and some girls' books and board games are downright insulting, implying that shopping and pursuing boys are the only valuable activities. While most people are aware of this sex-typing in toys, few know that there are also basic differences in infant and toddler handling (Jacklin, 1989) for boys and girls. For example, parents generally respond to a newborn girl's cries more quickly than they do to a newborn boy's. Perhaps the girl is perceived to be in distress, while the boy is simply exercising his lungs! Or perhaps it is early training in socially-accepted behavior: girls are allowed to cry and so their wailing is rewarded or responded to with attention; boys' tears are ignored in order to extinguish the "unmanly" behavior early on. Later in life, boys are permitted to express more aggression than girls: parents allow boys to hit, poke, and throw things at them, while frowning on such aggressiveness in their daughters. Girls frequently receive praise for "prosocial" behaviors such as helping, cooperating, sharing, boys much less so. When a girl in primary grades becomes frustrated with a task, her parents are likely to rush to help, yet they do not tend to help a son in a similar plight.

Given all this gender training, it's no wonder that children by age four or five begin to enforce sex roles themselves, with boys more rigidly committed to them than girls (O'Brien & Huston, 1984). By age seven, boys and girls have learned sex-role stereotyping: they can clearly identify careers as male or female, even though eight- to ten-year-olds are a little more flexible about occupational typing than children were twenty years ago. But girls still tend to prefer traditionally feminine careers; boys, traditionally masculine ones (AAUW, 1992). Girls are self-assured and outspoken as children, but around age eleven they begin to lose confidence in their abilities, their looks, and their personalities (Rogers and Gilligan, 1988).

Why do some girls lose confidence in their abilities while so often continuing to receive high grades? Most teachers are unaware of the many ways in which they differentially train girls' and boys' attitudes toward their own achievements. However, it is clear that girls learn to view their successes as caused by luck and their failures as due to lack of ability; boys learn to attribute their successes to ability and their failures to bad breaks.

How does such a self-view develop? Two educational researchers (Dweck & Gillard, 1975) discovered that most teacher feedback to boys is negative and focuses mainly on conduct and social behavior, with lack of effort being the usual criticism of boys: teachers consistently tell boys that they are not trying hard enough. Teachers' feedback to girls most often is positive, and seldom refers to effort: when girls fail at a task, teachers usually don't tell them they aren't trying hard enough. Thus, girls do not learn to associate effort with either failure or success, while boys learn, from being told to "try harder," that they have control over the results of their work. Such shaping is not limited to elementary education but continues throughout high school. More recently, it has been shown that from kindergarten through graduate school, males receive more attention than females, as well as more precise, informative responses (Sadker & Sadker, 1986, 1994). Boys are called on three times more often; girls are rewarded for sitting quietly.

Even in college, where so many gifted women can be found, professors shape achievement behavior differently for men and women (Bernard, 1976; Sandler, 1984). Men are called on in class more often than are women. Men are more frequently invited to become student assistants and to participate in research. Not surprisingly, many women increasingly feel left out as they progress through college. Bernard found that university professors respond to female students and even to female professors in two characteristic and negative ways: with put-downs and with avoidance. Put-downs include overt and subtle sexist comments in lectures, conversations, and recommendations.

Even more common is avoidance: many male professors passively neglect and resist women's academic efforts. Higher education, according to Bernard, seriously shortchanges women, providing for many of the gifted only a "null academic environment" without encouragement. Perhaps even more destructive to gifted women is the culture of romance, which insists upon the necessity of a romantic relationship and judges women only by the men with whom they associate. College campuses continue to insure that women are "educated in romance" better than they are educated for future career roles (Holland & Eisenhart, 1990).

The differential encouragement of independence and achievement of the behavior in school and college seriously hinders gifted girls and women. It seems incredible that a girl who has received straight As would attribute all of them to luck, but many girls do exactly that. It is likewise extraordinary that a qualified woman does not recognize when she has been discriminated against in employment, but instead interprets the rejection to mean that she must be less qualified—but this too, happens.

Sexism and Discrimination

"A woman needs to work twice as hard for half the credit."

"A woman's formula for success: Act like a man. Dress like a lady. Work like a dog."

"On the job market, a woman is worth 69¢ for every $1 a man is worth."

Such widely-quoted statements reflect the sexism and discrimination operating against women in the working world. To be sure, the climate has improved. The women's movement has raised awareness of inequalities in education and work. For a while, legislation improved the chances of a girl in the United States growing up to reach her potential. Title IX required that schools receiving federal funds make efforts to reduce disparate educational practices for boys and girls. Title VII's Affirmative Action legislation required that qualified female candidates be considered for higher education admissions and for jobs. Unfortunately, however, in the eighties there was little enforcement of these laws, and damaging forms of discrimination still exist.

Despite the large numbers of women in the workforce, sixty percent work in clerical, service, and traditional professions (Taeuber, 1991), and discrimination in employment is well-documented. Susan Faludi's *Backlash* (1991) shows convincingly how women's gains in corporate America were undone by the recession and the backlash against the women's movement.

While discrimination affects all women, it seems, except for women at poverty level, to affect gifted girls and women most adversely. A review by Sally Reis and Carolyn Callahan (1996) shows that sex role stereotyping is alive and well in gifted classrooms. Janis Jacobs and Victoria Weisz (1996) have confirmed persisting stereotyping of girl's abilities within families. Sexism and discrimination cause bright, achieving women to rise only so high as the "glass ceiling." Every highly achieving professional woman knows when she has reached that invisible upper limit in her ascent toward her career goal. Whether in business or academe, she has been accorded respect and has provided leadership in mixed-sex task groups and committees—up to that point. She has risen to positions of great responsibility and has encountered few setbacks attributable to her sex, or at least few that she could not overcome. However, as she advances she notes that the committee meetings and work groups number fewer women, minorities, and young professionals. Finally, she enters the board room to find only business suits and men's grey heads. She feels alone. She observes that when the men speak, it is to each other. When they seek information from her, they ask her supervisor or a male colleague next to her, "Has Mary got the budget from the subcommittee?" They avoid eye contact with her. When she speaks, they look puzzled and resume their conversations with each other. They interrupt her frequently when she does speak. Dismayed and bewildered, she begins to understand that she will not rise higher.

This ceiling effect is encountered only by women who are highly achieving, because in today's society, it is mainly at the very bottom and at the very top of the job prestige hierarchy that women receive such overtly unequal job treatment. Women in middle-prestige, moderate-salary jobs often are protected by affirmative action and other legislation and, more importantly, by the implicit agreement of employers and co-workers with new middle class values. Discrimination and negative attitudes toward women occur less often in middle management positions than they did a decade ago, according to recent studies of how women in management positions are perceived. But at top levels, business executives and public administrators know how to circumvent affirmative action. Statistics confirm that such men prefer to work with other men: since top-level hiring decisions are often risky, known quantities—i.e., men—are sought out. When a job opening occurs, they call their friends and ask about "good people." This has been called the "Old-Boy Network," or the male mentoring system; when the system acts consistently to exclude women, it is called discrimination.

For gifted women, who happen to be the most frequent objects of such exclusion, the discrimination comes as a rude surprise. They do not expect it, since many barriers have been removed from higher education and from entry-level professional positions. But the discrimination is real. An elderly female professor, in speaking to a student women's group, remarked, "Bright young women entering their first highly-paid jobs often say, 'I've never been discriminated against!' I want to say, 'Just wait.'"

Lack of Resources

Another major external barrier to achievement by gifted women is a lack of money for needs ranging from adequate schooling to neighborhood day care facilities. Inevitably linked to discrimination, a scarcity of funds is the primary barrier between the minority woman and achievement. In the last decade, poor women, particularly women of color, have become poorer, and the problems of African-American, Hispanic, and Native American women are compounded by sexism, racism, and poverty. With their lower earning power, women often cannot afford an education in a profession; compounding the problem is the fact that it has also become more difficult for women to get loans for medical school, law school, and other professional programs. But money problems also nag at women from other sides. Often, a woman's quickest road to poverty is divorce. The need for an immediate job—to pay for child care, home mortgage or apartment rental, food, transportation and utilities—often rules out training for a higher-level career position. Furthermore, women's opportunities to learn financial management skills have been generally lean—particularly long-term money planning for retirement and insurance programs. For mothers aspiring to careers, child care and help with household chores are indispensable, but reliable help tends to be expensive and hard to find. Thus, it is small wonder that women worry about jeopardizing safe, though lesser paying, traditional female roles.

Internal Barriers

Most of the research and writing on the internal barriers of women was done in the seventies and early eighties. Unfortunately, this work has often been used inappropriately to "blame the victim:" that is, women are accused of being their own worst enemies, exclusively and entirely at fault for not achieving their goals. At its worst, this kind of popular literature labels women with illnesses or deficits, as if women developed their misgivings about success in isolation from a society which told them at every turn that their achievement was unimportant or unacceptable. Equally inappropriate, in my opinion, is the literature which glorifies women's ambivalence about success as a valid "different voice," a good, constructive response which preserves intimacy. Therefore, I present these ideas, old and new, with some trepidation, because I don't wish to have my work used inappropriately, as Carol Gilligan's *In a Different Voice* (1982) has been, to perpetuate the status quo or to imply that it is simply up to women to change. I do want, however, to review these ideas in order to glean from them some ideas which can add to our understanding of gifted girls and women. The fact that the following internal barriers can be characterized as pathologies—which implies that gifted women are maladjusted in some way—may be because many subjects who experienced these barriers had sought psychotherapy in order to deal with unhappiness in their lives.

The Horner Effect

I first encountered the Horner Effect in college in my general experimental psychology lab. Our professor gave us a verbal learning experiment, handing to each student ten lists of simple words and ten M & M candies. Paired with a partner, we sat facing each other, one student slowly reading a list of words to the other, who was to repeat as many words as he or she could remember. When the entire list was memorized, the student won an M & M. Partners took turns reading and reciting until all the lists were read, at which time we were to count our M & Ms and write our score on the board. My first partner was a polite, smiling, blonde girl. We laughed as we flubbed words and cheered each other as we earned candy. I think I won more than she did.

We entered our scores on the board, and our professor announced a second experiment for us in digital dexterity. After a set of tiddlywinks was given to each student, the professor reassigned us to new partners. We were to play tiddlywinks for fifteen minutes, then to record our scores on the board. Now my partner was a beefy hippie in overalls with a full beard surrounding his grin. We played tiddlywinks, at first laughingly but then in mock seriousness. I thought I saw that my partner really wanted to win, so I didn't play very earnestly. Sure enough, I lost. Like a good sport, I went up to write our scores on the board.

Then came the surprise. These experiments were not about

verbal learning or digital dexterity at all. Rather, the whole activity was a demonstration of male/female attitudes toward competition. He purposely had assigned us to an even number of mixed-sex and same-sex partnerships, and involved us in two competitive games, one intellectual and one physical. "Let's see what the scores look like when we put them in same-sex and mixed-sex columns," he said, rearranging the scores on the board. Even without calculations the trend was clear: women's scores were much lower when they competed against men than when they competed against women.

"It's the Horner Effect," he said. "It's happened in every class today." Matina Horner (1972), psychologist, had first discovered this pattern in her achievement-motivation experiments similar to those my professor used. She observed that women characteristically under-achieved when competing against men. Despite exceptional ability, women would perform decidedly below their skills and, curiously, would usually be unable to explain why. The Horner Effect was later renamed the Fear of Success syndrome, for it was reasoned that the phenomenon occurred because the typical woman was afraid to win against a man in competition, for to win against a man was actually to lose. Lose what? Femininity, perhaps. Or his goodwill.

The Horner Effect, or Fear of Success syndrome, was confirmed throughout the seventies; then, in the eighties, the effect was observed to be lessened or even absent in psychological experiments. Some women—at least those young college women who are the most frequent research subjects—seemed to be changing. Had Title IX legislation, which encouraged more co-educational physical education and less sex-typed course selection, had an impact on girls? Did they, and do they, feel more comfortable with competition? Recent anthropological studies of boys and girls in competition and conflict, reviewed by Deborah Tannen (1990), show that girls do engage in competition and conflict with each other and with boys, but that they will compromise to preserve intimacy. Therefore, the Horner Effect may still live on in girls' and women's tendencies to negotiate and avoid conflict or competition when friendship or intimacy is at stake.

What is the impact of the Horner Effect on gifted girls and women? Since they are astute, gifted girls become sensitive to the conflicts for women in competitive situations much earlier than average girls do. While they may have been encouraged to be competitive and achieving with their classroom abilities, they conversely have often been discouraged from competition in traditional boys' activities, games, or sports that they may enjoy. The Horner Effect involves holding back one's efforts and dampening one's enthusiasm. Sadly, gifted girls have more ability than most to hide, making it more likely that they will have to work hard at hiding their gifts. Hence gifted girls are likely to be more aware of their underachievement, and even frustrated by it, although they may not know why they are underachieving. Terman's studies show the gifted girls and women have an even stronger need to please others than average women do. Even when a gifted woman understands how irrational or impractical it is to underachieve, she may continue to do so if she believes success will result in a failure of intimacy.

Therefore, fear of success seems to have its most powerful effect on the very women most likely to be successful. Their fears increase as they approach achievement and success. How curious that a bright girl or woman who is keenly in touch with social norms and who exhibits much potential should become progressively anxious as she nears the academic or career success for which she has yearned. As she anticipates the consequences of too much success, she slips to underachievement. She is puzzled by her underachieving, and usually feels intense, if undefinable, dissatisfaction with herself. This conflict is difficult and demeaning and requires great personal effort to cope with, even given an understanding of the issues.

The Cinderella Complex

Colette Dowling (1981) observed herself and others avoiding achievement. When she learned of the Horner Effect, she conceived a snappy title that included both fear of success and the desire to be cared for: The Cinderella Complex. In her book by that title, she advanced the theory that personal, psychological dependency is the chief force that suppresses today's women. The Cinderella Complex is a network of largely repressed attitudes and fears that detain women in a kind of half-light, retreating from the full use of their minds and creativity. "Like Cinderella, women today are still waiting for something external to transform their lives" (p. 31). Women caught up in the Cinderella Complex are "too angry to stay behind and too frightened to move ahead."

Though not based on a rigorous scientific study, Dowling's thought-provoking insights should not be ignored. She observed in her interviewees (mostly bright, middle-class women) the conflicts others have described as troubling gifted women. "Overhelped" as children, women are crippled by a subsequent sense of dependence on others, says Dowling. In adolescence, she observes, many women who had been intellectually encouraged by their fathers now felt betrayed by them. Fathers abruptly changed their opinions as their bright daughters' career goals grew. Why? Were fathers threatened by the achievements of daughters? Did they need to squelch their daughters, lest their daughters surpass them in achievement? Dowling quotes Simone de Beauvoir's description of her relationship with her father when she was a teen:

> *"I was obeying his wishes to the letter, and that seemed to anger him. He had destined me to a life of study and yet I was being reproached with having my nose in a book all the time. To judge by his surly temper, you would think that I had gone against his wishes in embarking on a course of study he had actually chosen for me" (p. 401).*

What about the mothers among Dowling's interviewees? Most were passive women who had made small contribution to the lives of the daughters. Jealous of their daughters' lofty goals, many had attempted to curtail them by encouraging their girls to seek the "right" boyfriends.

Dowling found that most of the women she studied acquiesced to the expectations of their parents and began to desire the total fusion of marriage. They learned to judge men by their competence to take care of them completely. Dowling describes single women who refused to commit themselves to permanent jobs or careers because they hoped that the right man would come along. Similarly, she describes married women whose dependency fed upon itself, so that with each passing year, they became less capable of pursuing their own goals. They seemed to base their self-worth on the man they had married.

Only crisis could shock these women out of submerging themselves in marriage and family, Dowling believed, and determined self-exploration, even psychotherapy, were essential for women to uncover and work through what she believed were often unconscious and severely limiting fears of independence. But in fact, many of the women Dowling observed had themselves first sought psychotherapy because they were especially unhappy with their prior life decisions. In other words, Dowling was studying women who by their own admission needed or wanted therapy of some sort. Perhaps their fears of independence were more extreme than those of women in general. Since they were not typical of all women, what may have been true for them cannot be assumed to be true for all women who do not reach their career goals.

Still, some research supports Colette Dowling's ideas. Studies (e.g., Holland & Eisenhart, 1991; Tangri, 1974;) show that girls who choose nontraditional or "pioneer" careers are not likely to be pressured by parents to date and marry. In addition, findings suggest that career-oriented women often come from homes that foster independence, achievement, and active exploration. These career-oriented girls generally have working mothers as models or mothers who are positive about careers, along with well-educated fathers who are proud of them.

It seems then that there is a Cinderella Complex at work when pressure to date is high, when independence, achievement, and exploration are discouraged, and when mothers and fathers are unsupportive about careers. Gifted women coming from such homes may be particularly at risk for experiencing the handicaps associated with the Cinderella Complex.

The Imposter Phenomenon

The Imposter Phenomenon offers yet another example of bright women's internal barriers to achievement. According to case studies by psychotherapists Pauline Clance and Suzanne Imes (1978) at Georgia State University, numerous bright female clients denied that they were intelligent despite significant successes and measurable accomplishments. The researchers describe the phenomenon this way: "Women who experienced the imposter phenomenon maintained a strong belief that they were not intelligent; in fact, they were convinced that they had fooled everyone." Such women believe that their high examination scores are attributable to luck, that some mistake must have been made when they were admitted to prestigious colleges and graduate programs, and that their successes on jobs are due to their work being overevaluated, the researchers found. The women they studied consequently feared that someone important would discover they were "intellectual impostors."

Clance and Imes point out the irony that since success for

women is contrary both to social expectations and to their own self-concept, women need to explain away their accomplishments—in this case by believing that they have fooled other people. How peculiar, that a bright woman can change her own self-image so that she denies her clear achievements and abilities even to herself.

Are there particular family dynamics that generate the imposter phenomenon? Clance and Imes identify two patterns. In the first, one sibling has been labeled the intelligent one; the future "imposter," who may be quite as intelligent, is given some other label, such as "the sensitive one." Nothing she undertakes will prove to her family that she is intelligent, even if she gets better grades than the "intelligent one." She begins to doubt her intellect and believes that her family is correct, despite contrary evidence.

In the second pattern, a girl has been given her family's full support. She has been persuaded by family to believe that she is superior virtually unto perfection. However, as the girl matures, she realizes that some tasks are in fact difficult for her, and she begins to distrust her parents' perceptions of her. She may hide the fact that she has to study because it would destroy the family myth that she can do everything with ease. Her difficulties now prompt her to believe that if she isn't a genius, she must actually be only average, or even dumb—and clearly an imposter.

Paradoxically, four common behaviors actually help these women maintain the belief that they are impostors. First is diligence: she works hard at her job in order to keep others from discovering that she is an imposter. Her efforts lead to praise and reward, which in turn frighten her into working even harder!

Second is a feeling of being phony that, Clance and Imes think, is often based in reality, for most of the women studied had tried to give answers that professors or supervisors wanted to hear, rather than what these women actually believed or knew.

Third is the use of charm and perceptiveness to win approval from superiors. A woman exhibiting this behavior may seek a mentor from among superiors she respects and enthusiastically pursue an intense relationship, hoping that the mentor will bring out her intellect and creativity. When the mentor does declare her to be superior to others, however, she cannot accept this fervently sought appraisal; the mentor's evaluation, she fears, is based entirely on her charm and not on her ability.

Finally, a woman can also maintain her belief that she is an imposter by avoiding any display of confidence in her abilities. She thus plays on the negative consequences of both fear of success and the Cinderella Complex: the imposter suspects that if she truly believes in her own intelligence and shows it, she will be rejected by others (especially men) and will be forced into a lonely life without being nurtured by others. Thus she convinces herself that she really is not that intelligent and so eludes risks.

Among the women in my own study, I found support for the imposter syndrome in women's and girls' negative views of their academic abilities, and in denying their giftedness. In general, women tend consistently to underestimate their abilities.

As a group, women also take few academic risks—especially in math, an area perceived to be reserved for men (Sells, 1980; Fennemia, 1990). Most girls and women deny entirely any ability in math and avoid courses that might prove or disprove this belief in their inability. This characteristic avoidance of math and math-related courses has a powerful impact on women's career development, particularly in today's modern technological society.

The "math filter," as it is called by Sells (1980), effectively prevents the majority of women from entering high-status, high-paying occupations. In a study at the University of California-Berkeley, only eight percent of women versus 57 percent of men had had four years of high school math. Yet four years of math were required to be eligible for three-fourths of CU's academic majors. Thus, avoiding math locked 92 percent of college women out of most of the numerous academic options.

The Self-Esteem Plunge

The American Association for University Women had always been active in promoting women's education, but the study they commissioned in order to study girls' attitudes and identity was one of the biggest initiatives ever undertaken (AAUW/ Greenberg-Lake, 1991). Sharon Schuster, then president of the AAUW, told me that the organization hoped to reach an understanding of the interaction of self-esteem, education, and career aspirations in adolescent girls and boys in today's society. The study they commissioned included three thousand children between grades four and ten in twelve locations nationwide. The major finding of the study was a self-esteem plunge for girls. Both boys and girls decline in self-esteem during the tumultuous teen years, but the drop for girls is much more dramatic. According to the report, "Girls, aged eight and nine, are confident, assertive, and feel authoritative about themselves. They emerge from adolescence with a poor self-image, constrained views of their future and their place in society, and much less confidence about themselves and their abilities. Sixty percent of elementary school girls say they are 'happy with the way I am,' a core measure of self-esteem. More boys, 67 percent of those surveyed, also strongly agreed with the statement. Over the next eight years, girls' self-esteem falls 31 percentage points, with only 29 percent of high school girls saying they are happy with themselves. Almost half of the high school boys (46 percent) retain their high self-esteem. By high school, this gender gap increases from 7 points to 17 points" (p. 4).

What does self-esteem mean to girls and boys? The biggest difference between girls and boys in the study was in their confidence about "doing things": more boys than girls felt they were pretty good at doing a lot of things. Boys were also more likely to speak out in class and to argue with teachers when they thought they were right. Twice as many boys as girls named their talents as something they liked best about themselves; girls were twice as likely to name a physical characteristic. The researchers also found that the boys were willing to dream bigger career dreams and more likely than girls to believe their own career dreams could come true.

Interestingly, the results were not the same across races. Black girls did not lose self-esteem as dramatically as white girls did, and in the area of personal self-esteem, Hispanic girls started out higher than the other groups and dropped further. In my talk with Sharon Schuster and colleagues, the suggestion has often come up that black girls' self-esteem does not plummet because their community supports their sense of personal worth. They do show increasingly negative feelings about school and work; perhaps their understanding of racism and its effects helps them to see that the negative experiences they have are not always the result of their own personal failings. Hispanic girls' plunge, a cause for alarm, seems to show that cultural influences as well as schooling and other societal forces are battering these girls' opinions of themselves.

Another important finding of the study was that family and school have a greater impact on self-esteem than the peer group. Pride in schoolwork, the belief that one is able to do many things well, and the feeling of being important in one's own family were the major contributors to self-esteem in this study. When self-esteem dropped, it was likely that it was because the girls perceived changes in these areas.

Finally, the AAUW researchers showed that there was a circular relationship among liking for math and science, self-esteem, and career aspirations. Girls who enjoyed math and science were likely to have higher self-esteem and aspirations, and girls with higher aspirations were likely to enjoy math.

A study as massive and important as this one ought to have made immediate waves in education, academe, and society, but sadly enough, the report was released on the same day that the United States bombed Iraq. The results of this study were eclipsed by international events for many months. Gradually, the findings have come to the awareness of the public, and there now is legislation at both the state and federal levels aimed at correcting some of the inequity.

Perhaps one of the true tests of the importance of research is the existence of opposition to it. Christine Sommers, in her book, *Who Stole Feminism* (1994), attacks the Greenberg-Lake/AAUW study, suggesting that the findings are exaggerated and that the research is the work of feminist extremists who do not understand that girls like their status and enjoy being who they are. I found these attacks puzzling: the AAUW, hardly an extremist organization, has a cautious leadership and a very high proportion of elderly women in its membership. The self-esteem studies and the reports which follow seem not to be advocating that we fix what isn't broken, but that we re-examine our complacency about the differences in boys' and girls' socialization, which are obvious to anybody, and that we consider what these differences mean for girls' happiness and fulfillment of potential.

A recent study performed specifically on gifted girls found a similar pattern of declining self-esteem (Klein and Zehms, 1996). Klein and Zehms found significant declines in total self-concept scores between grades 3 and 8 in a cross-sectional study. Girls' confidence in their behavior, their intellectual ability, school status, and popularity fell as they approached puberty.

The implications for gifted girls and women of the data at our disposal are great. We know from other studies that gifted girls, unlike average girls, do dream big dreams. We know they have extremely high self-esteem as children. If it is indeed true that the conditions of adolescence in our society provoke a plunge in self-esteem in girls in general, then the drop in positive self-opinions

170

for gifted girls must be even more dramatic, for they have further to fall. The study also points up the awesome responsibility teachers and parents have to protect and promote the self-esteem and aspirations of gifted girls.

The Process of Adjustment

Fear of Success, the Cinderella Complex, and the Imposter Phenomenon all focus upon women's deficits; current theories, however, are based on studies of women's differences and strengths. In fact, no single theory accounts for gifted women's underachievement. All barriers are at work for some gifted women, none for others, a combination of certain ones at certain times for most. The fact is that many patterns of adjustment characterize being female and gifted.

However, there is an internal barrier to achievement that ironically is not related to any unhealthy psychological state, even though it, too, often results in underachievement. Resulting from a healthy psychological state combined with an accommodating personality, this barrier is *psychological adjustment*, the process of resourceful adaptation to the environment, of compromising and adjusting in order to cope or to survive psychologically. Some people must make greater adjustments than others, and people with lower status must make greater adjustments than others. Carol Tavris (1991) points out that many of the differences in communication which we think are based on sex are actually based on status, with those who are different from the average often making the greatest adjustments. Communication theorists call this "code-switching": people who are both different and lower in status must learn to speak and behave like the more dominant group. From the earliest research on the gifted, it was clear that of all groups, gifted girls are the most adept at adjusting; in fact, gifted girls are of low status by virtue of their sex, and different by virtue of their intelligence. Hence, if the code-switching theory is true, they have indeed been required to adjust repeatedly to the dominant group, perhaps more often than anyone else. What makes their situation most poignant to me is that their giftedness must so often be applied to these extraordinary feats of adjustment, rather than to the attainment of their dreams.

An enlightening analogy can be learned from rehabilitation psychologists, who study and treat individuals coping with disability of various kinds. The adjustment to severe disability comes in stages much as adjustment to dying does: denial, bargaining, anger, and acceptance. In the stage of denial, patients refuse to believe there is anything seriously wrong. Amputees may refuse to acknowledge the stump of a leg. In bargaining, patients believe they can make a few changes, compromise in some way, and all will be well. When frustration mounts to a breaking point, patients experience rage at the condition, and anger sets in. Finally, acceptance: patients are at peace, having finally reconciled the dilemma and faced the impossibility of change, but having found positive, constructive ways of coping. Only when a patient has reached acceptance can he or she be considered ready for vocational/career rehabilitation. The amputee baseball player must willingly give up his dream of playing in the major leagues. The heart patient must turn down the prestigious but stressful administrative position that was once possible.

It may seem a peculiar comparison, adjustment to a disability and the career development of gifted women. However, when one examines the adjustment of gifted women to their often-restrictive roles as wives, mothers, teachers, and nurses, strong similarities appear, for gifted women often seem to be adjusting to the disability of being female. Denial is rampant in the teen years: nothing is wrong, there is no problem with being a female. The teenager says she will be a doctor, get married, and take off for eighteen years to raise children. Or, there is no problem with being gifted; it's perfectly all right when gifted women drop out of college to marry because their giftedness wasn't real.

Later comes the bargaining. The gifted woman will hold back on her education to put her husband through medical school if he will do the same for her. She will move to another city with him if he will move when she gets a big break. She will have a child if he will help out so she can finish her thesis.

The anger stage seldom reaches full flower in a gifted woman. More often, it is expressed in apathy, cynicism, or depression. After years of supporting her husband's education, she gives up on her own ambitions in mild irritation. It's too late to cope with being a student. After moving from city to city in response to her husband's promotions, she professes at least slight resentment that it will be too costly to find a satisfying job for her. After realizing that she must take primary responsibility for her child at the expense of her interests, she may feel angry with her husband, but only for a while, and she attempts to convince herself that she is more fulfilled than she actually is.

Acceptance comes when the anger has passed. She understands that she is gifted and has not really fulfilled her potential, but she also understands that she is a female, and that her experiences are simply typical for women in American society. She strives to find satisfaction in her achievements whenever she can, vicariously enjoying the accomplishments of those around her. She blames nobody and is generally able to feel good about who she is. She realizes that she has accomplished a lot within the limitations of her lifestyle.

And so it is her healthy adjustment that prevents achievement, her admirable self-acceptance that precludes self-actualization. Yet gifted women who have accepted the disability of being female often say they are happy women who enjoy their lives. Margaret Mead describes a scholar/mother who said she could not finish her research "because the baby cries so much." Mead felt she just as well might have said, "the baby smiles so much," for it is the pleasure of children, not always the burden of children, that has so often deterred gifted women from other work. And it is often the husband's love, not his oppression, that draws women away from accomplishment. A society that wastes female brilliance has made it the norm for gifted women to lead an average life, and gifted women have largely adapted to that norm.

Hence it would appear that this process of adjustment is more to blame for women's failure to achieve their potential than the other internal factors combined, though clearly all these forces interact. It seems imperative that psychologists study the process of adjustment in gifted women more closely. Do gifted women perceive their own development as researchers describe it? Are there any ways of intervening so that women don't give up too easily on pursuing their own goals? Can psychologists help gifted women to understand that accepting barriers too readily may lead to cheating themselves as well as society of the fruits of their talents?

References

American Association for University Women, *Shortchanging Girls, Shortchanging America*. Washington, DC: AAUW, 1991.

Bernard, J. "Where Are We Now? Some Thoughts on the Current Scene." In *Psychology of Women Quarterly*, 1, 1976, 21-37.

Candry, L. C. and Dyer, S. L. "Behavioral and Fantasy Measures of Fear of Success in Children." In *Child Development*, 48, 1975, 1417-25.

Clance, P. R. and Imes, S. A. "The Impostor Phenomenon in High Achieving Women: Dynamics and Therapeutic Intervention." In *Psychotherapy: Theory, Research, and Practice*, 15, 1978, 241-45.

De Beauvoir, S. *Memoirs of a Dutiful Daughter*. New York: Harper & Row, 1959.

Dowling, C. *The Cinderella Complex*. New York: Summit Books, 1981.

Dweck, C. & Gilliard, D. "Expectancy Statements as Determinants of Reactions to Failure: Sex Differences in Persistence and Expectancy Change." In *Journal of Personality and Social Psychology*, 32, 1975, 1077-84.

Fagot, B. J. "Sex-determined Parental Reinforcing Contingencies in Toddler Children." Paper presented at meeting of the Society for Research in Child Development, New Orleans, March, 1977.

Faludi, Susan. *Backlash: The Undeclared War Against American Women*, New York: Crown, 1991.

Farmer, H. S. "Environmental, Background, and Psychological Variables Related to Optimizing Achievement and Career Motivation for High School Girls." *Journal of Vocational Behavior*, 17, 1980, 53-70.

Farmer, H. S. "What Inhibits Achievement and Career Motivation in Women?" In *The Counseling Psychologist*, 6, 1976, 12-14.

Fennema, E. "Justice, Equity, and Mathematics Education." In E. Fennema and G. Leder (Eds.) *Mathematics and Gender*. NY: Teachers College Press, 1990, 1-9.

Fitzgerald, L. and Betz, N. "Issues in the Vocational Psychology of Women." In W. B. Walsh and S. H. Osipow (Eds.). *The Handbook of Vocational Psychology*. Hillsdale, NJ: Erlbaum, 1983.

Harmon, L. W. "Career Counseling for Women." In *Psychotherapy for Women*, E. Rawlings and D. Carter (Eds.). Springfield, Ill.: Charles Thomas, 1977.

Hoffman, L. W. "Early Childhood Experiences and Women's Achievement Motives." In *Journal of Social Issues*, 28, 1972, 129-56.

Holland, D. C. & Eisenhart, M. A. *Educated in Romance: Women, Achievement, and College Culture*. Chicago: University of Chicago Press, 1990.

Horner, M. S. "Toward an Understanding of Achievement Related Conflicts in Women." In *Journal of Social Issues*, 28, 1972.

Jacklin, C. Female and Male: "Issues of Gender." *American Psychologist*, 44, 127-133, 1989.

Jacobs, J.E. and Weisz, U. "Gender Stereotypes: Implications for Gifted Education." *Roeper Review.* 16, 3, 152-155, 1996.

Klein, A.G. and Zehms, D. "Self-Concept and Gifted Girls: A Cross-Sectional Study of Intellectually Gifted Females in Grades 3, 5, 8." Roeper Review, 19, 1, 30-33, 1996.

O'Brien, M. & Huston, A. "Development of Sex-typed Play Behavior in Toddlers." In *Development Psychology*, 21, 866-71, 1985.

Reis, S.M. and Callahan, C.M. "My Boyfriend, My Girlfriend, or Me: The Dilemma of Talented Teenaged Girls." *Journal of Secondary Gifted Education*, 2, 434-446, 1996.

Rogers, A. & Gilligan, C. *Translating Girls Voices: Two Languages of Development*. Cambridge, MA: Harvard University Graduate School of Education Project on the Psychology of Women and the Development of Girls, 1988.

Sadker, M. & Sadker, D. "Sexism in the Classroom: From Grade School to Graduate School." In *Phi Delta Kappan*, 68, 512, 1986.

Sadker, M. & Sadker, D. *Failing at Fairness: How America's Schools Cheat Girls*. New York: Scribners Sons, 1994.

Sandler, B. *The College Campus: A Chilly Climate for Women*. Washington, DC: American Council on Education, 1984.

Sells, L. W. "The Mathematics Filter and the Education of Women and Minorities." In *Women and the Mathematical Mystique*. L. H. Fox, L. Brody, and D. Tobin (eds.). Baltimore: Johns Hopkins University Press, 1980.

Sommers, C. H. *Who Stole Feminism: How Women Have Betrayed Women*. New York: Simon & Schuster, 1994.

Taeuber, C. (Ed.) *Statistical Handbook on Women in America*. Phoenix, Oryx Press, 1991.

Tangri, S. S. "Role Innovation in Occupational Choice Among College Women." In *JSAS Catalog of Selected Documents in Psychology*, 4, 1974 (MS. NO. 555).

Tavris, C. *The Mismeasure of Women: Why Women are not the Better Sex, the Inferior Sex or the Opposite Sex*. New York: Simon & Schuster, 1992.

Tresemer, D. *Fear of Success*. New York: Plenum, 1977.

Walsh, B. & Osipow, S. *Career Counseling for Women*. Hillsboro, N.J.: Erlbaum, 1993

Chapter 11

Gifted Minority Girls and Women

For most of the history of education, we have known very little about the needs of gifted girls, but we have known even less about those bright girls who are Native American, African-American, Asian-American, and Hispanic. There are just a few studies of minority gifted children (Kerr & Colangelo, 1992), and unfortunately most of the research focuses on how to identify gifted minority students through testing, rather than how to help them achieve their full potential. Some researchers have tried to create new norms for intelligence tests by including minority students among those used in the development of the tests. Some have tried to make the existing tests more usable by developing new techniques for interpreting the results, while others have simply created new methods of identification, but the sad fact is that the giftedness of many of our minority children is obscured by the physical and psychological effects of poverty and by the inferior schooling available to poor students. No amount of re-configuring tests can change the social conditions which prevent talent from emerging.

In my work, I have tried to avoid issues of testing and identification and instead tried to cast a wide net: that is, to use definitions of giftedness which are inclusive enough that children with great potential for achievement in any talent area are not missed when students are selected for special programs of education and guidance. This means trusting teachers of minority students to identify those who have that special spark; searching for students who have displayed leadership in their schools and neighborhoods; and asking students to identify peers who have the greatest potential for excellence. Through counseling workshops I have had the opportunity to meet and work with talented girls from many ethnic backgrounds: African-American young women from inner city St. Louis, Chicago, and Kansas City; Sioux young women in Nebraska; Pima, Navajo, and Apache young women in Arizona; Hispanic young women from urban Arizona. Most recently, my colleague Sharon Robinson and I received a National Science Foundation Grant to provide guidance and to study the needs of talented at-risk girls. This program, called the TARGETS project (Talented At-Risk Girls: Encouragement and Training for Sophomores), has allowed us to learn about almost all of cultural groups which exist in this diverse state.

In addition to my work in the counseling laboratory, I have also had the opportunity to collaborate with Nicholas Colangelo in a long-term study of minority students scoring in the 95th percentile or above on the American College Testing Assessment Program (Kerr & Colangelo, 1992; Kerr & Colangelo, 1993). In receiving the highest scores on their college admissions tests, these students have defied the expectation that minority students will not do well on standardized tests. What follows is a summary of my findings about gifted girls who are Native American, African-African, Hispanic, and Asian-American.

Gifted Native American Girls

It could be argued that this is the most neglected minority. Always listed last among minorities, always a small group about which not much is known, Native Americans are little understood by educators, perhaps because of sheer volume of information. Native American groups span the length of the Americas and belong to hundreds of cultural and language groupings, and so understanding the traditions and concerns of one tribe does not mean that one understands Native Americans. One tribe owns its land, always has, and is proudly independent; one has been forced to re-locate far from their original home; one lives in conditions of great poverty on the same land which once provided richly. One culture honors women and girls and their contributions to society; another minimizes their power; another is in transition, with many young women leaving the community. Very few things can be said in general about Native American gifted girls and women. However, there are some underlying themes in Native American culture (Herring, 1992): the belief in a harmonious universe in which every object and being has a sacred life; the belief that humans are part of nature, not superior to it; the belief that nature is sacred; the belief that each individual has rights and dignity; the belief that leadership is based on earned respect. These themes may affect bright girls growing up as Native Americans.

Gifted Native American girls may be reluctant to show their intellectual abilities because of a strong wish not to stand out, which is not just a preference but a cultural imperative. Many bright girls simply cannot do anything which brings attention to themselves as individuals, for in the extremely communal Native American culture, focus on the individual is not just in bad taste: it is wrong. For example, in order to encourage Pima girls to put themselves forward for a pageant featuring traditional and modern talents, it was necessary to stress the pride which the community would feel in the accomplishments of their young women.

Gifted Native American girls often feel rooted in their community so intensely that any educational program which threatens their ties to home may be rejected. For many, their religion and traditions revolve around specific places. Often the name of their tribe refers to this sacred place: the people of the river, the people of the mountain. Leaving the community means leaving one's religion and one's sense of belongingness behind, for she cannot bring her beloved, sacred natural places along. We found that some of the Native American girls who had opportunities for scholarships to a wide variety of prestigious schools did not wish to take advantage of them. It may be necessary to help gifted young Native American women find ways to maintain ties to home while they are in college. Honors programs at nearby universities or programs which understand and support the wishes of gifted Native American women to return to their homes are important.

179

Gifted Native American girls usually do not wish to be competitive or aggressive, in or out of class. Since their cultures usually stress co-operativeness and harmony, gifted Native American girls respond best to techniques and classroom strategies which emphasize quiet co-operation and friendly helping. My colleague, Sharon Robinson Kurpius, and I learned a completely new way to play Trivial Pursuit from a group of Navajo girls visiting our university: we all helped each other with the answers, and we all won.

The attainment of balance is an important goal to many Native American girls: balance between self and nature, body and spirit, masculine and feminine, inward and outward. To the degree that programs for the development of these bright girls' talents allow for the search for balance, they will be successful. Programs which go too far in either direction—for example, career programs emphasizing "dressing for success" or learning to "act like a man" or be self-sufficient—are probably doomed to failure.

We have also learned that the reservation is a different world, materially and spiritually, and that our usual occupational stereotypes do not hold up. On the reservation, a social worker might be seen as a "non-helper," because social workers have so often taken Indian children away from their families. On the other hand, an accountant might be seen as a "helper," because she might help everyone to figure out their tax forms so as not to get in trouble with the government. And the role of the physician or mortician might be viewed with horror by people such as the Navajo, who do not like contact with dead bodies. Therefore guidance counselors helping gifted Native American girls must understand the unique connotation of each educational and career goal.

Gifted African American Women

According to my study with Nick Colangelo, African-American gifted women are taking great strides in overcoming the effects of racism and sexism. The list of colleges they attend is a roster of America's finest higher education institutions: Harvard, Yale, Stanford, as well as the finest historically black institutions as Spelman and Morehouse. The AAUW study described earlier showed that alone among ethnic groups, African-American young women did not show a decline in self-esteem between eleven and seventeen.

It appears that many of these gifted girls are gaining confidence throughout childhood and putting that confidence to work in striving for ambitious goals.

However, several barriers to success continue to block gifted black girls from achieving their goals (Staples, 1988). The poverty of the inner cities and all of the related problems it creates; low expectations of academic performance; peer pressure from other African-American students which discourages academic achievement; difficulties in male-female relationships—all contribute to the burden of African-American gifted girls and women.

Poverty blocks all but the most fortunate African-American gifted girls from the education they deserve. The poorly-funded schools of the inner city seldom have special programming for gifted students. The lack of role models of successful black women discourages these girls from high aspirations. Often, African-American gifted girls are unaware of the availability of scholarships or of help for college planning; the road to success for many talented poor African-Americans has been the military, which may be an excellent choice because it provides job training and financial help with college. However, gifted girls need to be aware of all of their options, and in schools where guidance is also an unaffordable luxury, it is unlikely that the girls will find out about all alternatives.

Peer pressure to underachieve haunts many African-American gifted girls. In a racist society, achieving in school often seems like collaboration with white people in putting down black people—especially when the teachers and administrators are mostly white and the students are people of color. Gifted African-American girls need to be able to believe that their achievement is good for themselves, their families and their communities. It takes courage to raise a hand in class, score 100% on a test, and to apply for college scholarships when other girls are praised for their beautiful babies. Too often, gifted African-Americans are forced into "racelessness," with peers not accepting their achievement and whites not accepting their blackness (Helms, 1990).

Many gifted African-American women complain of difficulties in relationships with African-American men. First, there are too few, for many more black men than women die of the complications of poverty: homicide, accidental deaths, the lack of health care. Second, the humiliations many gifted African-American men have suffered sometimes make them doubly hard on the women they love. They may reject their partners' achievements or hold them to unreasonably high expectations. Finding and keeping love is com-

181

plex enough, but maintaining a relationship as well as one's career goals may be seem impossible under these conditions.

Gifted Asian American Women

Surprisingly, Asian-American gifted women in the ACT study were attending the least prestigious group of colleges of any of the ethnic minority groups. Apparently, they were either not seeking or not being offered scholarships to the highest-status colleges. Although it was not clear from our study which of these was the case, it has become clear that there is a new wave of racism toward Asian-Americans. They are frequently confused with Asian international students and lumped together in a category with people of diverse histories and cultures. A Japanese-American student may be expected by white students and teachers to have much in common with a recent arrival from Cambodia, when in fact all they may share are Asiatic features. Of greatest concern to educators is the increasing stereotype of Asian-American students as over-achieving, uncreative, obsessed with math and science. One Asian-American young woman in our study said, "I'm so tired of people expecting me to be such an intellectual. And I'm supposed to love math and be great at it. And I hate it!"

Another issue of concern to Asian-American gifted girls is the strong patriarchal nature of many Asian-American families. Sometimes the girls in the family are expected to subordinate their goals to those of their brothers. A strong father may command obedience and allow little opportunity for gifted girls to be nonconforming or assertive. On the other hand, when gifted girls are supported, they receive strong support indeed. Many Asian-American families value achievement highly, whether in girls or boys. Yet contrary to the stereotype of Asian-American families, no evidence of parents pressuring children into high achievement appeared in our study.

The honor and respect accorded elders normally does not affect a young Asian-American girl's achievements; however, upon marrying an Asian-American man, she may be expected to wait upon her parents-in-law, sometimes almost as a servant. One young woman in our counseling laboratory had a difficult time finishing her master's thesis because her mother-in-law, visiting for an extended period, required her complete attention.

Gifted Hispanic American Girls

The Hispanic population—people of Mexican, Central American, Cuban, Puerto Rican, and South American descent—is the fastest-growing minority in America. They too are extraordinarily diverse as a group, with Hispanic surnames sometimes being the only common element. However, regardless of subcultural distinctions, all Hispanics share discrimination on the basis of skin color and surname.

Like their Asian-American sisters, Hispanic gifted girls often come from strongly traditional patriarchal families that encourage traditional sex roles. Hispanic culture teaches, in addition to machismo for men, marianismo for women (Stevens, 1973). A girl is expected from childhood on to cultivate all the qualities of a good mother, to be feminine, nurturing, and patient. Sometimes these characteristics conflict with an achievement orientation, producing anxiety in a gifted girl who wishes to preserve her ties to her culture and yet to achieve her intellectual goals (Espin, 1985).

Families may also be very protective of their girls, discouraging activities considered unusual for girls or those that require going far from home. Most successful programs for bright Hispanic girls, like the Hispanic Mother-Daughter program at Arizona State University, take the close-knit nature of the Hispanic family into account.

One of the great strengths of the Hispanic family is that it often provides clear transitions from girlhood to womanhood, marking the transition with ritual and celebration. The great fifteenth birthday party provided to many Hispanic girls in the Southwest communicates to them their importance to their family and the community, building self-esteem in the process.

Guiding the Minority Gifted Girl

Rosie Bingham's and Connie Ward's (1994) excellent guidance suggestions for minority females can be adapted to gifted

183

minority females. Bingham and Ward suggest that helpers prepare themselves by opening up to the other culture, becoming familiar with a wide body of cultural knowledge, and being receptive to the girl or woman as their cultural teacher. Sharon Robinson and I found in our work with the gifted girls of the many tribes of Arizona that it was absolutely necessary to let the girls teach us about their culture. Reading as much as we could about Native Americans of the Southwest, while certainly a starting point, would not teach us all that we needed know about traditions of various groups. We simply told the girls that we wanted to understand their lives and their worlds, and we did whatever we could to be receptive. Sometimes that meant just listening, not asking endless questions! For example, we had each girl draw a picture of something she liked to do that was special to her, and then she would talk about her picture.

A second set of suggestions given by these authors had to do with assessment, and of the importance of understanding the young woman's racial or ethnic identification. A positive racial identification—that is, feeling good about being a member of one's race and understanding what that membership means—is usually associated with high self-esteem and good mental health. So, assessing the strength of a girls's ethnic or racial identification might help in guiding her toward her goals. It is also important to assess two important aspects of the family: what kind of support does the young gifted woman get from her family for her goals, and what familial obligations will affect her goals? We found that it is often these family issues which will determine if a poor Hispanic or Native American young woman will go to college.

I would add to Bingham's and Ward's suggestions the necessity for creativity in guiding minority gifted girls. Most of our counselors at the laboratory for Talented At Risk Girls could not find needed information in textbooks. The helper must be willing to exchange roles and become a learner; to try out new techniques that take into account both the helper's and the student's communication traditions; to try on a new worldview; to create with her a path that the young woman can follow to her goals while maintaining cultural connectedness.

References

Bingham, R. P. & Ward, C. M. "Career Counseling with Ethnic Minority Women." In W. B. Walsh and S. H. Osipow, (Eds.), *Career Counseling for Women*. Hillsboro, NJ: Erlbaum, 1994.

Espin, O. "Psychotherapy with Hispanic Women." In P. Pedersen (Ed.), *Handbook of Cross-Cultural Counseling and Therapy*, 165-171, 1985.

Helms, J. E. (Ed.) *Black and White Racial Identity: Theory, Research, and Practice*. Westport, CT: Greenwood Press.

Herring, R. D. "Understanding Native American Values: Process and Contents Concerns for Counselors." In *Counseling and Values*, 34, 134-137, 1990.

Kerr, B. and Colangelo, N. "Something to Prove: A Follow-up of Academically Talented." Presented at the Wallace Symposium for Gifted and Talented, Iowa City, Iowa, 1993.

Kerr, B., Colangelo, N., Maxey, J. and Christensen, P. "Characteristics of Academically Talented Minority Students." In *Journal of Counseling and Development*, 70, 5: 606-670, 1992.

Staples, C. "An Overview of Race and Marital Status." In H. P. M'Adoo (Ed.), *Black Families*, 187-189. Newberry Park: Sage, 1988.

Stevens, E. "Machismo and Marianismo." In *Transaction-Society*, 10, 57-63, 1973.

Chapter 12

Girls and Women with Specific Extraordinary Talents

Psychologists and educators have only recently begun to understand young people with specific extraordinary talent. The pioneering work of Julian Stanley and his colleagues at Johns Hopkins University sparked great interest in mathematically precocious students (Benbow & Stanley, 1984), who were found to be similar to academically gifted students in general yet who also had some unique needs. In 1983, Howard Gardner published his groundbreaking work *Frames of Mind: The Theory of Multiple Intelligence*, suggesting that we give up the notion of intelligence as being one unit. Interest in students with specific talents has been growing since then. Several of the talents which have been studied are verbal giftedness or writing ability, mathematical giftedness, spatial-visual giftedness and musical giftedness. In *The Handbook for Counseling Gifted and Talented* (Kerr, 1991), I summarized what was known about the psychological adjustment and development of young people in each talent area; I later explored the specific needs of girls in each talent area (Kerr & Maresh, 1993). Here are some of the facts Susan Maresh and I discovered about girls and women with specific talents.

Verbal Giftedness

Girls and women have always excelled in verbal ability, which does not bear the stigma for females that mathematical ability does. Nick Colangelo and I (1990) found twice as many female as male perfect scorers on the English subtest of the ACT. Writing and other verbal careers such as teaching have had a longer history of female participation than most other careers. And yet as in most other fields eminence in writing is largely earned by men.

According to Gardner, linguistic giftedness is among the later-developing abilities because its full flowering requires life experience, and precocious young talkers and readers do not necessarily become verbally gifted adults. Since girls are likely to speak, read and write earlier than boys, what appears to be verbal giftedness in a very young girl may in fact simply be evidence of this early developmental edge of girls over boys.

However, the verbally gifted girl certainly exists. She is more likely to suffer emotional and social difficulties than girls in other talent areas, according to one study, and appropriate guidance may be difficult for her to obtain. Her obvious career choices—writing, teaching English, translating foreign languages—are not a rich source of employment these days, and students of either sex are frequently urged not to prepare for them. In fact, only a very small percentage of students with perfect verbal scores planned to pursue careers in English (Colangelo and Kerr, 1990). Creative writing, of course, is a woefully difficult way to earn a living, let alone eminence. Sadly, many gifted girls are discouraged early on from fully developing their greatest gift.

Barron's study of successful creative writers (1972) revealed five common characteristics: high intellectual capacity; high valuing of intellectual and cognitive matters; high valuing of independence and autonomy; verbal fluency; and aesthetic reactivity. According to the California Psychological Inventory, writers are superior to the general population in social presence, self-acceptance, desire for social status, psychological mindedness and achievement through independence. They are significantly lower in achievement through conformance and tend to have low scores on socialization, on sense of well-being, and on desire to make a good impression. They are distinctly more introverted than extroverted; Bachtold & Werner (1973) found that women writers tend to be loners who preferred to work alone. All of these writerly characteristics are vastly different from the traditional societal and familial expectations of girls and women, and bright girls are seldom rewarded for the independence and non-conformity so necessary to the writer. Perhaps these social-role exclusions are to blame at least in part for the comparative lack of eminent women writers.

Another reason may be the fact that verbally gifted young women choose careers other than writing. Education at all levels, languages and translation, performance in radio, television, cinema and theater, and all areas of business may attract verbally talented females. Because verbally precocious young women tend to score very high on the artistic scale of vocational interest tests (Fox 1982), most careers which involve creativity, expressiveness, spontaneity and originality would meet the needs of verbally gifted young women. Careers primarily requiring linguistic abilities are historically the most open to women. Even though increasingly more young women are going into science- and mathematically-oriented careers, work requiring great verbal ability will probably continue to be the most attractive to gifted girls.

Unfortunately, many verbally gifted girls do not know the value of their gift. They may need help in identifying their talent and in understanding the link between ability and career. They may need encouragement in believing that their talents are rare enough and significant enough to earn them rewards in the job market. However, given the extreme independence, nonconformity, and desire for aloneness of verbally gifted girls, such guidance might not be well-received, and in fact verbally gifted girls may not seek out career guidance at all. Nevertheless, realistic encouragement can certainly help verbally gifted girls and women set and reach their goals.

Mathematical Giftedness

Mathematically gifted girls and women have been the subject of study by a number of researchers at Johns Hopkins University Study for mathematically precocious youth (Fox, Benbow & Perkins, 1983; Lubinski & Benbow, 1992). Mathematically gifted girls do differ from their less gifted counterparts in their interests, needs and aspirations, and they also differ from mathematically gifted male peers. Compared to average girls, these girls tend to have talented mothers who do not work outside the home; in fact, the mothers of many have Ph.D.s. Asians predominate among mathematically gifted girls, and even in the 1960s ethnicities other than the majority culture were very evident among female mathematicians (Helson, 1983). Clearly, mathematical interests are not reinforced in mainstream American culture among girls. Curiously, on vocational personality tests, mathematically gifted girls tend to score higher than average on both Investigative (scientific occupations) and Conventional (clerical occupations) Scales. Investigative people are idea-oriented and intellectually curious, while conventional people are conforming and cautious.

This surprising combination of investigative and conventional interests in mathematically gifted girls aspiring to non-traditional mathematics jobs concerned Constance Hollinger (1986), who said that the conformity associated with conventional career interests may work against the creativity required for higher level mathematics occupations. "While conventional attributes may serve the bookkeeper quite well, investigative attributes are essential to the higher level careers in mathematics" (p. 143). Hollinger was also concerned that the non-traditional math career aspirants might abandon their choice, for their high conventional scores revealed them as perhaps too conforming to pursue such non-traditional, stereotypically masculine careers. If these girls were to persist they would need extraordinary support for their choices.

Rena Subotnik (1988) studied the 1983 Westinghouse Science Talent Search Contest's winners, some of the most extraordinarily talented young scientists in the United States. She found the sexes differing in several important areas. Unlike the young men, the young women tended to attribute success to hard work and dedication rather than to intelligence or creativity. Furthermore, the young women were more concerned with the social impact of scientific research than were the young men; like Fox's study of mathematically gifted girls, this study revealed a distinct desire to improve the human condition or promote some social good among bright young women in math and science, with many more women than men choosing careers in these fields specifically to benefit others. However, curiosity was still the major reason that Westinghouse winners, both men and women, pursued science.

Most studies of mathematically gifted females focus on sex differences in mathematical ability (Eccles, 1984; Lubinski & Benbow, 1992). Despite the fact that such differences in mathematical ability appear to be diminishing rapidly with time, and that biological differences are known to account for only a very small proportion of the variance in scores between boys and girls, there is a disproportionate amount of discussion in literature and the popular media of the differences in mathematical ability among females and males. While it is true that far more young men than young women were shown to score at the very highest level of mathematical ability (Benbow & Stanley, 1983), it is not true that these differences in abilities are biologically dictated, as has often been automatically assumed.

In fact, the biological link is extremely tenuous: Benbow and Stanley based their hypothesis that males are biologically predisposed to do well in math almost entirely upon their findings of increased left-handedness and allergy problems—two characteristics genetically linked to males—among mathematically gifted youth. Their findings generated much discussion in the general public, a discussion which has had tremendous negative impact upon gifted girls and their attitude toward their own abilities. According to Jacobs and Eccles (1985), media reports of sex differences in mathematics influenced parental attitudes toward girls' mathematical ability, with mothers seeing their daughters' abilities lower than they had before the report, yet with fathers seeing their abilities as somewhat higher than before media reports of sex differences in mathematics. For whatever reason, gifted girls continue to have less confidence in their mathematical abilities than gifted boys do, and to see less relevance of mathematics to their own lives. The result is that a much smaller proportion of mathematically gifted girls actually pursue careers in math-related fields than do mathematically gifted boys.

Since the continued emphasis on sex differences in mathematics may discourage girls from considering mathematics-related professions, mathematically gifted girls need guidance which corrects stereotypes about mathematical ability and sex. In addition, they need continued encouragement to persist in mathematics course-taking. Math curricula need to be made more responsive to girls' social concerns. Finally, they need role models.Women teachers and mathematicians may be critical to the career development of these gifted girls.

Musical Giftedness

Although many women musicians have excelled as performers, very few women rank among the leading composers and conductors of orchestras (Piirto, 1991), and women in musical performance are far more readily accepted than those in leadership and creation. Trollinger (1983), studying creative female musicians during childhood, adolescence, and college years, found them to be solitary people who preferred creative activities above all other pursuits throughout the three periods. Parents were nurturing, with fathers particularly encouraging of creative and musical activities. Surprisingly, gifted female musicians did not have high participation in school musical activities. Like successful female visual artists and writers, successful female composers have been found to be more dominant and self-sufficient than their less successful female peers. Since female performers may not resemble female composers in personality, it is therefore important, in considering the career development of musically gifted women, to recognize the different needs of performers and aspiring conductors and composers.

Musical giftedness is one of the earliest-developing talents, perhaps because its flowering does not depend upon life experience and maturity. Many child prodigies are musical prodigies whose parents noticed their strong early interest and arranged for instruction. In fact, private lessons at an early age are critical to the development of musical talent (Bloom, 1985). Girls whose talent is neither identified nor nurtured at an early age may never manifest that talent.

Few schools provide special programs for musically gifted students. Although most high schools have a band or orchestra— which gifted female musicians may not choose to join—the development of musical talent is left up to parents. Musically gifted children are often not included in gifted programs. The traditional path to musical talent includes private lessons, practice, auditions, and performance. Suzuki methods of teaching music combine guidance with education (Gardner, 1983). How education and guidance for the musically gifted girl must differ from that of the musically gifted boy has not been investigated by researchers in the area of talent development. It is likely, however, that musically gifted girls need training and guidance which will develop their identities as musicians as well as developing the specific musical talent. In addition, mentors must help musically gifted girls get the recognition they deserve, particularly in high school.

Spatial-Visual Giftedness

Spatially and visually gifted students are often unhappy at school, where verbal and mathematical abilities are emphasized almost to the exclusion of any other talent. And school is not the only place they are neglected: the study of children with superior abilities in the visual arts now compares to the study of gifted children with superior intellectual abilities in the 1920s.

Gardner (1983) showed that spatial intelligence is made up of a number of abilities. These include the ability to recognize instances of the same visual element, the ability to transform or to recognize the transformation of one element into another; the ability to conjure up mental imagery and then to transform that imagery; and the capacity to produce a visual likeness of spatial information. These clearly are abilities needed by artists, photographers, inventors, and architects.

Studies of personality characteristics on standardized tests and on observational measures of both male and female artists show them to be aloof, reserved, introspective, serious, and nonconforming to contemporary social values (Getzels & Czikszentmihalyi, 1976). Their self-sufficiency is high, they prefer to make their own decisions, and they are seen as independent, subjective, intense and imaginative. They are both radical and experimental. The stereotypical "unconventional artist" is readily found among both men and women, and yet there are far fewer female visual artists than male.

Using the California Psychological Inventory, Barron (1972) studied young artists at the San Francisco Art Institute and at the Rhode Island School of Design. Profiles of both male and female art students showed that they were not interested in making a good impression on other people and were not well-socialized. They reported a high need to achieve success independently and were more flexible in outlook yet less cheerful than others. In the same study, the Minnesota Multiphasic Personality Inventory showed men and women art students scoring in the pathological ranges on all scales, perhaps simply an indication of their low need for conformity. They did not show other signs of overt psychosis and were far less rigid than other types of students. The women approached life vigorously and were unconventional, flexible, open, and independent. Less flamboyant, more naive, and more introverted than their male counterparts, these artists were nonetheless more adventurous, independent and willful than women in general.

Upon interviewing the art students, Barron (1972) discovered what the test did not reveal: the intensity with which the students pursued their chosen careers. Almost all of the men said their artwork was their life, was necessary for life, and was their main reason for living; in other words, "without painting I couldn't function." Conversely, only one woman indicated that her work was essential; the others commented that art was half of their lives, and their future families were the other half (p. 35). The men tended to view their work with passion and zeal, the women with distance and detachment.

Barron also pointed out a difference in self-image in the women that was not an indication of quality of work, for the women's art was equal to the men's. He wondered why women were not as intense as men in their pursuit of art as a career, especially since this intensity was critical to the ultimate successes of male artists. At any rate, Barron assumed in 1972 that regardless of their intensity as art students, women would eventually be sapped of creative energies by having children and would not continue as artists past motherhood. This archaic belief still exists among many leaders in the arts!

However, more girls than boys decide on art as a career before age ten. As those girls near adolescence, encouragement to continue with their choice may decline: Getzels and Czikszentmihalyi commented that art teachers in high school and beyond appraise male students on the basis of their personalities rather than their abilities and perceptual areas, but they appraise the female students based on the perceptual skills they display (Getzels and Czikszentmihalyi, 1976). This behavior may reflect a belief that a male artistic student will develop his vocation with time, while a female student who does not have an intense vocation to begin with will abandon her aspirations and settle for more traditional pursuits.

In the development of Talent Research Project at the University of Chicago, Sloane and Sosniak (1985) studied twelve men and eight women sculptors. Only a few sex differences in the development of these artists were described—one was that parents wanted their daughters to be happily married.

For a variety of reasons, few women become successful visual artists. A lack of intensity in pursuing their art may be one. Also, faculty attitudes toward women students may work against later success, with the personality characteristics of the men more highly valued than the real abilities of the females. Lastly, the expectation that a woman marry and have children, a belief advocated and communicated through parental values (Piirto, 1991), may seriously interfere with the single-mindedness required of the artist in pursuit of her art.

Summary

Understanding giftedness in girls requires knowing the impact of specific gifts. An extraordinary talent may affect a bright girl's mode of perceiving the world, her personality and identity, and her career and lifestyle development. Each talent area entails a different kind of education, mentoring, and career ladder. A gifted girl needs help in finding instruction to nurture her talent, a mentor to encourage her studies, a reliable method of entry into her chosen profession, and an abiding belief in her inevitable success.[1]

---

1   Many thanks to Susan Maresh for her research on spatially and visually gifted girls and women.

References

Bachtold, L. M. and Werner, E. E. "Personality Characteristics of Creative Women." In *Perceptual Motor Skills*, 36, 311-319, 1973.

Barron, F. *Artists in the Making*. San Francisco: Seminar Press, 1972.

Benbow, C. P. and Stanley, J. C. "Sex Differences in Mathematical Reasoning Ability: More Facts." In *Science*, 222, 1983.

Benbow, C. P. and Stanley, J. C. "Gender and the Science Major: A Study of Mathematically Precocious Youth." In M. W. Steinkamp and M. L. Maehr (eds.), *Women in Science*, 165-196. Greenwich, CT: JAI Press, 1984.

Bloom, B. S. *Developing Talent in Young People*. New York: Ballantine Books, 1985.

Colangelo, N. and Kerr, B. A. "Extreme Academic Talent: Profiles of Perfect Scorers." *Journal of Educational Psychology*, 82, 404-410, 1990.

Eccles, Jacquelynne. "Sex differences in Mathematics Participation." In *Advances in Motivation and Achievement*, 2, 1984, 93-137. JAI Press, Inc.

Fox, L. H. *Verbally Precocious Youth*. Baltimore, MD: Johns Hopkins University Press, 1982.

Fox, L. H., Benbow, C. P., and Perkins, S. "An Accelerated Mathematics Program for Girls: A Longitudinal Evaluation." In C. P. Benbow and J. C. Stanley (eds.), *Academic Precocity*. Baltimore, MD: Johns Hopkins University Press, 1983.

Gardner, H. *Frames of Mind: The Theory of Multiple Intelligences*. New York, NY: Basic Books, 1983.

Getzels, J. W., and Csikszentmihalyi, M. *The Creative Vision: A Study of Problem Finding in Art*. New York: Wiley, 1976.

Helson, R. (1983). "Creative Mathematicians." In R. Albert (ed.) *Genius and Eminence: The Social Psychology of Creativity and Exceptional Achievement*. London: Pergamon, 1983, 311-330.

Hollinger, C. L. "Counseling the Gifted and Talented Female Adolescent: The Relationship Between Social Self-Esteem and Traits of Instrumentality and Expressiveness." In *Gifted Child Quarterly*, 27, 4, 157-161, 1983.

Hollinger, C. L. "Career Aspirations as a Function of Holland Personality Type among Mathematically Talented Female Adolescents." In *Journal for the Education of the Gifted*, 9, 133-145, 1986.

Jacobs, J. E. & Eccles, J. S. "Gender Differences in Math Ability: The Impact of Media Reports on Parents." In *Educational Researcher*, March, 20-24, 1985.

Kerr, B. A. *Handbook for Counseling the Gifted and Talented*. Alexandria, VA: American Association for Counseling & Development, 1991.

Lubinski, D. and Benbow, C.P. "Gender Differences in Abilities and Preferences Among the Gifted: Implication for the Math-Science Pipeline." *Current Directions in Psychological Science*, 1, 2:62-67, 1992.

Munro, T. *Art Education: Its Philosophy and Psychology*. NYC: Liberal Arts Press, 1956.

Piirto, J. "Encouraging Creativity and Talent in Adolescents." In J. Genshaft & M. Bircley (eds.), *The Gifted Adolescent: Personal and Educational Issues*. Teachers College Press, 1991.

Sloane, K. D., & Sosniak, L. A. "The Development of Accomplished Sculptors." In B. Bloom (ed.), *The Development of Talent in Young People*. NY: Ballantine, 1985, 90-138.

Subotnik, R. F. "The Motivation to Experiment: A Study of Gifted Adolescents' Attitudes Toward Scientific Research." In *Journal for the Education of the Gifted*, 11, 19-35, 1988.

Trollinger, L. M. "Interests, Activities, and Hobbies of High and Low Creative Women Musicians during Childhood, Adolescent, and College Years." In *Gifted Child Quarterly*, 27, 94-97, 1983.

Chapter 13

Is Self-Actualization Optional?

Throughout *Smart Girls Two*, I have tried to make the point that many gifted girls and women are too well-adjusted (i.e., too accomodating and too responsive to others' expectations) for their own good. When confronted with the problem of gifted women's tendency to be too "well-adjusted, many say, "So what? So what if gifted women are so well-adjusted that they choose to be less than they can be? If they're happy, leave them alone." Some go even further: "If gifted women choose not to actualize their potential in the arena of some vocation, then they are merely being true to their own voice, a voice which calls for relatedness rather than accomplishment."

This chapter examines those arguments in light of recent literature on women's voices and women's development. First, I will present the ideas of cultural feminism, the belief that women are different from men and should be judged by their own standards, and that women have a different culture which should be respected and promoted. Carol Gilligan's *In A Different Voice* (1982) presents this theory. Then I will review the work of Deborah Tannen (1990), whose insights into women's and men's different styles of communication have implications for women's leadership. Carol Tavris's powerful case against cultural feminism made in *The Mismeasure of Woman* (1992) will be examined. Finally, new ideas which seem to integrate the different voices of women and the possibility of self-actualization will include the developmental theory of Linda Silverman and the theory of women's "wildness" and heroism captured in Clarissa Pinkola-Estes's *Women Who Run with the Wolves*(1992) and Kate Noble's *The Sound of the Silver Horn* (1994). This chapter ends with the conclusions I have reached about women, giftedness, and responsibility for self-actualization.

Different Voices

Carol Gilligan's Theory

Carol Gilligan began her research into the moral development of girls and women because she was dissatisfied with the major existing model of moral development, the Kohlberg theory. Lawrence Kohlberg had done a series of studies in the seventies in which he had questioned people—mainly male students at Harvard—about a number of moral dilemmas. He had rated their responses on a scale ranging from the most primitive, egocentric responses to what he considered the highest form of moral development: making decisions on the basis of universal principles of justice. Concern for others and the desire to please indicated only the third level of moral development. Yet Gilligan believed that is precisely the basis of many women's moral decisions, an ethics of caring about and not hurting others, and she was angry that moral decisionmaking of this sort was considered a lower form of development. Rather, she believed it was a different form of development, and that is how she arrived at the concept of the different voice: women are not inferior or superior to men in their moral reasoning. They are simply different.

Gilligan and her colleagues did not perform an extensive study of differences between males and females; in fact, most of her conclusions were based on a very small number of cases. In one of her major studies, women were asked how they made decisions about abortions. Of course, there could be no truly parallel group of men to be asked about this decision, a uniquely female experience. (Actually, most previous studies, even Kohlberg's, had found that men and women did not actually differ much in their moral reasoning, and there weren't significantly more women in the third stage in most studies.) Gilligan's book cannot be considered to be a scientific report, and she did not present it as one.

It seems to me that Gilligan was legitimately angry that the idea of making decisions on the basis of caring was considered a lower form of development. It also seems that she was concerned that women, whom she (and most of society) assumed to make decisions in this way, were once again in danger of being considered inferior to males. So she performed three very modest studies and used the very interesting responses to illustrate her ideas. I sympathize with her approach, because I have used it myself! However, the results of her work had unforeseen results.

An extraordinary scholarly and popular industry grew up around Gilligan's theory. She had defined two different approaches to moral reasoning: an ethics of care and an ethics of justice. She admitted that there was considerable overlap in how men and women responded (in fact, most of the differences in moral reasoning which appear in studies of moral dilemmas are class and race differences). She simply wanted it to be recognized that making decisions based on relationships and on concern for others' feelings was not an inferior form of reasoning. Unfortunately, her work was generalized far beyond moral reasoning. The popular press made it seem as if her work "proved" that there were basic differences in men's and women's intellectual processes, psychological dynamics, and personalities. Antifeminists used her work to bolster their arguments that men and women belong in separate spheres, and that independence is bad for women. Cultural feminists used her work to glorify the feminine aspects of women's culture such as nurturing and compromising, and to claim that women were actually superior to men. A great many books were published concerning differences in males and females, usually concluding that the differences were not bad, but instead simply worthy of being understood.

Deborah Tannen's *You Just Don't Understand*

While many popular books were published in the eighties and early nineties which delighted in discovering small differences between men and women and then drawing ridiculous conclusions, one book was based on careful research and was written in a reasonable tone: Deborah Tannen's You Just Don't Understand (1990). Tannen, a scholar in the area of communications, studies how people in different groups communicate differently, both nonverbally and verbally. Tannen shows, through vignettes revealing the misunderstood messages of men and women, the two sexes tending to communicate needs and feelings differently. Women, who often want to maintain intimacy and avoid conflict, tend to seek similarities or common ground by listening closely to the other, according to Tannen's research. Men, however, who often want to establish their position in a hierarchy, tend to use conversation competitively, gleaning for information about who's up and who's down. Tannen's studies reveal that women tend to listen, men to lecture; women to share feelings, men to express facts and opinions.

Tannen never implies that these differences are biological; instead, she shows how the differences start very early. She illustrates her descriptions of pre-school conversations with the hilarious "Pickle Fights" of girls in conflict over a plastic pickle, followed by the boys' struggle for same toy. The girl wanting the pickle claimed that it was another girl who actually wanted it, an indirect way of getting her way. The boys were direct: they simply plotted to take it from the boy who had it!

The fact that men and women communicate differently gives many opportunities for misunderstanding, Tannen believes, yet both methods can be effective, and men and women must learn how to understand the other and to be flexible in using different communication styles. The implication for women's actualization is not that women cannot assert themselves or demonstrate leadership in working toward their goals, but that they are likely to use compromises and strategies to increase intimacy with those they care about rather than strategies to increase power.

Unfortunately, Tannen's book has also spawned a large number of much less carefully researched and much more sensationalistic books that claim, for example, that the sexes—as though they were from separate planets—differ so greatly in their needs that their goals must be entirely different.

Carol Tavris's *The Mismeasure of Woman*

In one of the best and most reasonable books I have ever read about women and men, Carol Tavris (1992) examines the literature on sex differences and comes up with strong criticisms of those shoring up their political positions with psychological, sociological, or biological research. Her subtitle, "Why Women are Not the Better Sex, the Inferior Sex, or the Opposite Sex," perfectly describes her thesis. She shows that much research in these fields has concentrated on trivial sex differences, and that grossly inaccurate generalizations about men and women have often been based on small bits of information. People *want* to believe that men and women are inherently different, to justify women's not attempting equity in the world of work and men's discrimination against women.

Yet there is simply no evidence that men and women differ significantly on the personality dimensions that have so often been characterized as masculine or feminine; rather, men and women differ in their behavior in different contexts, and those contexts are shaped by societal status. The differing patterns of behavior which Carol Gilligan and Deborah Tannen have ascribed to women are really the patterns of behavior of low-status people. When men are in low-status, powerless positions, they also seek to connect with others, to reduce conflict, and to communicate indirectly. When women are in high-status, powerful positions, they seek to maintain their power, to communicate directly, and to engage in conflict. Tavris believes that labeling one kind of behavior feminine and another masculine obscures the fact that men and women are much more alike than they are different:

"This is one reason that I am so concerned about the current fashion for cultural feminism, the appealing theories that women have a natural ability to be connected, attached, loving, and peaceful, that they speak in a different voice, have different ways of knowing, or different moral values. Of course, many of the women who promote these ideas do so with the intention of raising women's self-esteem and promoting their welfare in society. Nevertheless, the philosophy of cultural feminism has functioned to keep women focused on their allegedly stable and innate personality qualities, instead of on what it would take to have a society based on the qualities we value in both sexes . . . Further, quite apart from their lack of research validation, these ideas get men off the hook

203

in family arrangements, ignore men's affections and attachments, and underwrite the ideology that women are best suited to certain kinds of jobs. At their worst, they distract us from the hard work we have to do, women and men together, to humanize jobs, foster children's welfare, save the environment, and combat corporate mindlessness" (p. 324).

Tavris also points out that both women and men can benefit from adding new behaviors to their repertoire. "Women do not need to stop being conciliatory in order to be leaders, or to stop caring for others in order to be autonomous. Connection and autonomy are both necessary in human life. The goal for both sexes should be to add qualities and skills, not lose old ones" (p. 325).

Wolves, Heroes, and Psyches: The Writings of Clarissa Pinkola Estes, Kathleen Noble, and Sharon Conarton & Linda Silverman

What qualities and skills should gifted women add to their self-conceptions? Three sources give similar answers, all deriving inspiration from the Jungian theory of archetypes, characters or events found throughout human cultural myths and rituals that help us understand the world and ourselves. Jungian theory also assumes that individuals are most mature when they learn to reconcile polarities: that is, to accept the opposite in themselves. Archetypes are helpful to the gifted woman who wishes to take on new qualities or behaviors and to grow beyond her current, limited visions of herself. For archetypes show, as do the stories of eminent women, that autonomy, strength, and courage have always existed in girls and women. Women who run with wolves, who go on heroic quests, who heal the soul—stories of these women exist in most cultures, and reclaiming and understanding the personal meaning of these archetypes can be a woman's first step to self-actualization.

Clarissa Pinkola Estes uncovers the archetype of *Women Who Run with the Wolves* (1992), relating stories told in many cultures of the girl baby who is adopted by wild animals, the girl child who runs away to be with the wild things of the forest, the woman who runs free among courageous peers. She shows how the characteristic of wildness is so very important to freeing women from their self-imposed restraints of domesticity and modesty, and that reclaiming the wolf does not mean rejecting the feminine. One learns from her book that nurturance can be fierce and that womanliness can encompass boldness.

The hero's quest describes contemporary women's search for self-actualization, according to Kathleen Noble (1994), who examines myths and legends to discover the hero's path. The Journey's Beginning is the immature woman's first tentative step toward defining herself. Next comes the Call to Awaken, which "asks us to leave behind our personal past and embark upon a journey that will change our lives forever" (p. 37). This can mean either literally leaving home or leaving the security of a familiar worldview. Next the hero meets the Dragons of Initiation, which Noble casts interestingly as the very experiences which contemporary women fear: confusion, depression, dependence, sexism, discrimination, saying "yes" to too many things, hardship, and loss. Along the way, Noble says, the woman hero needs allies to help her, for with help, she can face each dragon in its turn. Which she must do. Only through defeating these dragons can the hero reach her final victory of Transformation and Return. She changes forever when she sees that her former, limited self cannot meet the challenges of the quest and she integrates the courage, strength, and independence she has learned into her self. "The process of transformation invites us to participate consciously in the creation of our own selves" (p. 167). A self-actualized woman can return to her home, her people, and her society, ready now to transform them.

Sharon Conarton and Linda Silverman (1988) explain how that transformation comes to be in their own feminist theory of development. While many of their stages are similar to those of Kate Noble, the archetypal figure they choose as their hero is Psyche, the tragic and transformed woman who dared to look upon the face of Cupid, her lover, and then completed a heroic quest to reclaim her life and spirit and to become a healer. They trace women's development by analyzing the phases of Psyche's transformation. The ultimate stage of development, according to their conceptualization, is that of the healer. Psyche undergoes many hardships and faces many fears in the process of attaining the "healing ointments"; after this, she is ready to heal and transform others. In a way, their final phase of development is the full flowering of nurturance, beyond the nurturance of self and family to the nurturance of all humankind. Mother Theresa and Eleanor Roosevelt, as true healers of humanity, are fully self-actualized women in this view of development.

These readings represent the middle way between the world-view of the cultural feminists, who may believe that actualization of talent is optional for women, and those who expect women to simply act like men in order to actualize talents. This middle way—the way of the wolf-woman, hero, and healer—helps women become more than they are by encouraging them to take on new qualities and skills and by instilling in them a sense of responsibility to the world.

The Responsibility for Self-Actualization

It seems that whenever I suggest in my presentations that gifted women have a responsibility to actualize their gifts, someone always dilutes the issue by asking, "But aren't all girls gifted?"

Although it may seem late in this book to address this argument, it is in fact quite relevant here. Most arguments against special guidance or education for the gifted come from people who truly believe that all children are gifted, an appealing notion that simply isn't true. Even testing based on the theory of multiple intelligences does not assess everyone as gifted in at least one way. Talents are distributed along the normal curve, just like other human traits. A few people are completely lacking in special, innate talents—whether musical, mathematical, artistic, or scientific—many have some, and a few are gifted in almost all intellectual abilities. Every one is uniquely special; but only a very few are gifted with unusually high talents and abilities.

Girls with extraordinary talents in one or more areas, those who would be considered in the 95th-99th percentile of ability by experts in those fields, really are different in academic and guidance needs from those who are average. And I believe they are also different in their responsibility to themselves to develop their talents.

Next, I am often confronted with the question, "Shouldn't all girls be encouraged to do whatever they want with their lives?" I always remind the questionner that in American society, women are ostensibly free to do whatever they want with their lives, and that self-actualization is indeed optional in free societies. The more important question is, "What should we encourage girls to do with their talents?" Typically, adults are remarkably hands-off when it comes to this issue of guiding girls, in marked contrast to the strong guidance received by boys, most of whom are told nowadays that they can be anything they want, that having a career is fine and not having a career is fine, as long as they can afford not to work. Teachers and guidance counselors are so queasy about seeming to "place their values" on girls that they simply say nothing about the relationship of giftedness to self-actualization. However, it should be clear from all of the other material in this book that if giftedness is not carefully nurtured in girls, it is unlikely to blossom. The consequences of neglect are truly more severe for gifted girls. If a girl who is average in math decides not to major in mathematics or a math-related field, the loss is not great to her, to society, or mathematics. But if a girl who is extraordinarily gifted in math decides against math, the loss may be great indeed. She may have been the one to discover a new theorem; she may have been the one who found a way to understand gravity, or the cell; she may have had the happiness of doing the work for which she is uniquely suited. Therefore, it may be perfectly appropriate to encourage average girls to do whatever they want to with their abilities, but it may be irresponsible to take a similarly laissez-faire approach with a gifted girl.

I have come to believe that *the rarer the talent, the greater the responsibility of the both the individual and society to develop that talent.*

What, then, is the responsibility of the gifted young woman toward her own gifts? I believe it is the responsibility of every bright young woman, upon being made aware of her giftedness in one or more areas, to discover as precisely as possible the nature and degree of her giftedness. This may mean seeking further testing, or consulting with teachers in her areas of talent. My earlier research has shown that gifted women have a strong tendency to deny their giftedness. Although it may be expedient socially to be modest about one's abilities, it is intellectually irresponsible to pretend that achievement, aptitude tests, or intelligence tests mean nothing. Similarly, it is unwise to ignore the estimations of experts. When a music teacher says, "You have great talent, and you should continue with an individual instructor," that is important. When a professor writes on a paper, "This is excellent! Consider submitting it for publication," her estimation of the student's ability should not be dismissed.

What if a woman never learns of her gifts until later in life? Perhaps it's never too late to develop and enjoy those gifts. When a fifty-year-old college secretary asked me to give her an intelligence test, I advised her that the test, properly used, predicts future behavior, and surely her past academic and intellectual accomplishments would be reliable enough as indicators. However, she insisted, so I gave her the Terman Concept Mastery, one of the most difficult adult tests. She wept when she saw her results: her very-high-range scores were similar to those of professors and research scientists. "I always felt there was something . . . different . . . about me, but I didn't know what it was. Now there isn't much time left, but I want to get the education I should have had."

It is important for gifted women to explore their own giftedness well enough to be able to make decisions about nurturing their talents. It may never be too late to seek more education, to find mentors, and to find activities which challenge one's newly discovered, or re-discovered, abilities. Learning that one has a gift is the Call to Awaken, that rousing to the hero's journey described by Kate Noble.

For many gifted girls and women, the restlessness they feel within is a palpable need to learn, to develop, to explain, to challenge traditions.

We need a new psychology of giftedness which incorporates responsibility for the development of the gifts we have been given. Native Americans believe that our gifts do not belong to us, and therefore are no reason for pride. Instead, our talents are given to us so that we can share them with others. Many Christians believe in the concept of stewardship, the idea that we must preserve and extend what we are given because we are merely caretakers of that which we are given. Both of these viewpoints are preferable, I believe, to the notion that the development—or lack of development—of talent is a purely personal matter of little consequence to others.

I have observed in counseling talented adults that gifts seem to have their own insistence on acknowledgement. I never try to understand a musician separately from her music, or a scientist apart from her research, because if these outlets for talents are thwarted, the entire personality is threatened. Perhaps it is the power of the unrecognized gift which drives so many women in their forties to seek self-actualization. Whenever a gift makes itself known—to the twelve-year-old who suddenly discovers the beauty and strength of her artwork, or the forty-year-old who at last gives way to her urge to create—that experience should be treated with respect, awe, and a sense of responsibility. It is the beginning of a heroic journey. For the gifted woman, actualizing talents in a vocation is not simply acting like a man; it is her ultimate stage of development as a woman, a way of joining the wild women, heroes, and healers who define female courage and goodness. For the gifted woman, self-actualization should not be optional. Our world depends on her development.

References

Conarton, S. & Silverman, L. K. "Feminine Development Through the Life Cycle." In Dutton-Douglas, M.A. & Walker, L.E. (eds.) *Feminist Psychotherapies: Integration of Therapeutic and Feminist Systems.* Ablex (1988).

Estes, C. P. *Women Who Run with the Wolves: Myths and Stories of the Wild Woman Archetype.* New York: Ballantine Books, 1992.

Gilligan, C. *In a Different Voice: Psychological Theory and Women's Development.* Cambridge: Harvard University Press, 1982.

Noble, K. *The Sound of the Silver Horn: Reclaiming the Heroism in Contemporary Women's Lives.* New York: Fawcett Columbine, 1994.

Tannen, D. *You Just Don't Understand: Women and Men in Conversation.* New York: Ballantine Books, 1990.

Tavris, C. *The Mismeasure of Woman: Why Women are Not the Better Sex, the Inferior Sex, or the Opposite Sex.* New York: Basic Books, 1992.

Chapter 14

Programs Which Have Stood the Test of Time

Since 1985, when *Smart Girls, Gifted Women* was published, there has been a much-needed expansion of programs for gifted girls, some constructed around the ideas and suggestions in that first book. Some represent the combined efforts of concerned teachers, mothers, and community leaders who know that bringing gifted girls together—to share their feelings about their educational and vocational plans, to be exposed to role models, to gain college and career information—can lessen psychological barriers to achievement and raise aspirations significantly. However, since very few programs include an evaluation component, the long-term effects of such efforts are difficult to establish. In this chapter, some programs which have stood the test of time are presented, as well as some creative new ones that I have encountered. These include the diagnostic-prescriptive program of Project CHOICE; Lynn Fox's "Changing Attitudes" program for gifted girls; and the Guidance Laboratory approach, now tested at three different sites. The new ideas presented here are derived from interviews with directors of special, and effective, programs for girls.

Project CHOICE

From 1979 until the present, Elyse Fleming and Constance Hollinger at Case-Western Reserve University in Cleveland sponsored Project CHOICE: Creating Her Options in Career Education, a diagnostic-prescriptive program for talented adolescent women (Fleming and Hollinger, 1994.). The counselors were to diagnose barriers that stood in the way of gifted girls' achievement and to prescribe a series of activities to overcome those barriers. The program broadened the career options for participants by pointing out personal and cultural barriers likely to interfere with realization of potential. Project CHOICE was field-tested with gifted eleventh grade girls screened by counselors using a talent inventory and school records.

An initial diagnostic approach centered around a student questionnaire and an assessment of internal barriers. The questionnaire sought information about possible external barriers such as family structure, parents' occupation and education, parental aspirations for the child's exposure to role models, financial resources, and sex discriminatory practices. Internal barriers were examined through various measures of self-esteem, achievement motivation, assertiveness, and fear of success. The level of each student's career development was measured by the degree to which her career ideas were crystallized and by the appropriateness of those ideas.

A prescriptive plan resulted for each participant, indicating possible treatment of or solutions to internal or external barriers. Sometimes these strategies were individual, such as providing a student with a role model in the community; others were group strategies, such as referral to a "self-esteem" group.

The overall fourteen-week career development experience contained three career information workshops, student-selected role model experiences, and eleven group sessions in which the core curriculum was modified to meet the needs of each group member. This was one of the most comprehensive programs on record for guiding gifted girls. Follow-up evaluations five to fifteen years after participation in the program showed that the participants had achieved quite well compared to other gifted girls and women. Two-thirds had established a relationship with a significant other, and 27% had children, while simultaneously 71% were in career positions as business managers, professionals, and executives.

What was most impressive was that the group contained a group of poor African American girls who went on to college, graduate schools, and high achievement in careers (Hollinger, 1996.)

This program treats the gifted girl as a whole person as it helps reduce barriers. It serves as a model for those who wish to improve a gifted girl's chances for achievement.

Changing Attitudes for Gifted Girls

At Johns Hopkins University, Lynn Fox developed a program to direct junior high girls' attitudes and course-taking behaviors toward careers in science and mathematics. What is striking is how many components of it are now standard aspects of special math and science programs for girls. The American Association for the Advancement of Science now supports the idea of "girl-friendly" science (Kahle, 1985), an approach to science education which includes many of the creative ideas implemented in Fox's work-shops. Normally, girls drop out of math courses early in their education, thereby closing off many options; to stop this from happening, Fox's program (1976) initially provided social stimula-tion to motivate twenty-six Baltimore-area seventh grade girls who had scored extremely well on the SAT-M test, a mathematics achievement test for high school seniors.

The three-month course, taught by women instructors, was exclusively for girls. The informal structure stressed small group and individualized instruction, and cooperative rather than competitive activities. Since girls generally focus on social careers, teachers emphasized the ways in which mathematics could be used to solve social problems. Individual and family counseling encouraged girls to view themselves as competent in mathematics, and to overcome any math anxiety.

Two control groups, one of boys and one of girls, helped researchers assess the program's effectiveness. Students in these groups were pretested in algebra, values, and career interests; boys were found to be already more predisposed than girls to consider mathematics and science careers.

Only eighteen of the twenty-six girls attended the class on a regular basis, and eleven enrolled for Algebra II the following year. At the end of the first year, ten girls and no boys were accelerated by one year, and girls in the control group as well as all girls participating in the experiment were more advanced in math knowledge than boys in the control group. Two years later, 48 percent of the girls in the experiment were accelerated by one or more years, compared to nine percent of control-group girls. Control boys were accelerated at about the same rate as girls in the experiment.

The program was successful in challenging the girls to higher achievement in math. However, during that same three-year period, interest in math careers, after an initial rise, dropped off. In the absence of further encouragement from female role models, gains from the experimental treatment faded as time passed. However, a more recent study of this program by Olszewski, Kubilius and Grant (1996) demonstrated that accelerated summer math classes continue to provide greater gains and benefits to female participants than to male particdipants. Further, such summer math clases helped female participants maintain their gains and high aspirations.

The Guidance Laboratory Approach

Soon after the high school reunion that stimulated my interest in the career development of gifted women, the University of Nebraska-Lincoln agreed to support a new Guidance Laboratory for Gifted and Talented. The Guidance Lab, which would provide counseling services and a setting for research, was modeled on the successful Guidance Institute for Talented Students at the University of Wisconsin-Madison. Each Friday, ten to fifteen high school students from Nebraska came for day-long career guidance through vocational, personality, and values inventories, visits to university classes, career information, and individual and group counseling (Kerr, 1983). At the University of Iowa, I began applying guidance lab techniques at the Counseling Laboratory for Talent Development (Kerr & Erb, 1991). Here, we helped both high school and college-age gifted students to make career choices. Now at Arizona State University, I and my colleague Sharon Robinson Kurpius are re-shaping the counseling laboratory to meet the needs of talented at-risk girls (Kerr and Robinson Kurpius, 1995).

In Nebraska, counselors noticed that girls often had lower career aspirations than boys, and statistical analyses of their most-preferred careers confirmed this observation. How could Guidance

Lab counselors change gifted girls' attitudes? The ambiguous results of previous studies and programs were discouraging. Too many sex equity/career education programs had attempted and failed to interest young women in nontraditional careers and lifestyles. At an early session of the Guidance Lab, a counselor suggested tactfully but determinedly to a straight-A student that "secretary" was perhaps not an appropriate career aspiration for her. The young woman brushed a hand through her curls, straightened the cameo at her lacy neck, and smiled winningly at the counselor as she replied, "Oh no! I would like working with people in an office. Besides, my mom is really into Women's Lib, but I'm not!" It seemed that the gifted girls with low aspirations had heard feminist arguments for higher achievement—but hadn't bought them. They regarded the counselor's suggestion as women's liberation rhetoric, and a gifted sixteen-year-old can be one of the most narrowly focused and stubborn of all beings.

The sermons of feminism generally don't work with gifted adolescent girls, for several reasons. First, members of their generation recognize and reject rhetoric, even when they believe in the basic value of the points being made. Second, a feminist argument for higher aspirations is simply too abstract and alien for young women; they want concrete information about alternatives and are too young to be interested in political or philosophical implications of career decisions. Beside using feminist arguments, counselors also often make the mistake of suggesting arbitrary, high-paying, high-status careers as alternatives to girls' more traditional choices. If a gifted girl wants to be a teacher, a counselor is wrong to suggest engineering simply because of the better salary, but if a gifted girl chooses nursing, the counselor might suggest becoming a physician. In the latter case, alternatives must not be offered without first exploring what draws the young woman to nursing, which may be the study of medicine but could also be the opportunity to nurture, or the smaller investment of time and money to reach the career goal, or many other motives.

In the end, we realized that our lab at Nebraska needed new approaches involving neither rhetoric nor arbitrary suggestions. If young women could raise their aspirations from within—incorporating personality and deeply-held values—real change toward greater fulfillment of abilities might be possible.

The subsequent Career Aspirations program was designed as an intensive career education workshop for gifted female high school juniors. Many drove as far as 400 miles to spend a day at the Guidance Laboratory for Gifted and Talented. In addition to the variety of vocational, personality, and values tests and the campus tour of university classes in their interest areas, each girl met with an individual counselor who helped her set goals using the Personal Map of the Future. In addition, a group counseling session encouraged the girls to fantasize their Perfect Future Day, and then to discuss the barriers to attaining such a perfect day.

In this program, the formulated strategy of the individual counselor in raising aspirations is to establish clearly what the girl's personality traits and values are, then to raise her aspirations to higher-status careers that are appropriate within those traits and values. Thus, the gifted girl with a great desire to nurture who loves to work with children is encouraged to elevate her aspirations from child-care worker to child psychologist. The bright, enterprising girl who expresses a need for order and convention is encouraged to raise her aspirations from secretary to business woman.

The program's next step is for group counselors to then provide information about the long-term consequences of lifestyle decisions. Information based on research outlined in this book is described during the course of the discussion: Girls learn about the success of integrators, the greater satisfaction of Terman's professional women, and the negative effects of early marriage and childbirth on career achievement. The counselors do not preach; they simply share their knowledge about the lives of gifted women to help girls make their decisions.

In application, these Guidance Lab techniques seemed to work. When we compared the girls' aspirations before the Guidance Laboratory experience with their aspirations six to nine months later, we found significant change; a comparable group of gifted girls who had not attended the Guidance Laboratory experienced no change over the same period of time. Girls' career choices had gone from teacher to lawyer; from designer to architect; from X-ray technician to physician; from youth counselor to administrator for juvenile services. We were overjoyed! To our knowledge, it was the first time that gifted girls' attitudes to their own futures had been altered. We hoped that the girls continued to find encouragement in their new goals and that their changed aspirations led them to better educational opportunities (Kerr, 1983).

At Iowa, in working primarily with college-age gifted women, we realized that raising aspirations was not enough, for most already had high aspirations; what we found to be lacking was a commitment to those aspirations. Therefore, interventions designed to increase a sense of purpose were implemented. Students were shown how their profiles compared to those of eminent women. Counselors spoke passionately about falling in love with an idea, and they discouraged any high-status career that was inconsistent with the woman's deeply-held values, stressing that the surest way of falling in love with an idea is to base decisions on those values. Once again, results were exciting. Not only did students increase in their sense of purpose and in confidence in their identities, but over half changed to majors more in keeping with their values. Interestingly enough, most who changed majors did not lower their aspirations but rather chose work related more closely to service or creativity. The women, most of whom had been given practical or even cynical advice in the past, were excited by the encouragement to follow their dreams. Tired of being told to "dress for success" and to go for high-paying jobs just to get rich fast, they were delighted to know that their future work could be meaningful. (Kerr and Erb, 1991).

These counseling and guidance laboratories continue to be evaluated and improved (Kerr and Maresh, 1993).

Individual Counseling and Guidance

Individual counseling and guidance can help gifted girls and women change negative attitudes toward themselves and to raise their career goals. Currently, few psychologists or counselors specialize in the gifted and talented. However, the tremendous success of the book *Reviving Ophelia: Saving the Selves of Adolescent Girls* by Mary Pipher (1994) insures that professional helpers will take a new look at the conflicts experienced by adolescent girls in American Society. Mary Pipher, herself a compassionate therapist well-versed in the research on psychology of girls and women, gives advice which is relevant to all parents, teachers and counselors of gifted girls. It is hoped that the number of counselors and mental health providers who understand the needs of gifted and talented girls and women will grow as our society's interest in this population develops.

A few major centers for individual counseling of gifted and talented do exist. Notable among these are the Gifted Child Development Center in Denver, Colorado; the Guidance Laboratory for Gifted and Talented in Lincoln, Nebraska; SENG (Supporting the Emotional Needs of Gifted) at Kent State University in Kent, Ohio; the Counseling Laboratory for Talent Development at the University of Iowa and the TARGETS program (Talented At-Risk Girls: Encouragement and Training for Sophomores) at Arizona State University. A Gifted Resources Institute at Purdue University, while not focusing on the psychological needs of the gifted, does provide counseling. Similarly, various talent search programs—such as the Talented Identification Program at Duke University, and the Study for Mathematically Precocious Youth at Johns Hopkins University and at Iowa State University—will consult and make appropriate referrals for counseling. Linda Silverman provides a list of counseling and assessment services for gifted and talented in her book, *Counseling the Gifted and Talented* (1993).

Summary

Workshops and counseling programs for gifted girls and young women are proliferating across the country. The best programs use a combination of individual assessment, individual counseling, and group counseling. Bright girls need to fantasize about their future, to learn about their unique interests, needs, and values, and to set specific goals for their future. Only by establishing goals based on their most deeply held values can gifted girls find a meaningful path to their future.

An Interview with Kay North

I talked with Kay North at Coe College in Cedar Rapids, Iowa, in 1994. In *Smart Girls, Gifted Women* I had described the internal and external barriers to achievement for bright girls. Motivated to make a true difference in the lives of gifted girls, Kay envisioned a way to teach the skills needed to overcome these barriers. And so during the next few years Kay, Co-ordinator of Extended Learning Programs For Ames Community Schools, helped by her colleague, Sally Beisser, now an educational consultant and an instructor at Iowa State University, created the workshop of her dreams: "Go Power for Girls," a one-day workshop for fifth- and sixth-grade girls.

"We decided to develop this workshop because of our own personal experiences with fifth- and sixth-grade girls. So many of these girls wanted to pull out of their gifted education programs, and we took it personally! Then, I heard Linda Silverman and Sally Reis discussing the tendency of girls to drop out of gifted education as a national phenomenon. This was something that happened in every school.

"Then, I heard you speak at CONTAG at Coe College and was touched by your description of the internal and external barriers to achievement gifted girls face. Part of the workshop we developed centered around these barriers.

"The workshop is called 'Go Power for Girls' and we have made it open to all girls. We send invitations through teachers, and we make sure that ELP girls have invitations to send their friends. In this way we build a network. The workshop is on the teacher conference day, during the afternoon.

"The workshop begins with warm-up activities designed to help the girls understand some of the issues. We brainstorm the names of famous women. Then we brainstorm the names of famous men, and we discuss why it's so much easier to think of famous men. We look at advertisements and study how often women are shown in non-traditional or traditional roles.

"Then we lecture at them a little bit. We read to them the statistics on women's earnings and such from the AAUW book, Shortchanging Girls, Shortchanging America *(what a wonderful resource!) and we explain the internal and external barriers. We show a video from the Women's History Project called* A Woman's Place, *which shows women's true contributions throughout history.*

"Probably the most effective part of our program is when we bring in a panel of girls and young women to talk about achievement from their point of view. They discuss questions like 'What was tough about sticking it out in a gifted program?' The young women who were once students in Ames schools talk about majoring in math

and science at Iowa State University. They answer questions like 'Can you still be a cheerleader and take calculus?' I wish we could do more workshops with this panel. It really gets the girls' attention.

"We have found that fifth and sixth grade girls have a hard time making long-term goals, like planning for a career. Instead, it is helpful for them to set short-term goals like taking a math summer course or staying in gifted education. Now that we are extending the program to seventh and eighth graders, we may be able to include some long-term goal-setting.

"We need to do an evaluation. That's next. We know that young women come back and say the workshop had an effect, that it really raised their awareness. There's so much more we want to do!"

An Interview with Linda Lee-Boesl

After speaking in Rochester, New York, in 1991, I was approached by Linda Lee-Boesl, a teacher in a school for girls, Our Lady of Mercy High School. I had expressed concern about barriers to girls' recieving the education that they deserve. "Shouldn't girls be taught deliberate ways of communication that challenge traditional assumptions about women's intelligence?" she asked, and I heartily agreed that they indeed should. She then told me about the rules she had developed for effective communication in the classroom, which are printed here. A year later, Linda visited me at Arizona State University, bringing with her a treasure trove of ideas for enhancing the education of girls and young women. I interviewed her about her own motivations for her work and the nature of teaching strategies.

"I went to Nazareth College where I received a bachelor's degree in English, and I got my master's degree in English literature as a Danforth Fellow. It was in graduate school that I noticed how women behaved in class—for the first six weeks they didn't say anything! The competition was incredible in class, because it was full of boy wonders. My first husband

was a behaviorist, and I read all his journals. I learned about observing behavior, and I also learned about how verbal behavior can be modified. I was so frustrated with women's silencing themselves.

"My inspiration for developing new techniques for teaching young women comes from several sources. First, I like the company of young women. I enjoy the transformations that can occur with just a little help. Also, from theology, I had become concerned about the incompatibility of the demands of the church with the needs of women for a voice. I believed it was important to work within the church to help young women find their voices. Another part of my inspiration comes from my colleagues at Our Lady of Mercy, who gave me trust, who gave me freedom, and who understand what I do. At first, other teachers would not try my techniques. But they came to Bluestockings Club, our literary discussion group, and found that literature is a wonderful way of exploring new ways of communicating as women.

"My techniques for teaching young women involve, first, creating an environment in which women's voices are heard. I try to have images of strong women all over the room. I have an 'Odd Couples' display in which great women are paired with great men: Emily Dickinson and Robert Frost, Elizabeth I and Shakespeare, Billie Holiday and Langston Hughes. I make sure that there is evidence of women's culture throughout the room: fabrics, plants, teapots, art work of third world women, and music by women.

"Then I give them rules; I teach them how to behave as intellectual people with a fine, critical mind. We use rules for the method of shared inquiry, rules for marking a text in such a way as to 'own' it and rules for thinking and writing about literature. I add to these 'Rules for Real Women.'"

Rules for Real Women

When real women communicate:

1. They do not preface their opinions with self-effacing comments that dismiss the seriousness of their ideas.

2. They do not over-qualify their ideas in order to avoid taking responsibility for them.

3. They do not distract others with nervous mannerisms or irrelevant "chatter," and they make a point of looking the person in the eye, even, occasionally, calling him or her by name.

4. They do not speak too quickly or drop their voices at the end of a sentence in order to obscure their meaning; they avoid murmuring and whispering.

5. They do not apologize for holding an opinion that does not agree with others, and they do not expect others to convert to theirs. Their "goal" remains understanding, not "consensus."

6. They do not take responsibility for another's silence, for they realize that silence is often a respectful and creative response to understanding.

7. They do not interrupt the other person, and they avoid monopolizing the conversation.

8. They do not avoid asking questions about that which they have genuine doubt; neither do they ask superfluous ones about which they have *no* doubt.

9. They learn to listen "actively" by occasionally reflecting on the other's meanings; they make a sincere effort to truly hear.

10. They do not pretend to know something when, in fact, they do not. It is acceptable not to know; it is misleading to pretend otherwise. Neither do they feign ignorance.

Since learning of Linda Lee-Boesl's "Rules for Real Women," I have shared them with hundreds of girls and their teachers. These helpful rules make it possible for girls to be heard, and for them to benefit from the teaching they receive.

References

Fleming, E. & Hollinger, C. *Project CHOICE: Creating New Options in Career Education*. Boston: Educational Development Corporation, 1994.

Fox, L. H. "Sex Differences in Mathematical Precocity: Bridging the Gap." In. *D.P. Keating (Ed.), Intellectual Talent: Research and development*. Baltimore: The Johns Hopkins University Press, 1976, pp. 113-138.

Kahle, Jane *Women in Science*. Philadelphia, PA: Falmer Press, 1985

Kerr, B. A. "Raising Aspirations of Gifted Girls." *Vocational Guidance Quarterly*, 1983.

Kerr, B. A. & Erb, C.E. "Career Counseling with Aademically Talented Students: Effects of a Value-based Intervention." In *Journal of Counseling Psychology*, 38, 309-314, 1991.

Kerr, B. A. & Maresh, S. E. "Career Counseling for Gifted Women." In W. B. Walsh & S. H. Osipow (eds.), *Career Counseling for Women*. Hillsdale, N.J.: Erlbaum, 1994. 417-427

Kerr, B.A. & Robinson Kurpius, S. "Talented At-Risk Girls. Encouragement and Training for Sophomores." Final Report to National Science Foundation Model Programs for Women and Girls. Reston, VA: National Science Foundation, 1995.

Hollinger, C. "An Examination of the Lives of Gifted Black Young Women." In K. Arnold, K.D. Noble & R.F. Subotnik (eds.) *Remarkable Women*, Creskill, NJ: Hampton Press, 1996, 383-398.

Rosser, S.V. *Encouraging Girls in Math and Science*. Reston, VA: National Science Foundation, 1994.

Olsziwski-Kubilius, P. and Grant, B. "Academically Talented Women and Mathematics: The Role of Special Programs and support from others on acceleration, achievement, and aspirations." Chapter In K. Arnold, K.D. Noble and R.F. Subotnik (eds.) *Remarkable Women*, Cresskill, N.J.: Hampton Press, 1996, 281-94.

Pipher, M. *Reviving Ophelia: Saving the Selves of Adolescent Girls*. NY, NY: Ballantine Books, 1994.

Silverman, L. K. *Counseling the Gifted and Talented*. Denver, CO: Love Press, 1993.

Chapter 15

Guiding Gifted Girls

Chapter 7 presented evidence that gifted girls and women are basically psychologically healthy. If they underachieve, society should not label them victims of disorders but rather should recognize gifted girls and women as normal, whole individuals who simply may not be functioning at the upper range of their abilities. They live in a world that cannot easily accept or make use of their exceptional talents. Respecting their wholeness, those who would foster their growth must offer support that identifies talents, builds strengths, encourages confidence, and challenges with visions of personal and professional excellence.

Most parents underestimate their own abilities and thus have trouble believing that their child may be gifted, as though gifted were the same as genius. "Well, she's bright, but not gifted," parents concede. Since parental underestimation of talent is particularly likely for preschool girls, I would suggest to all parents that they reevaluate their notions—they may well have a gifted child.

But identification of the gifted is not enough. Many people believe that such children need no special help and can make it on their own. In reality, gifted girls in particular need the guidance of parents, teachers, and counselors throughout childhood, adolescence, and young adulthood to achieve maximum potential. But what sort of guidance is most beneficial? A number of helpful hints and specific recommendations can be offered.

Gifted girls whose intelligence is in the upper 3 to 5 percent live in a world mainly oriented toward the other 95 percent, where mediocrity and conformity are more valued than achievement. Gifted children need special support despite the myth that bright minds will find their own way. *Guiding the Gifted Child* (Webb, Meckstroth & Tolan, 1982), provides an excellent understanding of these issues and contains many practical suggestions about handling such common problems as motivation, discipline, sibling rivalry, stress management and peer relationships. It also discusses depression, identification of gifted children, and tradition-breaking. That book, and others like it, contain basic and necessary information. Recommendations specifically for gifted girls and women must go further, however.

The following suggestions, addressed to parents, are equally applicable to teachers and counselors. These guidelines are divided by age-group: preschool, primary, junior high, senior, college, and post graduate.

Preschool

An important principle for parents of preschool gifted girls to remember: If you don't want people to treat your girl like a fragile little flower, don't dress her like one. Lace dresses that are difficult to keep clean prevent girls from running, jumping, and climbing, and teachers moan when tears and stains inevitably appear. For school, dress your daughter for active play rather than inactivity on the sidelines. Dress your daughter in bold, bright, washable colors, not pallid pastels, if you want to help her communicate her adventurousness. One caveat: many pre-school girls insist on dresses, my daughter, Grace, included. We argued a lot until my husband and I realized that the whole point of the clothing was assertiveness, not costume, and that her assertiveness ought to be rewarded! So we let her wear dresses and insisted that she be allowed to get them dirty at school.

Choose nonsexist toys or at least a broad array of toys, so that your daughter is not limited to dolls. Encourage her interest in toys that allow manipulation of objects and active solution of problems. She needs practice to develop a sense of mastery and self-worth.

Toys are more sex-segregated now than ever. Try to explain to your pre-schooler that she is not limited to the pink aisles of the toy store. Don't discourage nurturant and quiet play, however! Simply make sure that other options are available and reinforced.

Choose child care cautiously; avoid day care centers or pre-schools that segregate girls and boys. Determine the child-care workers' attitudes toward sex roles. Look for facilities with men as well as women teachers. Often it will not be enough just to ask; you will need to observe how the teachers actually handle sex-role issues.

Be sure that day care centers/preschools do not rigidly enforce sleeping at nap time. Find a school that has "quiet time" instead, when children may lie quietly on cots and look at books or picture cards if they are not sleepy. Gifted girls seem to need afternoon alone-time more than sleep, and certainly they vary widely in the amount and types of limits and structure they need. You want a school that allows for individual differences.

Be sure that day care centers/preschools have plenty of books and that looking at books is encouraged. Many gifted girls want to learn the alphabet or to try writing, neither of which should be discouraged, since they are often indeed ready for such adventures. Also important is individual time with puzzles, mechanical toys, musical instruments, and art work, especially when the child seems interested in such activities.

Take your preschool girl to your place of work and explain your job to her. Explain the work of all the people she sees while shopping, traveling, and/or attending to household needs. Particularly, help her see women in leadership positions and in various occupations. *Take Our Daughters to Work Day,* a national event sponsored by the National Organization for Women the last week of April each year, is a great idea!

When she is about four or five, have her take such tests of intellectual ability as the WPPSI or the Stanford-Binet. These may be required for early admission to kindergarten or special preschool gifted programs. Even if they are not, they will give you reasonable objective benchmarks for comparing your daughter's abilities with those of other children. However, remember that scores are only moderately meaningful at this age.(These tests are more helpful in identifying children with deficiencies than they are in pinpointing children with superior abilities.) No test for preschoolers can adequately predict superior academic achievement in primary or later school, although school districts and educational programs persist in their use for this purpose.

To administer the test, select your own psychologist, one who has rapport with your daughter or who will take time to develop it. Then interpret the results cautiously, perhaps even assuming an underestimation of her true ability. Be alert to the development of extraordinary specific abilities. Musical and mathematical ability are early developing intelligences; have teachers or specialists in these areas evaluate your daughter's abilities if they seem special.

Take advantage of any preschool programs that may satisfy your gifted girl's hunger for intellectual stimulation or for an opportunity to exercise her abilities. As long as your daughter wants these activities and enjoys them, you're not "pushing." Try anything once, and see if she likes it—Suzuki lessons, karate, story hours, whatever sounds interesting.

Be alert to television programming. Sex role stereotypes in most children's and adult programming are worse than ever. Always discuss the meaning of girls' and boys' roles as seen on T.V., and let her know your feelings about what you are watching. Your comments can help inoculate your child against the pressures to conform to the average.

Take time to answer her questions. It is easy to let yourself become so busy that you have little left to give her, particularly when she seems to ask so many questions that your ears feel tired. Build in a few minutes of special time each day when she has your individual attention. This will help her feel that her curiosity is appreciated.

Elementary

Gifted girls are usually reading by kindergarten, and their interest in reading grows rapidly. Some parents notice their gifted daughter trying to teach herself. Find books, books, and more books for her. Choose books that portray women in many roles. Let her read all she wants, and help her when she asks. If her reading skills cause her to finish tasks well ahead of classmates, insist that she be allowed to read quietly until the others are done. A wonderful resource for gifted readers is *Some of My Best Friends Are Books* by Judy Halsted (1994).

Girls who are gifted in mathematical/logical reasoning often want math puzzles and problems to work with. Seek them out!

Teachers' school-supply stores are a treasure trove for games like these. A home computer may be a necessity, rather than a luxury, for the mathematically talented girl.

Girls with special talents such as visual arts and music need to understand and hone their abilities, but can do so only if they have the implements and instruments of their art. Individual lessons can be invaluable investments. How much do you push practicing? There is no single answer except to say don't force practice to the point that it seriously jeopardizes your relationship with your daughter.

Gifted primary school girls typically thrive on adventure and novelty. Camping, exploring, museum-hopping, and traveling all broaden the child's exposure to what is possible in today's world. If you have to take a short business trip, take her with you and then stop in a museum on the way back home.

Don't over-schedule so that every waking moment is pro-grammed. Gifted young girls need a private, special place: an attic, a basement room, a playhouse, or a treehouse. Fantasy and imagination develop well in such settings.

Don't push social relationships. For six-to-ten-year olds, books and play at one's own level are sometimes more interesting than other children are. Intellectual peer groups are useful, especially if you live in an area that has a gifted/parent group, but don't insist on participation. Chances are your daughter has the ability, but not a great need, to form close social relationships. Her friendships may become few and carefully selected, but quite intense.

If your girl is in a regular classroom, watch for signs of boredom and/or withdrawal: unwillingness to go to school, poor class participation, daydreaming, sadness. These signs suggest she needs more stimulation and opportunity through mentoring, indi-vidualized instruction, or acceleration. Remember that she may not complain or act out as a boy might, given the same needs.

Role models are important. Even in baby sitters, try to find an older girl or woman who is intellectually oriented, self-confident, and assertive.

Support your child emotionally, even when she is "thorny." A characteristic of gifted girls is their intensity, although usually it takes time and support for them to learn how to harness it. Show that you will love her even if she is not just like the other girls. Chances are that in the midst of her thorny times she doesn't find herself likable either, hence she needs more than ever your special support and encouragement.

Help her feel special and unique. Let her know you are delighted by her gifts and talents. Always be honest in regard to what you know about her abilities, and don't hide her giftedness from her, although you may acknowledge it in other words by telling her she is bright or curious. Gifted children are almost always aware that they are different, they but often don't understand how or why, or even whether the difference is good or bad. To open this area for discussion is important, and despite parents' worries it is not likely to give her an oversized ego.

Middle School

Try to conceal your astonishment when your uniquely gifted offspring suddenly wants to be like every other girl in her class. Pressures to conform are intense at this age. Try not to protest about her sudden desire to be "normal." Let her buy the faddish clothes and strange music. Within limits, let her go to the parties she wants to attend and try to avoid useless power struggles—particularly those you can't win.

Refuse, however, to cooperate in her attempts to evaluate herself primarily in terms of her attractiveness or her relationships. While you should be tolerant of her fluctuating self-image, continue to encourage her self-actualizing efforts—school work, activities, career planning. Though at times you may feel your efforts are useless, your continued support will help her develop a sense of personal worth and integrity independent of evaluations from others.

Insist that your daughter continue taking math and science courses if they are optional. Whether she performs outstanding work in such courses is not the issue. Basic knowledge in these subjects preserves her options for choices later in her life.

She may go through periods of being exceedingly self-critical, particularly as she becomes aware of the conflict between "fitting in" and developing herself as an independent person. Receptive listening and gentle advice are needed. Perhaps she can talk also with some bright high school and college women about these issues.

Help keep her career aspirations high by encouraging continuing exploration of careers. Biographies are helpful reading. Volunteer work in the right settings can provide experience-based career education.

Begin to talk with her about "falling in love with an idea." When her whole culture pressures her toward falling in love with a guy, teach her that she can find meaning through her work first, and then be prepared to find love.

High School

With most gifted girls, your efforts will begin to have positive results, although you may still have many days when you feel your help is useless. You can expect at least brief episodes of a rekindled interest in academics and careers. When that happens, be ready to reinforce them lavishly. Support and encourage these spurts in growth.

Consider all-female schooling. The evidence is clear that all-girl high schools can provide a more equitable, encouraging education. Make sure, however, that it is not a "finishing school," but instead one which is focused on achievement and excellence.

Help your daughter find college and scholarship guides, as well as good career information. The family's clear interest and expectation that she will attend college is of inestimable value. Talk about colleges and postgraduate education at the dinner table. Accompany her to college social and sports functions, and to the college guidance and placement services.

Seek competent, nonsexist career guidance that includes assessment of vocational interests, personality, and values. Take advantage of any high school or college counselor with a special interest in gifted girls. Otherwise, find a career guidance specialist in private practice through your state gifted association.

Senior high gifted girls need to complete four full years of math in order to assure all career options. If four years of math are not available through the high school, try to find evening courses at a local community college.

The need for a mentor continues. If your daughter has become especially talented in a specific area, find a coach or instructor in her area. A woman may not be available in some male-dominated area, but a man can also be an appropriate mentor, so seek the best available instructor without regard to gender.

Your gifted daughter will particularly need to understand the implications of her giftedness on her relationships at this time in life. Help her to understand that she has choices in romantic feelings, that she can deliberately choose boyfriends with whom she can communicate easily. Sometimes gifted girls find they have relatively few boys from which to choose. As parents, you too must be realistic about her narrow range of choices for relationships with men, and help her develop patience.

Keep her self-esteem high by showing her your admiration and the admiration of others. If she has body-image problems, help her to see herself realistically and to find the beauty that is within her. If her belief in her abilities declines, show her concrete evidence of her giftedness: test-scores, products, even precocious drawings and writings from childhood.

The pitfalls of pregnancy and early childbirth and marriage may be avoided by providing accurate sex education and discussions about marriage. Being gifted doesn't mean she knows all about sex, which is a very powerful urge in high school and is embedded within rapidly changing relationships. Also, help her make the difficult, future educational decisions that are likely to be independent of relationship decisions.

Gifted girls are full of activity and intensity. When possible, prevent her from spreading herself too thin and becoming an exhausted teenager. Encourage her to focus on excellence in a few areas rather than trying to be perfect in everything.

A particularly helpful technique for promoting perspective is to ask her to imagine her life ten years from now. What would be the perfect future day for her? Then, help her to examine what barriers she sees that might prevent such a day, and how she might overcome those barriers.

College

Try to find an all-women's college or a serious, academically oriented coed institution with a high proportion of tenured female faculty. Evidence indicates that women's colleges produce more women scholars and leaders. Co-ed colleges with high proportions of women faculty at least provide more role models.

Encourage your daughter to seek career counseling early in her college program so that she can avoid the frequent changes of major common to "multipotential" students. Suggest that she find a mentor even if she must begin as an unpaid assistant to a potential mentor; perhaps she can find such sponsorship in her academic advisor.

Help her to understand the internal and external reasons that women's grades slip in college. In all likelihood she is quite able, but is she willing to compete with male students? Are her professors nonsexist, or do they seem to favor male students? Suggest that she practice speaking up in class. She will want to be sure her professors notice and respect her, but she can only accomplish this if she is reasonably assertive. Share with her some of your successes in being assertive.

Share with her the dangers of the culture of romance. Help her keep problems with relationships in perspective. She will need to understand that the traditional college dating system is not likely to lead her to satisfying relationships with men since the emphasis is typically on popularity, good looks and conformity. Suggest that she seek men and women friends in those campus organizations that have goals more closely in tune with her own.

If she becomes involved in unusual campus groups, don't panic. Gifted young women are often very idealistic or even iconoclastic. Membership in slightly fringe groups provides them an opportunity for intellectual independence and testing values. Most eminent women needed this stage.

Initiate values-centered discussions. In what way is she seeking meaning and purpose in life? How is she planning to make a difference? Her ideas often will be awkward, incomplete or unrealistic. Nonetheless, it is important that you indicate your confidence in her growing ability to contribute importantly to society.

Make your home a safe haven. With their intensity, gifted young women often overextend themselves and have intellectual or emotional crises. Sometimes college can be lonely and frightening, especially if your daughter is younger than most, or farther from home than others. A home base to return to is extremely reassuring and helpful.

Postgraduate or Professional School

By now your gifted daughter's education may extend beyond that of both parents. Her interests may be esoteric and far from your area of expertise, which could become a barrier between you. Maintain your curiosity and interest in her work. She still needs your emotional support.

She may be feeling a need for financial independence. Many

of her peers are now working at full-time jobs, making more money than she. Help her out as much as she will let you, and discourage her from passing up educational opportunities because of the cost. What may seem like a large amount of money to her now—for special lessons, for tuition to a prestigious graduate school—will be well worth the investment.

Discuss with her the hazards of being underemployed and underpaid, and encourage her to familiarize herself with what she rightfully can expect in various positions. She may need to learn new on-the-job interpersonal skills to prevent others from placing barriers in her path, or to prevent herself from hindering herself by her own behaviors.

Her self-doubts may recur. Having set high standards for herself, she may fall short and begin to feel inadequate, even depressed. Believe in her always, but especially when she doesn't believe in herself. You have reared a woman with a fine intellect and extraordinary talents, who also happens to have the cultural "disability" of being female. If you continue to be a supportive parent with high expectations for your daughter, you can help her maintain her aspirations even in a society that discourages her achievements.

References

Halsted, J.W. *Some of My Best Friends Are Books.* Scottsdale, AZ: Gifted Psychology Press, 1994.

Webb, J.T. Meckstroth, E.A. and Tolan, S.S. *Guiding the Gifted Child.* Scottsdale, AZ: Gifted Psychology Press (1982).

Chapter 16

Conclusion

So what became of the little girls I remembered from my school, so scrupulously trained for the destiny of "the leaders of tomorrow"? Sixteen years have now passed since Mary asked me that troubling question at our ten-year reunion, and much has changed for all of us. However, like gifted women everywhere, we have been, for the most part, flowers who bloomed in the spring.

The girlhood of those women in my study was full of promise. Their lives were full of bright achievements and big dreams. But their childhood dreams flickered, their hopes for achievement dimmed, and their lives at twenty-nine and thirty-nine differed little from women of average intelligence. At twenty-nine, most were homemakers, teachers or nurses; only a few were professionals. Yet they were still decidedly easy to identify as gifted people. Their articulate, introspective letters and comments told both of their special qualities and their unfulfilled hopes.

At age 29, all but a few of my former classmates were careful to deny their giftedness and to minimize its importance. Only a few claimed to be unhappy with their current situation; most were positive and cheerful about their lives. They portrayed themselves as self-assured, self-accepting women. At 39, my classmates had begun to accept the fact of their giftedness, but were still very ambivalent about it. Now the group fell into very different categories. One group had transformed their lives, creating a career or business to which they were able to apply their considerable talents. Another group had committed themselves to the traditional occupations they had chosen, finding creative vocations in teaching and homemaking. Another group, which had been career-oriented all along, were in the prime of their vocational lives. Finally, a new group had emerged, a group of women defined by their struggle for economic and psychological survival: this overwhelmed group seemed trapped by their limited education and early choices which somehow got them off track. They lived in environments indifferent to their giftedness and to their dreams for themselves.

My review of the research confirmed that my St. Louis classmates were quite representative of gifted women generally. They had been more adventurous and curious than was characteristic of less gifted girls; within the interests they professed, they were more like boys than other girls. As other studies had shown, my classmates, too, had excelled in elementary and secondary schools, usually surpassing boys in academic achievement. Adolescence struck this group harshly as giftedness, careers and dreams were set aside—not unlike findings involving gifted adolescents in other studies. The girls redirected their energies into such traditional achievement as finding boyfriends and showing concern about their popularity.

Although they had shown strengths in math and science, these young women typically chose the more standard feminine humanities and social science courses. Those who did attend college often entered traditional women's fields, such as teaching and nursing. Entering college in 1969, most of them probably found themselves in institutions with little commitment to developing the talents of women. They had few role models on campus, and few opportunities for mentoring.

Ten years after high school, the proportion of my Sputnik school group in homemaking and traditional occupations matched Terman's decades-earlier group of gifted women almost exactly. Twenty years after graduation, there were pleasant differences—and some ominous ones—from the Terman group. The "transforming women," the committed traditionals, and the continuing professionals had shown that they could make use of their giftedness in resourceful, determined ways. Even among the homemakers, few were "traditional" in the sense of having little interaction with the larger world. The overwhelmed gifted women, however, were a group which has not appeared in any of my previous research: a group of women whose profound talents could not keep them afloat in a downsizing economy with failed support systems. They were the lost women of our generation, a great reservoir of talent thoroughly ignored or laid waste by our society.

Underachievement and underutilization of gifted women is *fact*. When I looked to my classmates and to the literature for explanation, I found that the attitudes and overt discrimination of our culture had created an environment that was hostile to feminine achievement. My classmates and others knew that employment usually translated into underemployment. The Horner Effect or Fear of Success may have prompted the most feminine of the group to underachieve when in competition with men. The Cinderella Complex may have affected the most dependent of the group, sending them into a determined search for someone to take care of them. And the Imposter Phenomenon may have drained the success of a few high achievers who doubted themselves. A plunge in self-esteem may have prevented them from perceiving their own giftedness. However, most women in our group, as most gifted women, did not suffer from psychological disabilities. Paradoxically, most of them were hurt by their tendencies to be well adjusted, easy going and accommodating. They adjusted to the disadvantage of being female, accepting broken aspirations much as a patient caught in a no-choice predicament accepts fractured limbs. However, some picked themselves up after losing earlier opportunities, and created new lives within the limits that now existed.

What about those in our group who committed themselves early to a career and managed to overcome societal barriers to their success? Characteristics that distinguish them from their peers also are similar to those found among eminent women. Those who achieved had stubbornly held to their dreams. They probably received more intellectual nourishment as children and more time alone to digest knowledge. They were not as conforming or popular as others. Being marginal socially may actually have helped them maintain both independence and some sense of their aspirations. They had mentors and counselors who helped them. They stayed single, chose a lesbian lifestyle, or married men who supported their achievements. Most important, they fell in love with an idea, took responsibility for themselves, and thus derived strength.

It is a national tragedy that so few of gifted women have attained eminence while the remainder accept obscurity. How long can society continue to squander the brilliance of gifted women? How long will gifted women stand on the threshold of self-actualization, not taking steps that would fulfill their dreams because they might inconvenience someone?

Do gifted women owe the world and themselves more than cheerfulness, compliance, and children? Is self-actualization optional? This is the question with which I have struggled since I began this project. From a popular point of view, women should be free to do whatever they wish with their lives, whether they are gifted or not. Any choice they make, from this point of view, is equally valuable. From conservatives who believe that women's traditional roles are ordained by God to new feminists who believe all women's work, including work in the home, should be valued (and paid for), there is general agreement that <u>any</u> choice is all right.

But what if that choice only <u>looks like</u> a choice? What if gifted women never really make one deliberate choice to give up their original dreams, but instead make a series of small decisions, somewhat reluctantly, which add up to the loss of their original potential? What if society prevents gifted women from making a legitimate choice of vocation by denying them accurate information about the type and extent of their talents and by providing them with none of the resources they need to pursue a career within the context of a fulfilling family life? And what if gifted women are nice enough and smart enough to make do with whatever limits have been imposed upon them, and to defend their lifestyle as being the product of their own free choice?

For gifted women to fulfill their potential and their responsibilities to society, there are two requirements. First, the gifted woman must be willing to accept her giftedness and to understand it as a promise to be fulfilled. Second, society must take substantial responsibility for guidance of gifted girls and for creating situations that nurture, direct and inspire intellect among gifted girls.

What then must be done for gifted girls? First, we must find them. The field of gifted education offers old and new techniques for identifying gifted and talented students. I. Q. tests, creativity tests, musical auditions, art competition—all help to discover the gifted. The new techniques truly cast a wide net. However, gifted girls also need very specific information about how their talents compare to those of others. For instance, they need to hear, "You read faster and more accurately than 95% of people your age." With their social camouflage, gifted girls are not always easy to identify. However, we need to find them.

Second, we must nourish them by providing as much reading or computer time or music as they crave. It may mean skipping a grade or accelerating within subject areas or, if these are not possible, seeking enrichment opportunities in the regular class-room. Individualized instruction through tutoring or coaching can provide the stimulation the gifted girl needs. Where at all possible, an all-female educational environment may make a tremendous difference in the amount of nourishment a gifted girl or young woman receives.

Third, we must guide them. The most striking feature of the education of my group of gifted peers was the total lack of guidance. Gifted girls will not get by on their own. Ideally, they should have access to skilled counselors who will provide them with the emo-tional support, with comprehensive information about career edu-cation, and with the specialized strategies that can help raise and maintain high aspirations. Parents and teachers can also augment gifted girls' needs for personal and career guidance by shaping their adventurousness, seeking information about future alternatives in their areas of interest,and always challenging them to be more and do more than they thought they could.

Fourth, we must love them. Being smarter, more sarcastic or cynical and sensitive to the point of tears can make a gifted girl hard to love. But such qualities also make great love all the more necessary. A gifted girl whose intelligence places her into a minus-cule percentile will feel alone easily. The thorniness of some gifted girls may largely be reactions to the lack of friendliness or absence of love they sense from others. When the gifted girl's cynicism melts it is because of a warm and caring relationship. Unusual sensitivity of gifted girls means they need more reassurance to help them through times of sadness; if such reassurance takes place, they are capable of great compassion toward others.

Finally, we must make room for them. Whether it is "a room of one's own" or a job of one's own, gifted girls and women need the opportunity to do what they love to do—to learn and to work. In classrooms across the nation, girls' contributions are treated as less important than those of boys. In so many families, the intellec-tual and emotional needs of gifted girls go unmet because the family has other priorities, and because gifted girls are so accepting of their families' other priorities. Everywhere in society one can find gifted women who are under-employed, taking the jobs they can get and hoping one day for a chance to prove what they can do.

Gifted women have revitalized the arts, humanized the sciences, and changed our history. Our daughters can shape the future if only we challenge them, guide them, and preserve their hope.

Associations and Advocacy Groups for Bright Girls and Gifted Women

- American Association for Gifted Children
  C/O Talent Identification Program
  Duke University
  1121 W. Main St. #100
  Durham, NC 27701

- American Association of University Women
  1111 16th St., NW
  Washington, DC 20036

- American Psychological Association
  Division 35 (Women)
  750 1st St. NE
  Washington, DC 20002-4242

- The Association for the Gifted (TAG)
  Council for Exceptional Children
  1920 Association Drive
  Reston, VA 22091

- The Gifted Child Society
  190 Rock Rd.
  Glen Rock, NJ 07452

- Mensa, Gifted Children Program
  C/O Roxanne H. Cramer
  5304 1st Pl., N.
  Arlington, VA 22203

- National Association for Gifted Children
  1155 15th St. NW, #1002
  Washington, DC 20005

- National Association of State Boards of Education
  Council of State Directors of Programs for the Gifted
  Suite 340
  701 N. Fairfax St.
  Alexandria, VA 22314

- National Association of Women in Education
  1325 18th St., NW #210
  Washington, DC 20036

- National Coalition of Girls' Schools
  228 Main St.
  Concord, MA 01742

- National Coalition for Women and Girls in Education
  1625 K St. NW #300
  Washington, DC 20006

- National Organization for Women
  1000 16th St. NW #700
  Washington, DC 20036

- National/State Leadership
  Training Institute on the Gifted
  and the Talented
  Hilton Center
  900 Wilshire Bldg. #1142
  Los Angeles, CA 90017

- National Women's Political Caucus
  1275 K. St., NW Suite 750
  Washington, DC 20005

- National Women's Studies Association
  C/O Deborah Louis
  University of Maryland
  College Park, MD 20742

- Supporting Emotional Needs of Gifted (SENG)
  405 White Hall
  P.O. Box 5190
  Kent, OH 44242

- The World Council for Gifted
  and Talented Children, Inc.
  University of Toronto
  Faculty of Education
  371 Bloor St. W.
  Toronto, ON, Canada

Appendix

Questions & Answers

As director of counseling laboratories for gifted students at three universities, I have counseled hundreds of gifted girls, gifted women, and parents of gifted girls. Much of the content of this book has grown out of my counseling and research work at the Guidance Laboratory. Since many problems recur, I have addressed here the most common questions, grouped into problems of childhood, adolescence, and adulthood.

Problems of Childhood

Q. Our three-year-old daughter shows signs of gifted-ness; she is verbally far ahead of her peers; she has many creative ideas, and her energy level is very high. Even though we have been very careful about bringing her up in an egalitarian home, our concern is that she is so very feminine. She plays only with girls and seems only interested in girls' toys. We want her to develop all her talents, not just traditionally feminine ones.

A. It is natural for preschoolers to gravitate to their own sex, and it is inevitable that they will learn sex-role behavior of the dominant culture from the peer group. The T.V. advertisements during children's programming promote sex-role stereotypes; media images of women often portray them as weak, silly, passive, and compliant. You cannot completely protect your child from these stereotypes and images because they are everywhere.

You can, however, help her develop an independent mind and the strength to refute cultural stereotypes. Be openly critical of sexist advertising and programming; explain in simple terms why they are wrong: "Those police are all men, but women are police too." Soon she will pick up the habit. A three-year-old I know well said of the popular cartoon series, "Hey, Mommy, where are all the woman Smurfs?" However, never be critical of her desire to play with dolls, dress up, or play house. You would only make her ashamed of her femininity, which is precisely what you want to avoid! Instead, provide her also with alternative games and toys that she may choose when, if ever, she desires. Some types of toys given to gifted girls may also be important in their developing mastery skills. Toys that have multiple functions, use different levels of skill over time, and encourage use of strategy and imagination are those to which gifted boys tend to devote much time and energy: Legos, erector sets, building sets, trains, puzzles, games with elaborate rules or use of strategy, science kits, and arts and crafts projects. If girls are also given such toys, one important outcome can be their development of the types of visual-perceptual-motor skills, problem-solving skills, alternate strategies, risk taking abilities, and persistence behaviors that underlie successful performance in math, the sciences, and other traditionally male roles.

Finally, continue to encourage your daughter's independence by helping her see that her successes result from her efforts and not from luck; always praise trying. Teach her that her ideas count by listening to them and by putting her suggestions into effect. Make it clear that you know she has important things to say, and show her how to get others' attention through polite but firm assertion.

In this way, you will add to those important qualities of nurturing, cooperation, and even temperedness, and the equally important qualities of independence, achievement-orientation, and assertiveness.

Q. My gifted nine-year-old girl doesn't want to do anything but read. She sits inside even in the summer and reads all day. What can we do to get her outside?

A. First, it's important to understand that the period between seven—when most high I. Q. children become capable of reading really interesting books—and eleven—when adolescence begins—is a time when gifted girls are most likely to enjoy being alone and to enjoy reading more than any other leisure time activity. This doesn't mean that your daughter is going to be a cloistered bookworm when she grows up; it most likely means that she is feeding an intellectual curiosity that is as yet unblemished by social anxiety. For her, reading most of the time is probably okay.

If you're worried about her getting fresh air and exercise, you might try two strategies. Build a tree-house (really!) where she can read outside. Suggest nature books and stories about people exploring the outdoors or enjoying sporting adventures to encourage her participation in such active events.

Q. Our third grade girl hasn't had any close friends since kindergarten. She plays alone, even at recess. We don't think it's by choice, but she won't talk about it. If we try to force the subject, the discussion ends in tears. We wish she could be in gifted classes, but our school doesn't have any at her grade level.

A. Gifted girls often do prefer to play alone, but it sounds as if your daughter is unhappy about her situation. She may be ashamed to talk with you about it because she knows her isolation makes you unhappy. Many possible reasons can explain the social isolation of gifted girls: others may resent their good grades; they may be dissimilar in appearance and behavior at a time when conformity is very important; they may lack "friendship skills" such as ability to listen and to give compliments and share toys and treats; they may pick the wrong kids to approach; they may talk about topics or suggest play that is too advanced for other children. Sometimes gifted children try to organize or boss the other children, or with their intensity will attempt to be the center of activity through making up complicated games or rules. Talk with her about friendship skills, empathy, sharing, and tolerance. Role playing is often particularly helpful for promoting understanding of how others see her.

You may never be able to identify the causes. What you can do is this: if she seems to feel pressure to make friends, take the pressure off. Let her know that you don't consider friendships to be achievements that she must attain. Tell her that bright girls do sometimes have periods of loneliness, but that these times don't last forever; a time will come when she will find friends like herself.

Continue your search for intellectual peers—boys or girls—and try to arrange for them to meet. Many parents of gifted groups exist, even in small cities, though they may be identified as Friends of the Museum or the Inventors' Council. Find out where the nearest group is and see if they have a children's play group.

Do help your daughter develop similarities to other children. Make sure she has clothes and toys like the other girls if she wants them. Many parents who dislike kids' fads refuse to allow their children to participate, but I think this may hurt gifted children more than it protects them from the crassness of consumerism. You don't need to go overboard; just ask her if there are any things she would like, and mildly go along with choices.

Help her learn friendship skills by allowing her to bring small treats or toys for friends and to give gifts of compliments. Many parents of gifted children feel that this is "buying friendship." It may very well be that, but it happens to be how friendships are formed in children's culture.

Make sure that all of these strategies are not unilaterally announced and instituted by you; instead, suggest them to your daughter objectively and allow her to choose to try them if she wishes.

Q. As a homemaker, how can I possibly help my highly gifted daughter? At ten years old, she already seems to have read more than I have. I feel I am not a good role model for her. I was not able to pursue my education because of family responsibilities.

A. There is no need for you, as a mother, to be an exact role model for your daughter, nor is there evidence that gifted girls with professional mothers are any more accomplished than those whose mothers are home-makers. A mother can be a role model, or she can be a supporter of her daughter's ambitions. If you are willing to show interest in your daughter's enthusiasms, to help her find special tutoring and role models she might need, and to show her your love and acceptance when she feels different and alone, then you will have been a very great help to her indeed.

Q. Our eight-year-old gifted daughter loved school at first, but now she says she doesn't like it "because there's nothing to do." She is often sick before school and sometimes has to leave school feeling ill when there is apparently nothing physically wrong. She also has nightmares at night. Her home life is happy, her teachers like her, and she has nice friends. I'm puzzled.

A. Boredom is the single most common school problem of gifted and talented students in the regular class-room. Boys will show their boredom by disruptive

249

behavior and disorderly work. Girls, on the other hand, often show no overt sign, smiling and participating even when they are irritated by the repetitiveness of it all. Their anger comes out in daydreaming, psychosomatic illnesses, bad dreams, and nervous habits. Investigate the possibility that your daughter must have a chance for more challenge. Consider moving her up a grade or more, getting tutoring for part of the day, or better still, attending a school with special classes for the gifted. If you aren't sure how bright she is, have her tested by a competent child psychologist.

Q. What is the effect of acceleration and grade-skipping on gifted girls? Can these practices be harmful?

A. Grade-skipping and acceleration are far less harmful than the alternative—staying in the regular classroom. In fact, at both our Guidance Laboratory and Wright State University's SENG, acceleration often has been found to be a treatment of choice for gifted children with certain kinds of emotional problems. Gifted girls, who mature earlier than boys, probably adjust to grade-skipping more easily than boys. Acceleration or early entrance into school, when applied appropriately, can hardly be anything but helpful.

Q. My little girl has such wild, crazy ideas. She wants to talk about space travel, ESP, and fantasy tales. She dresses like a nut and talks in foreign accents. Every day she's into something new and strange. I hate to say this, but I do wish she'd be a little more normal, especially in social situations.

A. My first impulse is to tell you to enjoy your delightful little eccentric while you can because, sadly, what puberty doesn't accomplish, peer pressure will to make your daughter less "different." Your daughter's interests are not unusual among gifted children. Think of it this way: certain subjects allow gifted kids intellectual sensations they crave. For instance, an interest in space travel and ESP gives a gifted child the sense of wonder and possibility that is nearly impossible to achieve in a world where there are no new geographical frontiers. An interest in funny clothes and accents allows a gifted child to "try on" personalities and so to explore human nature and potential. So what seems like wild and crazy ideas actually serve the important function of training your girl's intellectual curiosity and sharpening her empathy.

On the other hand, gifted girls who are smart enough to impersonate cockneys and cowgirls also are smart enough to impersonate nice little girls. So when you have those few situations in which you need an imaginary nice little girl (reunions with aged, wealthy relatives, for instance) you might ask your daughter to trot out her "Pollyanna" role for an afternoon.

Q. My daughter is such a perfectionist it scares me. Won't this lead her to put too much stress on herself?

A. Perfectionism is a common characteristic of gifted children, a trait many seem to be born with. At the Guidance Laboratory we have seen casual, easygoing parents who are amazed to have reared a child obsessed with neatness and order, "doing things right," and scoring 100% on all school tasks. Unfortunately, I've heard educators blaming this on parents who drive their kids too hard and expect too much. But often this just isn't the case; in fact, most parents of perfectionists would be relieved if their children would just relax a little. Although some perfectionistic parents may "infect" their children, I believe that most of the time perfectionism in gifted children begins with a predisposition for fastidiousness, coupled with a learned fear of failure.

Fear of failure is the result of lack of experience with failure. Many gifted children who have been unchallenged in school become addicted to the As that come so easily. As the years go by with straight-As piling up, many gifted children become more and more person-

251

ally invested in maintaining these grades, which have become a part of their identity. These children will eventually avoid taking any course or participate in any activity in which they can't shine. The life of the perfectionist, who must go on obtaining imaginary As long after the days of report cards are over, is really a very stressful one.

What can you as a parent do? First, work with your girl's inflexible and fastidious personality by helping her to enjoy or at least tolerate imperfection: model humorous, tolerant responses to your own and others' mistakes and messes; encourage her to be a slob once in a while (camping out is a good occasion for this); and teach her compassion for those who couldn't possibly attain perfection even if they wanted to. Second, help her to overcome her fear of failure by allowing opportunities to fail—or at least not be the best. This may mean encouraging art, music, or sports activities—whatever doesn't guarantee an A—and then showing her how to enjoy an activity for its own sake, not for the final result. Noncompetitive games, such as "New Games," cooperative 4-H group projects, and creative hobbies, all can be helpful in overcoming perfectionism.

Q. Our daughter is depressed and always puts herself down. She says she's tired of being weird and different.

A. Depression happens when people feel that nothing they do can improve their situation—when they feel helpless and ineffectual. It sounds as though social isolation is the key to your daughter's depression; she feels trapped by her role as a "weirdo" and doesn't want to try any more to be like the others. And the more intelligent she is, the harder she has had to try. Talk with your daughter to be sure that she, too, believes her isolation is the root of her sadness. If so, she may benefit from the special programs that have helped many gifted children to feel better about themselves and to overcome isolation. Summer camps for gifted, summer enrichment programs, scholars' academics, and Saturday schools all provide gifted children with opportunities to interact with their intellectual peers and to be with adults who don't expect them to "act normal"! I like to see gifted girls who felt weird and unloved blossom in these special environments. It's comforting to know that from even such a temporary environment of support many gifted children can reenter their old environment with the confidence and strength they need to "tough it out" for the rest of their time in school. Summer friends make great penpals, too.

Q. Our daughter tries to cram twenty-eight hours into each day. I'm worried she'll end up with nervous exhaustion.

A. The activity level of most gifted children is usually more exhausting for the parents than for the children themselves. Gifted children often sleep less, play harder, and demand more parental attention than average children do. The major concern I have about gifted girls is the frequency with which they lack focus for all of their activities. Most middle and high schools seem to encourage the blind accumulation of in-school and out-of-school activities as a sign of female popularity and success. Gifted girls often become overinvolved, participating in so many school activities that they become ill from lack of sleep and good eating habits or from the stress resulting from spreading themselves too thin. Whereas boys will blow up or just quit what they're doing when overloaded, I've observed that gifted girls will go until they are felled by mononucleosis, pneumonia, or other exhaustion-related disorders. You can prevent this by insisting that your daughter try to focus and limit her interests. I think that enormous energy directed toward a few cherished goals is always less stressful than energy indiscriminately spread over a variety of unrelated activities. I think it would be unwise to try to enforce rest periods or quell all that energy; simply help your daughter to channel it more effectively.

Problems of Adolescence

Q. *We were pleased when our daughter's high school began to offer calculus this year because she has been identified as mathematically gifted and has excelled in this area. The course is offered as a final period elective, which falls at the same time as her cheerleading practice. As a result, she doesn't want the course. What can we do?*

A. Your daughter's high school administrators assume that cheerleaders don't take calculus. Take issue with this stereotype, but don't expect the schedule to change in time to benifit your daughter. Give her the best possible information about her loss if she were to discontinue mathematics, the key to numerous high paying, prestigious careers. Even journalism, psychology, and law require substantial mathematics. Medicine, engineering, life sciences, and natural sciences are closed to people without high school, undergraduate, and graduate math courses.

Second, it is always unwise to "drop out" even for a year from mathematics; it is too easy not to go back to math.

Third, a course in calculus will have a much greater impact on your daughter's chances for admission to a first-class college or university than participation in cheerleading. Without being overly critical of this enjoyable activity, try to point out that, in this case, it may be an investment in time that will not pay off. If persuasion fails, you have two other choices: refuse to give permission for her to attend cheerleading, or locate a night course or summer course in calculus.

Q. *We are horrified by our daughter's choice of boyfriends. She is about to enter college, and we don't like to think about the types she'll bring home. All of her boyfriends are either troublemakers or weirdos. One of*

them is involved with drugs, one has been in trouble with the law, and one shaves his head and plays in a band. She is a good girl, always pleasant and easy to be with. We can't understand her attraction to these boys.

A. *Gifted girls often enjoy dating odd, nonconforming, or down-and-out types, for the simple reason that they are more interesting. Gifted girls are usually aware that they are not yet seeking a lifemate, and are mainly interested in challenging and stimulating relationships. Gifted girls like to "reform" drunks, encourage creative companions, and egg on daredevils.*

However, it is important to assure yourself that her boyfriends are not abusive, pathological, or serious violators of the law, so talk with her straightforwardly about them. Once you are assured that she is happy in and about these relationships, you can probably relax; as she matures, she will naturally select more appropriate partners. Try to avoid making her choose between you and her friends, or to criticize her so that she avoids talking with you. Your relationship with her is extremely important and should be the most long-lasting. If you find, however, that the relationships make her troubled and unhappy, she needs your help. If they put her in physical or legal jeopardy, she needs your guidance. Share your fears and your understanding of her feelings about her friends. Let her know you understand how frustrating friends can be when they show so much promise but can't measure up to our expectations. Offer your continuing help.

Q. *Our thirteen-year-old is hanging around with a terrible bunch of girls. She has friends her own age and ability in her grade, but she has become enchanted with some older girls who overdress, wear hideous makeup, and think of nothing but boys. We're afraid her school work will suffer since these girls are not interested in academics at all.*

A. *If her school work isn't suffering yet, it may not at*

255

all. *Gifted girls are often perfectly able to associate with "nonacademic" friends and continue to do well in school. The early teen years often find gifted girls seized with a sudden desire to be incredibly "normal," and their intellectual peers of the same age may not be "normal" enough.*

You do need to be prepared for the possibility of her lowering her career aspirations as a result of peer pressure. If she suddenly develops a desire to be a beautician, you may need to do a little at-home career education! Simply remind her always that you have confidence in her ability to realize her potential, and have a counselor or teacher explain her potential to her.

Q. Our daughter has switched college majors at least three times. We're beginning to worry that at seventeen she wasn't ready for college.

A. *It is more likely that multipotentiality, not immaturity, is the problem. Many gifted students have problems with multipotentiality—the ability to select and develop any number of career goals. People are always telling them "You can be anything you want to be," but that is precisely the problem. Most gifted college students who play "musical majors" are struggling with multipotentiality. For gifted women, it is a special problem because then they are more likely to experience self-doubt and to give up on ever finding a career goal. Self-doubt, lack of clear focus, and criticism by others make it more likely that they will then drop out.*

We must deal with gifted girls' multipotentiality early in life by teaching them focusing, values clarification, and goal-setting skills in junior high and high school. If multipotentiality is a problem in college, good career counseling with a professional can help her to narrow her interests and weigh the pros and cons of her goals. As a parent, make sure you show understanding of your daughter's embarrassment over her intellectual riches.

Problems of Gifted Women

Q. What kinds of relationship problems are related to giftedness in women? It seems that gifted women have more trouble finding the right kind of men.

A. The most frequent relationship problems we see at the Guidance Laboratory are related to romantic expectations. Often a gifted woman's intellectual maturity far outstrips her maturity about feelings and relationships.

Just because women are intellectually mature and gifted doesn't mean that they haven't bought the American romantic myth lock, stock, and barrel. The myth goes something like this: "When the right man comes along, he will sweep you off your feet. You and he will be intensely attracted to one another and will not be able to bear to be apart. You will agree on everything, and you will share all your deepest feelings with one another. Neither of you will ever need anybody else ever again. He will be strong and protective, and you will be nurturing and supportive. You will both be completely faithful to one another in all ways. You will marry in a perfect wedding, have perfect children, and have a happy home life. You will continue to be madly in love with one another. You will grow old together, sharing every experience. You will both die on the same day, in each other's arms."

Every sentence of this myth is wildly untrue, but every sentence has been believed sincerely by many gifted women. As long as gifted women wait for the "right men" to come along, they will be alone. As long as gifted women assume that they must be physically attracted to a man in order for love to occur, they will lose a great many opportunities for true intimacy based on friendship. If gifted women decide they like less intelligent men because many gifted men may be sarcastic and argumentative, then they may be condemning themselves to a lifetime of boredom. If a gifted woman opts for a man who will take care of her instead of a man who will demand her strength and independence, then she is forging her own chains. If she expects the kind of perfection in her marriage and family that she has been able to attain in her work, she will be disappointed. If she does not first and finally learn to live on her own as a separate individual, defining herself through her own values, goals and career, she will be nothing if he is not there.

The romantic myth has done incalculable damage to gifted women because no matter how hard they try, they cannot live it; unable to fulfill the expectations of the myth, they live in constant anxiety and frustration. The research and accounts of eminent women clearly show that gifted women must often temper their intensely idealistic relationships and should attempt at least somewhat to rationally and pragmatically consider their decisions about relationships.

Q. As a gifted woman, how can I find a suitable partner?

A. *Love through work and ideas, the key for eminent women, is appropriate for most gifted women. To find the right mate, stop looking. Find the dream, the movement, the work to which you can commit yourself wholeheartedly. Strive for excellence in your chosen field, and associate with others who share your passion and are committed to excellence. Explore your idea or serve your people. When you no longer feel you need a partner—when your work and your community created by your work are enough—then you will be ready for true intimacy.*

Q. Why do gifted women want romantic relationships so much? Why aren't they happy with collegial or companionable relationships with men?

A. *Gifted women sometimes confuse intimacy with achievement. Gifted women are often very achievement-oriented; they want to be the best and have the best. They have often bought into society's belief that a woman's highest achievement is a relationship with a man. They also have astutely determined the kind of man who, in the eyes of society, is best to possess: he is handsome, strong, masterful, and aggressive. They do this figuring much in the way they used to psych out what they needed to do in class to get an A, only now they are trying to get an A from society for catching the "right kind of guy."*

But the right kind of guy in society's eyes is often exactly the wrong kind of guy for most gifted women, who seem happiest with the supportive, easy-going men who seem definitely unromantic to women brought up on a diet of Cosmopolitan, best selling novels, and Burt Reynolds movies. Such men are less threatened by gifted women's achievements and more willing to share domestic responsibilities so that a combination of career and family becomes manageable. They are also more likely to place more emphasis on their partner's ideas and values than on their physical attractiveness, and are more likely to see women as their equals. In the friendly, interdependent relationship of equals, a gifted woman can attain true intimacy, not in the hollow achievement of landing "the perfect man."

One final note relative to several of the questions and answers about relationships: I cannot emphasize too strongly the fact that marriage and having children are not required for gifted women to have satisfying lives. Single, childless, gifted women are among the happiest of this population. A community of friends, a life of one's own, a sisterhood of independent women are reasonable possibilities and hold promise of a satisfying single lifestyle for gifted women.

Q. As a homemaker, I resent the emphasis on steering gifted girls away from the traditional woman's role of wife and mother. Surely we need gifted mothers at home if there are to be gifted children. This is the road I've taken, and I'm proud of it.

A. This question embodies so many similar concerns of women who have found life satisfaction in the traditional women's roles. However, I also find many problems in this comment. First, as the biographies of gifted women have shown, there is no evidence that gifted children are the product of, or must be raised by, gifted mothers. Second, we do not discourage girls from marriage and family at the Guidance Laboratory; in fact, we point out that they can have a career and a family. Most professional positions such as college professor, physician, and lawyer allow the freedom to take time off and to arrange a flexible schedule. So if girls have high aspirations, they are more likely to have time for family later than if they are forced to work in lower level jobs to supplement family income. Finally, it is important for you to understand the resentment you feel. It is hard not to want our daughters to make the same choices we did. But a gifted girl who is deciding to be primarily a homemaker is probably making a choice that will not lead to great satisfaction: the research is unequivocal about this. Homemakers feel under attack right now, and many feel defensive about their own lifestyle. It is important to leave the options open for your daughter, even if you didn't have those options for yourself.

Q. At thirty, I am dead-ended in my career. I work as a sales representative for a film distributor. I hate my work. It is a family-owned business, and I have no chance for promotion. I am paid so poorly I can hardly keep up with my rent. Worst, I feel humiliated to be working in a job a high school graduate could do; I have a masters degree in art history. There are no jobs in art history, the only thing I really care about.

A. These are very harsh times for gifted young adults— especially gifted young women. Underemployment is a bitter and exasperating condition, robbing even the strongest individuals of self-esteem and creating an inner rage that feeds on itself. In fact, it is hard not to be angry at everyone: your employer for taking advantage of you, your friends and family for not understanding why you are so unhappy ("You have a job, don't you?"), and your society for ignoring and wasting your gifts.

If you give in to your despair and settle for this life, you join the people who are selling you short. It is important for you to reconsider your situation, and then act. First, rethink: you must learn to distinguish between your job and your career. Sales is your job; art history is your career. A job is something someone gives you to do in return for money; a career is something only you can give yourself. It is a rare gifted woman whose job really matches her career.

Of course, you will want to continue to seek a job that more closely approximates your career. Until that time, you should be spending your limited free time in building your career in art history. What question or problems in art history fascinate you? What needs to be done in the field of art history? What about art history do you care about?

Then act: if you cannot afford to be formally enrolled in a research program, do your own research. Seek people who are interested in the same problems that you are. You don't have to have a job in art history to attend art history conferences and to associate with art historians socially. You don't have to have a job in art history to do committee work for a professional association. Your knowledge, rather than your job title, are the most important career credentials.

Nobody can take away your career as an art historian, because it is your basic identity. However, fatigue from a forty-hour job can rob you of energy you need to actualize your ideas. Conserve your energy! Work competently at your job, but don't exhaust yourself—it is a bad investment of time. Don't feel that you must involve yourself intensely in social relationships at work, because you need to save yourself for friends who have interests more like yours. If you use your spare time for involvement with your career, you will find that you have more energy than you thought, and you will begin to feel better about who you are.

Index

A

H

I

T

U

V

W

Y

Z